Beyond Software Architecture

Advance praise for *Beyond Software Architecture*

Luke Hohmann is that rare software technologist who views software development from the viewpoint of the end user. He passionately believes that one hour spent with an end user is worth many hours making software architectural choices or days documenting perceived user requirements. Most of what is written about software development focuses on methods used to design and develop robust software. Luke's latest effort, *Beyond Software Architecture*, illuminates the more mundane aspects of creating true business solutions by supporting the user throughout the lifecycle of the software product. By concerning himself with creating business value, Luke tightens the connection between a software application and the business function it performs.

—Bruce Bourbon
General Partner, Telos Venture Partners

There are two kinds of people that read the Dilbert comic strip: folks that take a moment to marvel at how accurately it reflects life at their company before moving on to the next comic strip, and folks that think Dilbert is an amusing reminder that high tech companies can and *should* be better than Dilbert's world. Anyone in the first group should stick to reading comics. This book is for people in the latter group.

—Tony Navarrete
Vice President, Diamondhead Ventures

Luke brings a proven methodology to the challenge of software development. In *Beyond Software Architecture,* Luke provides practical and proven techniques that all development executives can employ to improve the productivity of their software organization.

—G. Bradford Solso
CEO, Taviz Technology

Beyond Software Architecture is the first book I have read which contains an insider's perspective of both the business and technical facets of software architecture. This is a great book to get marketers and software managers on the same page!

—Damon Schechter
CEO, LOC Global
author of *Delivering the Goods*

There are books on technical architecture and books on product marketing, but few, if any, on how architecture and marketing information must be integrated for world class product development. *Beyond Software Architecture* provides this valuable bridge between technology and marketing—it explains how to deliver quality products that are profitable in the marketplace.

—Jim Highsmith
Director, Cutter Consortium
author of *Adaptive Software Development*

Product development managers, marketing managers, architects, and technical leads from all functions should read this book. You'll see a pragmatic view of how to define and use a product architecture throughout a project's lifecycle and a product's lifetime.

—Johanna Rothman
Rothman Consulting Group, Inc.

Luke Hohmann has captured the essence of product creation in his latest book. He cleverly discusses the need for both the marketing and engineering roles in product creation and ties the two together building a good foundation for understanding and executing successful product creation.

—Lee Sigler
Principal, 360 Market View, Inc.

Finally a book that deals with those often ignored but critical operational issues like licensing, deployment, installation, configuration and support. *Beyond Software Architecture* is the "What they don't teach you at Harvard Business School" book for anyone who develops software products—or buys them.

—Mary Poppendieck
Managing Director, Agile Alliance
President, Poppendieck LLC

Luke Hohmann delivers a passionate, articulate wake-up call to software architects: it ain't just technical any more! Technical architectures have profound business ramifications, and ignoring the business ramifications of portability, usability, configuration, upgrade and release management, security, and other architectural choices can not only lead to project failures, but ultimately to nasty lawsuits from disappointed customers. *Beyond Software Architecture* is a must-read for successful software product managers!

—Ed Yourdon
Author of numerous books and articles on software development

Beyond Software Architecture is not just for software engineering professionals! Executives and product managers will find that the book provides the necessary background to make informed decisions about the software that their companies build. I have found that the book is a useful tool for building consensus between management and engineering, because it discusses business and customer-related issues without delving too deeply into implementation details.

—David Chaiken
Vice President, Systems Architecture
AgileTV Corporation

Product marketing influences product architecture. This shouldn't be a surprise, yet most texts on software architecture are silent on this fact. This may be because we lack the language for distinguishing between the technical aspects of an architecture and the marketing aspects. *Beyond Software Architecture* provides the language to draw this important distinction, and provides strategies for overall architectural success.

—Dave W. Smith

Beyond Software Architecture, as the title implies, successfully addresses the often neglected aspects of developing total solutions. Hohmann demonstrates both passion and depth for the broad set of topics discussed.

—Craig Priess
Director Product Management, Resonant Software

Looking through my technical library, it's apparent that many books are obsolete, casualties of technical innovation and change. There are a few, however, that remain and continue to be relevant. Adding Luke Hohmann's new book, *Beyond Software Architecture: Creating and Sustaining Winning Solutions* expands that selection and fills an important gap. It is the first book that I recall presenting a holistic approach to software creation. Going beyond the technical aspects by weaving together and linking critical business and marketing development in such a way to elevate and show how both technical and marketing processes must coalesce to create a winning solution. The topic's importance extends beyond programmers, designers and other technical staff, just as does its content. For marketing professionals, it shows how their decisions and strategies can impact technical decisions. For consumers, it can give them insight on the best ways to work with software manufacturers. For the software entrepreneur, it offers a plan for creating a successful venture. The content, at just the right amount of detail, is presented in easy-to-understand language and in such a way that the information is easy to retain and apply. The topics are timeless. The book will be relevant for a long time.

—Clay Miller

I highly recommend this book. As a former software company CEO and founder I have worked with many software engineers and had a number of VPs of engineering report to me. Luke was and is one of the best. He is not only a great engineer, but has a keen grasp of the strategic business issues that must drive good code and architectural decisions. I consider *Beyond Software Architecture* required reading for anyone building software systems.

—Kevin Rivette
Executive Advisor, BCG Consulting
author of *Rembrandts In The Attic*

Perhaps you've met, or worked with, or heard speak at events, or read the writings of someone who expects reverence because he commands academic knowledge of the latest software patterns, technologies, or development processes and tools. So what, you say. Suppose you take such knowledge for granted. Suppose that knowledge is the minimum qualification for a member of your team. Then what? What separates a real contributor to the success of your project and organization, from the average bookish expert of the day? In *Beyond Software Architecture*, Luke Hohmann writes of the stuff that makes up those answers. Installation and upgrade. Configurability and customization of your software. Integration with other software. Usability. Logging. Interdepartmental processes and release management. Business models, licensing, and deployment choices. The stuff that makes software development much bigger, and much messier, than UML diagrams of some pattern implemented with components. The stuff that makes software development real. Luke knows because he's been in the trenches, trying to make businesses successful. He spends his time doing it more than writing and talking about it. But now he distills his insights and shares the benefit of his experience. If you're like me, you'll find yourself nodding your head and underlining passages as you read this book. Luke's observations will resonate with you. Your organization, and the software development profession as a whole, can benefit from using the vocabulary and ideas in this book. So you'll want to recommend it to others, which is exactly what I'm doing here.

—Randy Stafford
Chief Architect, IQNavigator, Inc.

Hohmann's book provides a unique perspective on how the many and subtle technology decisions shape the economic and strategic landscape. Corporate strategists in many industries will find these insights enormously valuable.

—Martha Amram
Strategic Advisor and Consultant
author of *Value Sweep* and co-author of *Real Options*

Luke put his tremendous experience to good use by eliminating the us versus them approach of marketing and engineering departments. This book is a must for every senior engineer, software architect, and product manager. With the practical advice in this book they can concentrate on beating the competitors.

—Heinrich Gantenbein

I once was a QA manager for Luke Hohmann. I can tell you the guy knows competitive software development. He was in the trenches with us, working through technical problems and sweating the difficult business decisions. He's uniquely qualified to write about both the business and technical side of software architecture, and this book successfully bridges both worlds. The result is a seminal handbook for product managers and directors of software engineering.

—James Bach
Founder, Satisfice, Inc.

Too many times my firm is asked to resolve a dispute that could have been avoided had the companies involved with the dispute more clearly defined their business and licensing models before the contract was signed. In *Beyond Software Architecture*, Luke Hohmann clearly explains how to avoid unnecessary and costly disputes regarding business and licensing models. This is a must read book for senior product managers and technical executives.

—Rob Sterne
Founder, Sterne, Kessler, Goldstein and Fox
International Authority in Intellectual Property

Luke Hohmann's excellent BSA communicates essential hard-won insights from a rare individual—both architect and business leader—who shows us that architecture is more than describing layers; it's about creating winning solutions through understanding, and resolving the market, business, and technical forces.

—Craig Larman
author, *Applying UML and Patterns: An Introduction to OOA&D and the Rational Unified Process*

By stepping back and evaluating the interaction between business drivers and software development, *Beyond Software Architecture* provides the perspective to create a winning solution. This book is a practical guide for achieving quick time to market solutions through the identification of pitfalls and suggests pragmatic alternatives to effective solution development. Real life examples provide an instructional view of the life cycle phases, including clear roles and responsibilities, as seen by the entire project team. Knowing when to give up the ghost, seek the help of others, or simply leverage a proven model, *Beyond Software Architecture* explores the alternatives and identifies key decision points. A must read for software architects and product managers seeking an understanding of the challenges and dynamics of a successful software development effort, and a winning solution—the first time.

— Mark Welke
High Availability Marketing Manager, Hewlett Packard

The thing you need to consider when creating a great application is "Everything." Great applications do not usually come from a single great idea, great architecture, or great appreciation of the customer's need. Instead they come out of a unique confluence of a large number of factors encompassing marketing, technology, psychology, support, economics, legal factors, and more. While many books address individual aspects of software application development, Luke Hohmann's book, *Beyond Software Architecture*, addresses a very broad range of topics, all of which should be addressed in the creation of every application, but often aren't. I would recommend that anyone involved in the creation of a software application read this book as a guide to the things that need to be considered in the process. No book can cover "everything," but this one is a laudable attempt.

—Jim Gay
One Jump Consulting

A successful software product's technical architecture must align with the realities of the marketplace. While the goal is obvious, marketers and technologist often find themselves in two warring camps, separated by a chasm of incompatible attitudes and expectations. If you want to close this gap and focus on product success, this book is required reading for both sides.

—Dave Quick
Architect, Integrated Solutions Development Group, Microsoft, Inc.

As a technologist who has transitioned to product team leadership, this book distils many of the lessons I've learned through study, trial, and error. As someone who still bridges the gap between software development and executive management, I found this book a great refresher and filled with little "oh yeah!" insights. And, as I continue to work with teams to manage and develop new products, I'm sure I'll use it as a reference and a teaching resource, bringing the "big picture" into view and avoiding costly pitfalls. Anyone managing product development or marketing, aspiring to manage, or unhappy with current management should definitely read Hohmann's work.

— Todd Girvin
President, Optiview Inc.

The Addison-Wesley Signature Series ◢◣

The Addison-Wesley Signature Series provides readers with practical and authoritative information on the latest trends in modern technology for computer professionals. The series is based on one simple premise: great books come from great authors. Books in the series are personally chosen by expert advisors, world-class authors in their own right. These experts are proud to put their signatures on the covers, and their signatures ensure that these thought leaders have worked closely with authors to define topic coverage, book scope, critical content, and overall uniqueness. The expert signatures also symbolize a promise to our readers: you are reading a future classic.

THE ADDISON–WESLEY SIGNATURE SERIES
SIGNERS: KENT BECK AND MARTIN FOWLER

Kent Beck has pioneered people-oriented technologies like JUnit, Extreme Programming, and patterns for software development. Kent is interested in helping teams do well by doing good — finding a style of software development that simultaneously satisfies economic, aesthetic, emotional, and practical constraints. His books focus on touching the lives of the creators and users of software.

Martin Fowler has been a pioneer of object technology in enterprise applications. His central concern is how to design software well. He focuses on getting to the heart of how to build enterprise software that will last well into the future. He is interested in looking behind the specifics of technologies to the patterns, practices, and principles that last for many years; these books should be usable a decade from now. Martin's criterion is that these are books he wished he could write.

TITLES IN THE SERIES

Test-Driven Development: By Example
Kent Beck, ISBN: 0321146530

User Stories Applied: For Agile Software Development
Mike Cohn, ISBN: 0321205685

Patterns of Enterprise Application Architecture
Martin Fowler, ISBN: 0321127420

Beyond Software Architecture: Creating and Sustaining Winning Solutions
Luke Hohmann, ISBN: 0201775948

Enterprise Integration Patterns: Designing, Building, and Deploying Messaging Solutions
Gregor Hohpe and Bobby Woolf, ISBN: 0321200683

Beyond Software Architecture

Creating and Sustaining
Winning Solutions

Luke Hohmann

✦✦ Addison-Wesley

Boston • San Francisco • New York • Toronto • Montreal
London • Munich • Paris • Madrid
Capetown • Sydney • Tokyo • Singapore • Mexico City

The publisher offers discounts on this book when ordered in quantity for bulk purchases and special sales. For more information, please contact:

    U.S. Corporate and Government Sales
    (800) 382-3419
    corpsales@pearsontechgroup.com

For sales outside of the United States, please contact:

    International Sales
    (317) 581-3793
    international@pearsontechgroup.com
    Visit Addison-Wesley on the Web: www.awprofessional.com

Library of Congress Cataloging-in-Publication Data

Hohmann, Luke.
    Beyond software architecture: creating and sustaining winning solutions / Luke Hohmann.
        p. cm.
    ISBN 0-201-77594-8 (pbk. : alk. paper)
    1. Computer software. 2. Computer architecture. I. Title.
    QA76.754.H65 2003
    005.1—dc21   2002152562

Text printed on recycled and acid-free paper.

ISBN 0201775948

7 8 9 10 11 12 CRS 07 06 05

7th Printing   September 2005

To Jena—
I'll write another book!

To Jaren and Cres—
Thank you for going to bed early and sleeping so well.

I love you all more than you'll ever know.

Luke

Contents

Foreword by Martin Fowler

Architecture has become a very slippery word in the software business. It's hard to come up with any solid definition of what it means. I see it as a fundamentally subjective term—when people describe their software architecture they select the important parts of their systems, how these parts fit together, and the key decisions they made in designing their systems. Architecture is also seen as a technical issue, with the implication that the key decisions that need to be made are technical decisions.

In talking with Luke over the last few years I've really enjoyed the fact that he talks about the kinds of things that are often sadly omitted from most architectural discussions—yet are every bit as important. Such things as the marketing view of a system, licensing terms, branding, deployment, billing. All of these issues have important technical and business implications. Senior technical people need to think about this stuff, or otherwise a technically capable system could fail to be good business decision.

Many of these issues matter most to people who sell software to other entities. But even if you're an architect of an in-house IS shop these issues are just as likely to trip you up. Licensing agreements with your vendors can make a big difference to the costs of the software you deploy, billing may become important if your business decides it wants to introduce a charge-back scheme, branding helps affect your visibility to the business side of your company.

Luke writes from the perspective of someone who has dealt with both the technical and business sides of software development. It's a duality I find appealing because it's led him to ponder issues that often don't get talked about. He shows that it's often the things you don't think to worry about that hurt you the most and in the process provides the advice you need to deal with them. As a result this book is a much needed compliment to the technical aspects of software design.

Martin Fowler,
Series Editor

Foreword by Guy Kawasaki

First, you have to understand that I think writing software is more art than science. How is it, then, that I would write a foreword for a book that is focused on the nuts and bolts, instead of the creative?

The creative process of both art and software is highly overrated. Clear your mind of visions of sitting around in a comfy chair as the software muse penetrates your mind and thousands of lines of elegant code flow effortlessly from your brain. If you've created software, you know it isn't like this.

Art is hard. Debugging is even harder. This is a book that will help you and your team become better artists. It is about discipline, teamwork, perspiration, and, yes, inspiration. I hope you read it, and it enables you to create great art (a.k.a. software) that changes the world.

Guy Kawasaki,
CEO
Garage Technology Ventures

Preface

Many excellent books have been written on software architecture. These books, which, among other things, define, classify, and describe software architectures, define notations for representing and communicating architectural choices, and provide guidance on making good architectural decisions, have enduring value. Unfortunately, while these books may help you build a successful *architecture,* they fall short of the goal of helping you create a *winning solution.* To create a winning solution, you need to move beyond subsystems and interfaces, beyond architectural patterns such as Front Controller or Pipes and Filters, and beyond creating third-normal-form relational databases. You need to move beyond software architecture and move toward understanding and embracing the business issues that must be resolved in order to create a winning solution.

An example of one such business issue concerns technical support. It is inevitable that some of your customers are going to have a problem with your software. The choices you've made long ago in such areas as log file design, how the system is integrated with other systems, how the system is configured, or how the system is upgraded will determine how well you can solve their problems. *Beyond Software Architecture* helps you move beyond software architecture and toward creating winning solutions by discussing a wide range of business issues and their interrelationship with architectural choices.

This book presents a unique perspective that is motivated and informed by my experiences in creating single-user programs costing less than $50; software systems used in academic research; utilities to diagnose and fix problems associated with internally developed systems; and distributed, enterprise-class platforms costing millions of dollars. Along the way, I've played a variety of roles. I've been an individual contributor, a direct manager, and a senior member of the corporate executive staff. At various times I've either worked in or led engineering, product marketing and management, quality assurance, technical publications, and first- and second-line support organizations. I've managed teams and projects across multiple cities and continents.

The common thread tying all of this software together is that it was created to provide value to some person. Research software, for example, serves the needs of the researchers who are trying to understand some phenomena. Enterprise application software, dealing with everything from customers to supply-chain management, is designed to serve the needs of a well-defined set of users and the businesses that license it in a sustainably profitable manner. Similar comments apply to every other kind of software, from games to personal contact managers, inventory management systems to graphic design tools.

The issues identified and discussed in this book affect every kind of software. Their presentation and discussion occur most often in the context of enterprise application software, where I have spent most of my professional career. While they have no universally accepted definition, enterprise applications typically meet one or more of the following characteristics:

- They are designed to support the needs of a business, at either a departmental or larger organizational unit.

- They are relatively expensive to build or license ($50,000–$5,000,000 and up).

- They have complex deployment and operational requirements.

- They can be operated independently, but the needs of the business are often best served when they are integrated with other enterprise applications.

Even if you're not creating an enterprise application, you will find this book useful. Creating sustainable software solutions—meeting customer needs over a long period of time through multiple releases—is a challenging, enjoyable, and rewarding endeavor, certainly not limited to the domain of enterprise applications!

Although I will often refer to software architecture and discuss technical matters, my discussions won't focus on such things as the best ways to diagram or document your architecture or the deeper design principles associated with creating robust, distributed Web-based component systems. As I said earlier, there are plenty of books that address these topics—in fact, almost *too* many, with the unfortunate side-effect that many people become so focused on technical details that they lose sight of the business value they're trying to provide.

Instead of concentrating on purely technical choices, *Beyond Software Architecture* helps you create and sustain truly winning solutions by focusing on the practical, nuts-and-bolts choices that must be made by the development team in a wide variety of areas. I have found that focusing on practical matters, such as how you should identify a release or integrate branding elements into your solution, reduces the often artificial barriers that can exist between developers and the business and marketing people with whom they work.

These barriers prevent both groups from creating winning solutions. I cringe when engineers take only a techno*logy* view without due consideration of *business* issues, or when marketing people make "get-me-this-feature" demands without due consideration of their underlying technical ramifications. When either side takes a position without due consideration of its impact, the likelihood of creating and sustaining a winning solution drops dramatically.

What is especially troubling is that these arguments seem to be made in support of the idea that technical issues can somehow be separated from business issues, or that business issues can somehow be separated from technical issues. At best this is simply wrong; at worst it can be a recipe for disaster. Developers are routinely asked to endure the hardships of design extremes, such as a low-memory footprint, in order to reduce total system cost. Entire companies are started to compete in existing markets because investors are convinced that one or more technological breakthroughs will provide the competitive advantage necessary for success. Not surprisingly, investors are even more eager to invest when the technological breakthrough is accompanied by a similar breakthrough in the business model being offered to customers.

Managing the interrelationship between technology and business will be a recurring theme throughout this book. Handle only the former and you might have an interesting technology or, perhaps, an elegant system,—but one that ultimately withers because no one is using it. Handle only the latter and you'll have a paper solution that excites lots of people and may even get you funding—but one that doesn't deliver any sustainable value. Handle both and you'll have a winning solution. While creating new technologies or elegant systems can be fun, and designing sophisticated new software applications or business models can be exciting, both palc in comparison to the deep satisfaction that comes from creating winning solutions and sustaining them.

Acknowledgments

Thanks to all of the people that have helped me create this book. I am especially indebted to Don Olsen, Haim Kilov, Rebecca Wirfs-Brock, Myron Ahn, Rob Purser, Ron Lunde, Scott Ambler and Dave Smith for their detailed reviews. Steve Sweeting, Craig Larman, Todd Girvin, Erik Petersen, Sandra Carrico, Adam Jackson, Tony Navarette, Chris Reavis, Elisabeth Hendrickson, James Bach and Alan Shalloway all provided detailed reviews of one or more chapters. Some of you were especially critical, and the book is better for it.

A very special thanks goes to Bob Glass for working with me to create the title. Once again a phone call was better than a lot of e-mail.

Ron, I imagined that writing a chapter with you would be fun. It was!

Steve Dodds, Lee Sigler, and a host of students and colleagues have provided me with inspiration and friendship as I undertook this project.

Special thanks to my good friend and original publisher Paul Becker, who patiently waited for me to complete it. Paul, it has been a few years since I completed my first book. Thanks for your willingness to wait until I had something to say.

I am deeply indebted to the superb professionalism and hard work of the Addison-Wesley production and marketing organization. They took a raw manuscript and helped shape it into a book. Thanks to Mary O'Brien, Elizabeth Ryan, Marilyn Rash, Chris Guzikowski, and Dianne Wood.

I have undoubtedly forgotten to mention one or more individuals who have helped in the creation of this book. This was, by no means, intentional. I'm also certain that there are several areas in which the book can be improved based on your experience. Tell me what I've missed, or how I can improve the book—and I will.

Luke Hohmann
luke@lukehohmann.com

Chapter 1

Software Architecture

The foundation of a winning solution lies in the architecture that creates and sustains it. This chapter defines software architecture and examines how architectures are created and evolve through use. Along the way I'll discuss the role of architectural patterns, timeless principles of design, various motivations that shape the architecture, and conclude with a discussion of the interrelationship that exists between the architecture and the team that creates and sustains it.

Defining Software Architecture

Software architecture is a complex topic. Because of its complexity, our profession has produced a variety of definitions, each more or less useful depending on your point of view. Here is a definition from my first book, *Journey of the Software Professional:*

> A system architecture defines the basic "structure" of the system (e.g., the high-level modules comprising the major functions of the system, the management and distribution of data, the kind and style of its user interface, what platform(s) will it run on, and so forth).

This definition is pretty consistent with many others for example, [Bass], [Larman], and [POSA]. However, it lacks some important elements, such as specific technology choices and the required capabilities of the desired system. A colleague of mine, Myron Ahn, created the following definition of software architecture. It is a bit more expansive and covers a bit more ground than my original (2002, personal communication).

> Software architecture is the sum of the nontrivial modules, processes, and data of the system, their structure and exact relationships to each other, how they can be and are expected to be extended and modified, and on which technologies they depend, from

which one can deduce the exact capabilities and flexibilities of the system, and from which one can form a plan for the implementation or modification of the system.

We could extend these definitions from the technical point of view, but this wouldn't provide a lot of value. More than any other aspect of the system, *architecture* deals with the "big picture." The real key to understanding it is to adopt this big picture point of view.

Alternative Thoughts on Software Architecture

While the previous definitions of software architecture are useful, they are far too simplistic to take into account the full set of forces that shape, and are shaped by, an architecture. In truth, I doubt that any single definition of software architecture will ever capture all of what we believe to be important. To illustrate, this section raises some issues that aren't often covered by traditional definitions of software architecture but are nonetheless quite important. Unlike the previous definitions, which focus on the "technical" aspects of architecture, consider that these focus on some of the most important "human" and "business" issues, which are all part of the big picture.

Subsystems Are Designed to Manage Dependencies

Having managed distributed teams that have spanned the globe, I've found that an important criterion in decomposing subsystems is having the simplest possible dependencies among development organizations. By simple, I mean manageable based on the people who are creating the system. In work with my consulting clients, I've found that, contrary to "technical" justifications, many architectural choices regarding subsystem design are based on creating easily managed dependencies among groups of developers. The practical effect of these choices is that subsystems are rarely split across development organizations.

Subsystems Are Designed According to Human Motivations and Desires

Many books on architecture remove far too much of the human element from the architectural design process. For example, architectural patterns are a wonderful place to begin the design process, but creating an architecture isn't just taking some form of starting structure, such as a pattern, and objectively tailoring it to the needs of the business. You have to understand and take into account the hopes, experiences, dreams, fears, and preferences of the team charged with building the architecture. Subjective and objective decision making collide as the technical structure of the architecture shapes the social structure of the team and vice-versa.

To check this, ask yourself if you've ever been involved in a project where you wanted to work on a particular aspect of the architecture because you knew you could

Designing Subsystems to Create a Sense of Wholeness

Few developers want to be so specialized in their work that all they do is analysis or design or coding or bug fixing. More often than not, developers want to be associated with the full range of development activities: working with customers or product managers to clarify requirements, developing analysis and design artifacts and implementing them, fixing bugs, tuning performance, and so forth. I think of this as a strong desire for a sense of "wholeness" or "completeness" relative to our work. This desire has deep implications, and good designs are often chosen so that the teams building them can fulfill it.

The concept of wholeness means different things to different groups, and it is important for managers to understand how a given team interprets it. In one client-server application, we considered several alternative designs for the client. I'll use two of them to illustrate how we interpreted wholeness and how it influenced our design choice.

In the first design, one team would be given responsibility for "customer-facing" issues and the other would be given responsibility for "infrastructure" components. In the second design, each team would have both customer-facing and backend infrastructure components.

While the first design may have been a bit easier to manage on paper, it left the infrastructure team demoralized, feeling that they would not be full participants in the release process. Specifically, they wouldn't be working directly with product management, technical publications, or potential customers. They had done this in prior releases and wanted to keep doing it in the current and future releases. As a result, we chose the second design, as it was the only choice that allowed both teams to achieve the sense of wholeness that they felt was important. For them, this included interaction with product management and full participation in the release process.

do a better job than anyone else (confidence based on experience); you wanted to learn the underlying technology (desire); you thought that doing a good job might earn you a bonus or promotion (aspiration); or you were concerned that no one else on the team had the requisite skill or experience to solve the problem *the right way* (fear).

Give in to Great Architectures

I use the phrase "give in" when an architect or development team subordinates, to the extent that they can, their experiences and expectations about what they think is right, and instead let the forces of the problem domain guide them in the realization of the architecture. Some people claim that this is not a problem and that they or their team always create an architecture solely based on an objective understanding of the customer's problem and its best technical solution. The operative word, of course, is *best*.

Your opinion of best may not match mine, which is probably more heavily influenced by my experiences than by the problem domain–unless my experiences are born from this domain. One aspect of "giving in" to a great architecture is continually assessing if the decisions we're making are designed with the customer and their needs first, and our willingness to change prior decisions when we find they're not.

Beauty Is in the Eye of the Beholder!

We all have many definitions of successful software architectures. While a company may feel that a system is successful because it is powering a profitable product, the developers who have to maintain it may cringe because of its antiquated technical architecture. Alternatively, many truly elegant technical solutions fail for any number of reasons. In addition, we all have our own opinion on architectural elegance. Two of my most skilled developers had very different philosophies regarding stored procedures in databases. I was confident that both could create a good solution to just about any database-related problem you could throw at them, but I was equally confident that their designs would be different and that both could justify their own design while validly criticizing the other's. Few developers can escape the aesthetics of their design decisions.

Why Software Architecture Matters

Software architecture matters because a good one is a key element of your long-term success. Here are some of the ways that architecture influences success. Not all of them are equally important, but all are related to your architecture.

Longevity

Most architectures live far longer than the teams who created them. Estimates of system or architectural longevity range from 12 to 30 or more years, whereas developer longevity (the time a developer is actively working on the same system) ranges from 2 to 4 years.

Stability

Many benefits accrue from the longevity of a well-designed architecture. One of the biggest is stability. Architectural stability helps ensure a minimum of fundamental rework as the system's functionality is extended over multiple release cycles, thus reducing total implementation costs. It provides an important foundation for the development team. Instead of working on something that is constantly changing, the team can concentrate on making changes that provide the greatest value.

Degree and Nature of Change

Architecture determines the nature of change within the system. Some changes are perceived as easy; others are perceived as hard. When easy correlates strongly with the *desired* set of changes that improve customer satisfaction or allow us to add features that attract new customers, we usually refer to the architecture as "good."

In one application I worked on, the development team had created a plug-in architecture that would extend the analytic tools that manipulated various data managed by the system. Adding a new tool was relatively easy, which was a good thing because it was a major goal of product management to add as many tools as possible.

Profitability

A good architecture is a profitable one. By profitable, I mean that the company that created the architecture can sustain it with an acceptable cost structure. If the costs of sustaining the architecture become too great, it will be abandoned.

This does not mean that a profitable architecture must be considered elegant or beautiful. One of the most profitable architectures of all time is the Microsoft Windows family of operating systems—even though many people have decried it as inelegant.

It is important to recognize that the profitability of a given technical architecture often has little to do with the architecture itself. Take Microsoft, which has enjoyed tremendous advantages over its competitors in marketing, distribution, branding, and so forth. All of these things have contributed to Windows' extraordinary profitability.

This is *not* an argument for poorly created, inelegant architectures that cost more money than necessary to create and sustain! Over the long run, simple and elegant architectures tend to be the foundation of profitable solutions.

Social Structure

A good architecture works for the team that created it. It leverages their strengths and can, at times, minimize their weaknesses. For example, many development teams are simply not skilled enough to properly use C or C++. The most common mistake is mismanaging memory, resulting in applications that fail for no apparent reason. For teams that do not require the unique capabilities of C or C++, a better choice would be a safer language such as Java, Visual Basic, Perl, or C#, which manage memory on the developer's behalf.

Once created, the architecture in turn exhibits a strong influence on the team. No matter what language you've chosen, you have to mold the development team around it because it affects such as things as your hiring and training policies. Because architectures outlast their teams, these effects can last for decades (consider the incredible spike in demand in 1997–1999 for COBOL programmers as the industry retrofitted COBOL applications to handle the Y2K crisis).

How Many People Will It Cost to Replace This Thing?

One of the most difficult decisions faced by senior members of any product development team is when to replace an existing architecture with a new one.

Many factors play into this decision, including the costs associated with sustaining the old architecture, the demands of existing customers, your ability to support these demands, and the moves of your competitors. Creating a formal set of rules for knowing when to replace an architecture is impossible, because there are so many factors to consider, and each of these factors is hard to quantify. The following rules of thumb have served me well.

If you feel that your current architecture could be replaced by a development team of roughly half the size of the existing team in one year or less, you should seriously consider replacing your current architecture with a new one. In very general terms, this rule allows you to split your team, putting half of your resources to work on sustaining the old system and half of your resources on creating the new system, with minimal increases in your cost structure.

The resources assigned to create your architecture may not all come from your current team. Bluntly, creating a new architecture with fewer people often requires radically different development approaches. Your current team may not have the required skills, and may be unwilling or unable to acquire them. Thus, every manager must be ready to substantially change the composition of his or her team before undertaking an architectural replacement.

While replacing one or two people is often required, it is lunacy to try to replace everyone. The older and more complex the system, the more likely you'll need the services of one or two trusted veterans of its development to make certain that the new system is faithfully implementing the functionality of the old. There *will* be skeletons, and you're going to need these veterans to know where these skeletons are buried.

All of the traditional adages of "being careful" and "it is harder and will take longer than you think" apply here. You *should* be careful, and it probably *will* be harder and take longer than you estimate. People usually forget to estimate the total cost of replacement, including development, QA, technical publications, training, and upgrades. Economically, a good rule of thumb is that it costs at least 20 percent of the *total* investment in the old architecture to create a functionally equivalent new one *if you are using experienced people, with no interruptions, and a radically improved development process*. If you're on your fourth iteration of a system that has been created over five years with a total investment of $23 million, you're probably fooling yourself if you think that you can create the first version of the new system for less than $3–$5 million. More commonly, the cost of creating a functionally equivalent new architecture is usually between 40 and 60 percent of the total investment in the original architecture, depending heavily on the size of the team and the complexity of the system they are replacing.

Boundaries Defined

During the architectural design process the team makes numerous decisions about what is "in" or "out of" the system. These boundaries, and the manner in which they are created and managed, are vital to the architecture's ultimate success. Boundary questions are innumerable: Should the team write its own database access layer or license one? Should the team use an open-source Web server or license one? Which subteam should be responsible for the user interface? Winning solutions create technical boundaries that support the specific needs of the business. This doesn't always happen, especially in emerging markets where there is often little support for what the team wants to accomplish and it has to create much of the architecture from scratch; poor choices often lead the development team down "rat holes" from which it will never recover.

Sustainable, Unfair Advantage

This point, which summarizes the previous points, is clearly the most important. A *great* architecture provides a technically sophisticated, hard to duplicate, sustainable competitive advantage. If the technical aspects of your architecture are easy to duplicate, you'll have to find other ways to compete (better service, superior distribution, and so forth). Architecture still has an important role: A good architecture may still help you gain an advantage in such things as usability or performance.

Creating an Architecture

A *software architecture* begins as the result of the collective set of design choices made by the team that created the very first version of a system. These early beginnings, which might be sketches on a whiteboard or diagrams created in a notebook (or on a napkin), represent the intentions of this first development team. When the system is finished, these sketches may not represent reality, and often the only way the architecture can be explained is through a retrospective analysis that updates these initial designs to the delivered reality.

The initial version of a software architecture can be like a young child: whole and complete but immature and perhaps a bit unsteady. Over time, and through continued use and multiple release cycles, the architecture matures and solidifies, as both its users and its creators gain confidence in its capabilities while they understand and manage its limitations. The process is characterized by a commitment to obtaining honest feedback and responding to it by making the changes necessary for success. Of course, an immature architecture can remain immature and/or stagnate altogether without feedback. The biggest determinant is usually the market.

I've been fortunate to have been part of creating several new product architectures from scratch, and I've learned that the way architecture is actually created is a bit different from the recommendations of many books. These books tell us that when the system is completely new and the problem terrain is somewhat unfamiliar, designers should, for example, "explore alternative architectures to see what works best." This is sensible advice. It is also virtually useless.

There are many reasons that this advice is useless, but three of them dominate. Any one can be strong enough to prevent the exploration of alternatives, but all three are usually present at the same time, each working in its own way, sometimes in conjunction with the others, to motivate a different and more pragmatic approach to creating a software architecture. These forces are not bad—they just *are*.

The first force is the lack of time in a commercial endeavor to truly explore alternatives. Time really is money, and unless the first version is an utter disaster, the team will almost certainly need to ship the result. They won't be able to wait! The strength of this force usually results in hiring practices that demand that the architect of the initial system have sufficient experience to make the right decisions without having to explore alternatives. In other words, hire someone who has already explored alternatives in a different job.

The second force, and one that is considerably stronger than the first, is the nature of the problem and its surrounding context, which dictate a relatively small set of sensible architectural choices. A high-volume, high-speed, Web site is going to have a relatively standard architecture. An operating system will have a slightly different but no less "standard" architecture. There probably isn't a lot of value in exploring radically

When You Know It's Going to Fail

As you gain experience with different architectures, you can sometimes spot disastrous architectural choices before they are implemented. Then you can either kill the proposed architecture and send the design team back to the drawing board or kill the project. Killing the project may seem a bit drastic, but sometimes this is required, especially when poor choices substantially change the new system's economic projections.

In one assignment, the engineering team decided that a full J2EE implementation was needed for a problem that a few dozen Perl scripts could have easily handled—if another part of the application was also modified. In a classic case of "resumé-driven design," the technical lead, who fancied himself an architect, managed to convince several key people in both development and product management that the J2EE implementation was the best choice. The architecture was also beset with a number of tragically flawed assumptions. My personal favorite was that CD-ROM images of up to 600Mb of data were expected to be e-mailed as attachments! In the end I became convinced that there was nothing to salvage and ultimately killed both the architecture and the project. We simply could not create and release the desired product within the necessary market window (that period of time when a product is most likely to find a receptive customer).

different high-level architectures, although there is often some use in exploring alternatives for smaller, more focused, portions of it. These explorations should be guided by the true risks facing the project, and should be carefully designed to resolve them.

The third, and strongest force, is architectural "goodness," which can only be explored through actual use of the system. Until you put the architecture into the situation it was nominally designed to handle, you don't really know if it is the right one or even if it is a good one. This process takes time, usually many years.

Patterns and Architecture

The net result of the forces just described is that the creation of the initial architecture must be grounded in a thoroughly pragmatic approach. The emerging discipline of software patterns provides such an approach. Software patterns capture known solutions to recurring problems in ways that enable you to apply that knowledge to new situations. Good patterns have been used in several systems, and the best patterns have been used in dozens or hundreds. Someone, and often, several people, have taken the time to research, understand, and carefully document the problem, and a proven way to solve it, so that others can leverage the experiences learned from systems that are known to work. A software pattern is "pre-digested" knowledge.

Architectural patterns capture fundamental structural organizations of software systems. Primarily addressing the technical aspects of architecture presented earlier in this chapter, they provide descriptions of subsystems, define their responsibilities, and clarify how they interact to solve a particular problem. By focusing on a specific class of problem, an architectural pattern helps you decide if that kind or style of architecture is right.

The pragmatic approach when creating a software architecture is to explore the various documented patterns and choose one that is addresses your situation. From there, you must tailor the architecture to meet your needs, ultimatcly realizing it in a working system. The tailoring process and the design choices made are guided by the principles described later in this chapter. If you are familiar with architectural patterns, you might want to read the remainder of this book as a way to "fill in the gaps" in each one. For example, every software architecture can benefit from a well-designed installation and upgrade process or sensibly constructed configuration files. The goal is to use all of these approaches to create and sustain winning solutions.

Architectural Evolution and Maturation: Features versus Capabilities

Although much emphasis is placed on the initial creation and early versions of an architecture, the fact is that most of us will be spending the majority of our time working within an existing architecture. How a given architecture evolves can be more fascinating and interesting than simply creating its initial version. It is through evolution that we know where we have success, especially when the evolution is based on direct customer feedback. On a personal note, I've faced my greatest managerial challenges and had my most satisfying accomplishments when I've been able to work with software teams in modifying their existing architecture to more effectively meet the needs of the marketplace and position their product for greater success.

This process, which involves both evolution and maturation, is driven by actual use of the system by customers. Many companies claim to continually request customer feedback, but the reality is that customer feedback is most actively sought, and most thoroughly processed, when planning for the system's next release. The next release, in turn, is defined by its specified required functionality as expressed in the *features* marketed to customers. Whether or not these features can be created is dependent on the underlying architecture's capabilities. The interplay of requested or desired features and the underlying capabilities required to support them is how architectures evolve over time.

What makes this interplay so interesting is that it takes place within continual technological evolution. In other words, customer feedback isn't always based on some aspect of the existing system, but can be based on an announcement about some technology that could help the customer. In fact, the source of the announcement doesn't have to be a customer, but can quite often be the development team. Regardless of the source or context, it is useful to think of architectural evolution and maturation in terms of features *and* capabilities.

A *feature* or *function* (I use the terms synonymously but prefer *feature* because features are more closely related to what you market to a customer) defines something that a product does or should do. The entire set of requested features defines the requirements of the product and can be elicited, documented/captured, and managed through any number of techniques. In case you're wondering what a feature *is*, here is a time-tested definition from *Exploring Requirements: Quality Before Design* [Weinberg and Gause, 1989]: "To test whether a requirement is actually a [feature], put the phrase 'We want the product to . . .' in front of it. Alternatively, you can say, 'The product should . . .'" This approach shows that a wide variety of requirements qualify as features. Here are a few examples:

- *Supported platforms.* "We want the product to run on Solaris 2.8 and Windows XP."
- *Use cases.* "The product should allow registering a new user."
- *Performance.* "We want the product to provide a dial tone within 100 ms of receiving the off-hook signal."

Note that, as descriptions of features, use cases have an advantage over other forms of documentation because they can put the desired feature into a specific context. The most useful context is based on the goals of the actors involved in the use case—what they are trying to accomplish. Once you know this, and you know that the system can fulfill these goals, you have the data that product management needs to create the value proposition, which informs the business, licensing, and pricing models.

Features are most easily managed when clearly prioritized by marketing, and they are best implemented when the technical dependencies between them are made clear by the development team. This is because features are usually related, in that one often requires another for its operation. As stated earlier, because the system architecture determines how easy or hard it is to implement a given feature, good architectures are those in which it is considered easy to create the features desired.

Capability refers to the underlying architecture's ability to support a related set of features. The importance of a capability emerges when marketing is repeatedly told that a class of related features, or a set of features that appear to be unrelated on the surface but are related because of technical implementation, is difficult or *impossible* to implement within the given architecture. Examples in the sidebar on page 12 illustrate this point.

The interplay between architectural maturation and evolution is a function of time and release cycle. It is uncommon for the development team to implement most or all of the desired features in the very first release, especially if the product manager specifies requested features in a well-defined, disciplined manner. If all of the desired features aren't implemented in the first release, they often come along shortly thereafter. Because there aren't a lot of customers to provide feedback, the team is likely to continue working on the leftover features from the first release and complete them in the second. The focus of the team is on completing the total set of desired features, so there is usually little time or energy spent on changing the architecture. Instead, the initial architecture matures. Certainly some changes are made to it, but they are usually fairly tame.

After the system has been in continuous operation for three or more release cycles, or for two or more years, the initial features envisioned by its creators have typically been exhausted and product managers must begin to incorporate increasing amounts of direct customer feedback into the plans for future releases. This feedback, in the form of newly desired features or substantial modifications to existing features, is likely to mark the beginning of architectural evolution, as the development team creates the necessary capabilities that provide for these features.

Of course, not all architectural evolution is driven by customer demand. Companies that proactively manage their products will look for new technologies or techniques that can give them a competitive edge. Incorporating key new technologies into your evolving architecture can give you a sustained competitive advantage. Chapter 3 discusses this in greater detail, and Appendix B includes a pattern language that shows you one way to organize this process.

Architectural maturation and evolution are cyclical, with each phase of the cycle building on the previous one. New capabilities are rarely introduced in a mature state, as it is only through actual experience that we can know their true utility. Through feedback, these capabilities mature. In extremely well-tended architectures, capabilities are removed.

There is a special situation in which the maturation/evolution cycle must be broken and where capabilities dominate the development team's discussions. This is when

Architectural Capability or Feature Agility?

In one system I managed, users could search and collaboratively organize documents into folders. New documents also arrived from external sources on a regular basis. One set of requirements that emerged concerned storing and executing predefined queries against new documents. Another set comprised the notion that when one user modified the contents of a folder another user would receive an e-mail detailing the modification. Both feature sets required the architectural capability of a *notification mechanism*. Until this capability was implemented none of the desired features could be realized.

The primary target market of this system was Fortune 2000 companies, and the original business model was based on a combination of perpetual or annual licenses accessed by a named or concurrent user. While these business models are standard in enterprise-class software, they prevented us from selling to law firms, which need to track and bill usage on a metered basis for cost recovery. Working with my product managers, we realized that we could address a new market segment if we provided support for a metered business model. Unfortunately, it was far easier to define the new business models than to implement them, as they required substantial changes to the underlying architectural capabilities. Instead of simply counting the number of named or concurrent users, the development team had to create several new capabilities, such as logging discrete events into secured log files for post processing by a billing system. Until this was done we were unable to address this newly defined market segment.

A different system I managed was responsible for creating trial versions of software. Trialware is a powerful marketing tool, created by applying special tools to software after it has been written to add persistent protection to it. Customers of this system asked for increased flexibility in setting trial parameters. Unfortunately, this seemingly simple request was not supported by the underlying architecture, and I had to initiate a major design effort to ensure that the right capabilities were added to the system.

A common example of the difference between features and capabilities is when product marketing requests that the user interface be localized in multiple languages. Each language can be captured as a separate feature and is often marketed as such, but unless the underlying architecture has the necessary capability for internationalization, supporting multiple languages can quickly become a nightmare for the entire organization. There are many other examples, especially in enterprise applications: workflow, flexible validation rules, increasing demands for customizations, to name but a few.

you must undertake a complete redesign/rewrite of an existing system. Although many factors motivate a redesign/rewrite, one universal motivator is the fact that the existing system does not have the right capabilities and adding them is too costly, either in terms of time or in terms of development resources. In this situation, make certain your architect (or architecture team) clearly captures the missing capabilities so that everyone can be certain that you're going to start with a solid new foundation.

The motivation for redesign/rewrite (the lack of underlying capabilities) often finds its roots in the delivery of new features to a growing customer base as quickly as possible. Quite simply, success can breed failure when is not properly managed.

Architectural degradation begins simply enough. When market pressures for key features are high and the needed capabilities to implement them are missing, an otherwise sensible engineering manager may be tempted to coerce the development team into implementing the requested features without the requisite architectural capabilities. Usually many justifications are provided by everyone involved: Competitors will beat the team to an important customer, or an important customer won't upgrade to the next version, delaying critically needed revenue. Making these decisions is never easy.

The almost certain outcome of this well-intentioned act is that the future cost of maintaining or enhancing new features will be quite high. Additionally, because the underlying architectural capabilities have not been added to the system, any other new features depending on them will find themselves in the same predicament. Worse yet, the cost to morale will likely reduce the effectiveness of the team, further compounding the problem—especially if the alleged "market pressures" turn out not to be so pressing.

The result is that implementing new features results in the team taking on a technical debt that must be repaid in the future.[1] The principal of this debt is the cost associated with creating the right underlying capability. It simply won't go away. The interest is the additional burden of sustaining a feature in an architecture that can't support it. This interest increases with every release and increases again as customers continue to demand new features. If things get bad enough—and they can and do—the team might eventually have to scrap the entire architecture and start over. Servicing the debt has become too high.

While sometimes there really is a critical market window and a shortcut must be taken, or you simply must implement a given feature for an important customer, more often this is just an illusion fostered by impatient and harried executives looking for a supposed quick win.

As people mature, they often become wary of taking on unnecessary financial debt. You cannot wish away debt but have to pay it. When a given set of desired functions require a significant new or modified architectural capability, avoid debt whenever you can. When it comes to implementing needed capabilities, the phrase "Pay me now or pay me later with interest and penalties" truly applies.

---

1. Ward Cunningham is the first person I know of to refer to this as technical debt.

Entropy Reduction: Paying off Technical Debt after Every Release

In the heat of battle a development team will usually need to make some compromises on the quality of the code and/or its implementation to get the product finished. It doesn't matter if this team is "agile" or not. To get the product shipped you have to focus on shipping it. This usually means making compromises (hacks, ugly code—you get the picture.).

No matter how they get into the code base, unless these compromises are removed the quality of the source base will degrade. After the product is shipped some reasonable amount of time needs to be devoted to improving the source code. I call this "entropy reduction" (ER). A development organization realizes several crucial benefits from the ER process, a few of which are itemized below in no particular order.

- It maintains a focus on source-level quality. Developers know the importance of a very fundamental level of source code quality. The company reduces risk associated with an unmaintainable code base.

- It reinforces good will in the development team. Great developers wince when they compromise the source code in order to ship the product. They'll do it, but they won't like it. If you don't let them go back and clean up, they will become "dead" to quality. If their sense of quality dies, so do your products.

- It substantially improves the maintainability and extensibility of the system.

- It allows the team to clearly understand the specific sets of behavior within the system and makes them aware of the possibilities of really changing it.

- It ensures that any inconsistencies relative to things like the coding standard are addressed.

Entropy reduction is *not* about making substantial changes to the architecture or adding lots of new features. The goal is to hold the external behavior of the system constant while improving its internal structure.

Entropy reduction is usually scheduled after a major release, roughly every 9 to 12 months for most products. Within these release cycles your team should be refactoring their source code as needed. Entropy reduction is often about handling refactorings that were postponed so that you could release your system or avoided because they were deemed too big or complex.

It is important to establish appropriate rules or guidelines when initiating an ER session. The most important is the requirement that no new features or capabilities be added during ER. To help enforce this rule, try to keep product management from becoming involved. Keep ER as a pure development activity.

Functional tests, if they exist, of course need to run. Do *not* ship the product after ER without a full and complete regression test.

Teams vary in their willingness to engage in ER. Those that embrace it are easy to manage. Those that enthusiastically embrace it may be trying to use the process to change the architecture. Be wary! Teams that have had their sense of quality and their desire to tend their architecture beaten out of them by poor management may have to be forced to do it ("I know that this ER thing sounds weird, but this is just the way that I do things, and since what we've done in the past isn't producing the results we want we're going to try something new").

Before engaging in ER the team should create and peer-review a plan that details the specific modules and/or functions they're going to improve. This is important because sometimes a team will propose changes that are a bit too big to accomplish in a one to two week period, which is the amount of time I normally allow for an ER session. To help ER run smoothly here are some best practices that have worked well for me.

- *Use code tags.* Code tags are a way of identifying sections of the source code that should be fixed in a future ER session. I've had teams use "TODO," "REDO," or even "HACK" to alert readers of the source that something should be fixed. Finding the tags is easy.

- *Establish a rhythm.* The rhythm of ongoing releases is very important to me. Successful teams develop a nice rhythm, working at a good pace during the majority of the development. It's like a brisk walk—sustainable but fun. Near the end, they work as needed, including 80-hour work weeks, to hit the release date. The sprint to the finish. After the release the team recovers. They rest or work on ER (which *should not* be mentally challenging).

- *Time-box the ER activity.* One to two weeks works best. I once tried three weeks, but the process was too hard to control—new features were being added. If you need four weeks or more for productive ER, look in the mirror and say, "The architecture is dead."

- *Don't ship the result.* You could be making changes all over your code base. Just because your automated unit tests pass, you still can't ship without a full regression test.

- *Choose your language carefully.* I've used the terms "technical debt" and "entropy reduction" to mean the same basic thing. Different people hear these words in different ways, so consider if the phrase "entropy reduction" will work for your team before you use it. If it won't, consider something else, like "technical debt payback," or "architectural improvement."

- *Use ER to reinforce other values you deem important.* You can use ER to instill a whole host of values, including source code quality, the importance of finishing on time, responsible management ("incur a little technical debt now and you'll get the time to pay it back after the release"). You can associate cultural artifacts with the first ER session, like a "chaos" game or a toy (a symbol).

> • *Don't commit unless you can deliver.* If you promise an ER session, make certain you can deliver. I almost lost all credibility in a turnaround situation when the CEO of my company told me that I couldn't do an ER session because he had promised a new feature to a key customer. It took some stringent negotiation, including a few heated meetings, but in the end we had the session before we attempted to deliver the promised feature. Avoid this pain and make certain you have appropriate senior executive buy-in for ER.

Architectural Care and Feeding

In addition to architectural maturation and evolution, which are driven by features and the capabilities that support them, the development team must also care for and feed their architecture. An architecture is like a carefully designed garden. Unless you tend it, it will soon become unruly, overgrown with the wasteful vestiges of dead code. Ignore it long enough and you'll find that your only recourse is to make massive—and very costly—changes to correct the neglect. Architectural care and feeding isn't about adding new features or capabilities; it is about keeping the features and capabilities that you've got in good shape.

Consider the following care and feeding forces that shape the architecture. Many of them are discussed in greater detail in subsequent chapters.

Technological Currency

Every complex application interacts with a wide variety of fundamental technologies. Staying current with technological advances as your product evolves ensures that you won't have to engage in expensive redesign. Technological advances are often the key to providing additional benefits to your users. The result? A double win. It doesn't hurt your marketing department either, as the phrase "new and improved" will actually mean something.

Technological Debt

Developers are constantly struggling to release the system on time while creating appropriate long-term solutions. Successful software teams know when and how to compromise on technical issues in order to hit the ship date. More bluntly, successful software teams know when they need a potentially ugly hack to get the system to a shippable state. The problem with hacks is not in the current release (which needed them to ship) but in subsequent releases, when the so-called *compromise* makes itself known, often exacting a heavy toll to fix it.

These compromises are another kind of technical debt, similar to that incurred when you implement a feature without the underlying capability. Part of architectural care and feeding is paying down this debt.

Known Bugs

Every complex application ships with bugs, which you can think of as pestiferous weeds. Leaving them in your garden, especially when they are big enough to be seen, can take an unnecessary toll on your development staff. Give them some time to fix the bugs they know about and you'll end up with happier developers—and a better architecture. You also foster a cycle of positive improvement, in which every change leaves the system in a better state.

License Compliance

Complex applications license critical components from a variety of vendors. As described above, as they upgrade their technology you respond in kind to keep pace. Of course, sometimes you may not need their new technology and are better off directing your development efforts elsewhere. Watch out though: Wait too long and you risk falling out of compliance with your component vendors. Remember to review each vendor's upgrade. Know when you must upgrade your architecture to maintain compliance. License compliance is discussed in greater detail in Chapter 5.

I invite you to add your own categories for architectural care and feeding. Be careful not to confuse radical changes in feature sets that require similarly radical changes in architectural design with the kinds of changes described above. Scaling a departmental application designed for 100 users to an enterprise application that can handle 1,000 users or converting an application whose business model is based on an annual license to one based on transaction fees is *not* the kind of architectural change I'm talking about! Such changes require fundamentally new capabilities and substantial modification of the architecture.

Principles First, Second, and Third

Creating, maturing, evolving, and sustaining an architecture are guided by the design choices made by architects and developers. All choices are not equal. Some are downright trivial and have no bearing on the architecture; others are quite profound. All software developers, and architects in particular, must hone their ability to recognize better design alternatives. This means, of course, that we must have criteria for evaluating design alternatives and that we must apply them as best we can. The following principles for good architectural design have stood the test of time.

Encapsulation

The architecture is organized around separate and relatively independent pieces that hide internal implementation details from each other. A good example is a telephone billing system. One part of the system, such as the switch, is responsible for creating, managing, and tracking phone calls. Ultimately, detailed transaction data are created for every phone call (who called whom, for how long, and so forth). These data are fed into separate billing systems, which manage the complexities of calculating a precise fee based on the contract between the telephone company and the customer.

Within each of these broadly encapsulated systems are other encapsulations that make sense. For example, the billing system is likely to have separate modules for calculating the basic bill, calculating any discounts, calculating appropriate taxes, and so forth.

Interfaces

The ways that subsystems within a larger design interact are clearly defined. Ideally, these interactions are specified in such a way that they can remain relatively stable over the life of the system. One way to accomplish this is through abstractions over the concrete implementation. Programming to the abstraction allows greater variability as implementation needs change.

Consider a program originally designed to write output to a file. Instead of programming directly to the interface provided by a file, program an output mechanism to the abstract interface, which in many languages is referred to as an output stream. This allows the program to direct output to a file stream, the standard output stream, an in-memory string stream, or any other target consistent with this interface, even, and especially, those not yet envisioned by the original developer. Of course, what is most important is defining the initial interface, something that can almost only be done well through experience.

Another area in which the principle of interfaces influences system design is the careful isolation of aspects of the system that are likely to experience the greatest amount of change behind stable interfaces. ODBC and related APIs provide an example of this principle in action. By programming to ODBC, a developer insulates the system from a common dimension of change: the specific selection of a database. Using ODBC a developer can switch relatively easily from one SQL-based database to another. Bear in mind that this flexibility comes with its own special cost—you give up the "goodies" that are present in vendor-specific APIs.

Loose Coupling

Coupling refers to the degree of interconnectedness among different pieces in a system. In general, loosely coupled pieces are easier to understand, test, reuse, and maintain, because they can be isolated from other pieces of the system. Loose coupling also promotes parallelism in the implementation schedule. Note that application of the first two principles aides loose coupling.

Appropriate Granularity

One of the key challenges associated with loose coupling concerns component granularity. By *granularity* I mean the level of work performed by a component. Loosely coupled components may be easy to understand, test, reuse, and maintain in isolation, but when they are created with too fine of a granularity, creating solutions using them can be *harder* because you have to stitch together so many to accomplish a meaningful piece of work. Appropriate granularity is determined by the task(s) associated with the component.

High Cohesion

Cohesion describes how closely related the activities within a single piece (component) or among a group of pieces are. A highly cohesive component means that its elements strongly relate to each other. We give the highest marks for cohesion to components whose elements contribute to only one task.

Parameterization

Components can be encapsulated, but this does not mean that they perform their work without some kind of parameterization or instrumentation. The most effective components perform an appropriate amount of work with the right number and kind of parameters that enable their user to adjust their operation. A sophisticated form of parameterization, referred to as "inversion of control," occurs within frameworks and plug-in architectures. This is where one component hands over processing control to another.

Deferral

Many times the development team is faced with a tough decision that cannot be made with certainty. Sometimes this is because of technical reasons, as when the team is trying to choose a library to perform a specific function and are not certain which vendor can provide the best performance. Sometimes it is because of business reasons, as when the product management team is negotiating with two or more technology providers for the best possible terms.

By deferring these decisions as long as possible, the overall development team gives themselves the best chance to make a good choice. While you can't defer a decision forever, you can quarantine its effects by using the principles of good architectural design.

Creating Architectural Understanding

Let's return to the definitions of software architecture provided earlier. An important criterion for the development team is that they have *some* way to identify, describe, communicate, and modify their understanding of the architecture, without resorting to the source code. One or more models must exist in order for the team to actually operate at the "big picture" level. There are a variety of models for doing this, and I've had good success with several of them. Recently, I adopted the Rational "4+1" model, which captures several of the most useful models in one convenient approach (see the references for other models you may wish to consider).

Based primarily on resolving the needs of key participants in the software process, the Rational 4+1 model recommends four primary views of the architecture, as shown in Figure 1-1. Philippe Kruchten, the creator of 4+1, defines these views as follows:

- *Logical view.* The logical view provides the *static* snapshot of the relationships that exist among objects or entities in the development of the system. This view may actually have two or more representations, one of the *conceptual* model and the other of the realization of the model in a database schema.

- *Process view.* The process view describes the design's concurrency and synchronization aspects.

- *Physical view.* The physical view describes the mapping of the software onto the hardware, including distribution of processing components created to achieve such goals as high availability, reliability, fault tolerance, and performance.

- *Development view.* The development view describes the software's static organization in its development environment.

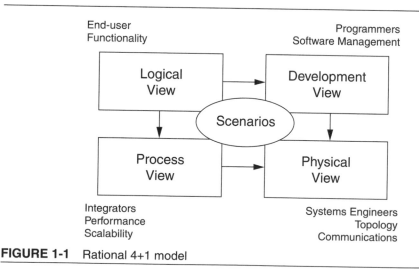

FIGURE 1-1   Rational 4+1 model

Software designers can organize their architectural decisions around the four views. To make the system easier to understand, each view can be described in the context of few key use cases (all of the use cases constitute the "+1" architectural view.

In truth, this approach should be referred to as "*n*+1", because nothing in it restricts the architect to just four views. Indeed, all of the major disciplines for representing software architectures explicitly recognize the need for multiple views for correct architecture modeling. As near as I can tell, *no one* dogmatically requires that you use exactly *three* or *five* views. Instead, they encourage you to understand the communication properties of a given view and then use this view as needed.

This shouldn't be surprising, as the concept of multiple models of complex systems is quite common. I have both built and remodeled homes and in the process have learned to carefully read the many models of the home produced by the architect—from the site plan to the electrical plan to the lighting plan to the elevations and to the plumbing plan. The specialized and skilled workers creating a home need all of these models, and to the extent possible I want to make certain that they will result in a home I will like.

The value of plans, like the various viewpoints of architecture promoted by Rational and others, is that they provide artifacts of relatively enduring value to the team. More generally, the parts of the architecture whose capture is worthy of your time, energy, and money deal with the relatively stable aspects of the problem, the problem domain, the business model (see Chapter 4), and the idiosyncratic aspects of the technical solution that exist between all of these things.

The Team

The architectural creation, maturation, and evolution process cannot be separated from the team associated with each release. In this section I will share some thoughts on the interplay between the architecture and the team. A more complete discussion can be found in my book, *Journey of the Software Professional* [Hohmann, 1996].

It is natural to first consider the initial development team. Remember that, as the creators of the first system, these people are making design choices based primarily on their experience. While subsequent teams must deal with the choices made by this first team, in some way or another, the first team has no such constraints (this is one powerful reason so many developers are drawn to working on new systems). Because of this, any new architecture, even one based on an architectural pattern, will reflect the idiosyncratic experience of its creators. The number of people involved in creating the architecture, and their relationship with each other, will also profoundly affect the initial architecture. Simply put, there is no way to isolate the team from the architecture.

Experience has shown that creation of the initial architecture should be by as small a team as possible, to minimize communication overhead and to maximize team cohesion. As subsystems are defined, planned, or retrospectively justified, the team will naturally allocate responsibilities to reflect the skills of its members. Suggestions for the initial team range from as few as three to a maximum of ten. My recommendation is three to five, with one identified as the architect, primarily to keep the team moving (see Chapter 3 for a more complete description of the role of the architect).

With the release of a successful initial architecture, the team often grows to accommodate additional requests for features and capabilities. It is natural to grow the team within the initial architecture's boundaries. Perhaps the user interface, which was once handled by one developer, is expanded to need three. Or perhaps the database, which originally could be managed by a single developer, now needs two. In this manner subteams spontaneously emerge in a way that reinforces the initial architecture. The advantage to this model is that the original team member, who is now part of the subteam, can carry over the overall design and share it with new subteam members.

The process of growing the team continues until the team and the architecture have stabilized or until some management-induced limit has been reached. Some companies limit the size of any given team to a specific number of people in order to maintain a fluid, open, and collaborative approach to communication. Other companies allow teams to grow as needed to meet the needs of the system. I consulted on one defense department contract in which the development team consisted of more than 150 C++ developers, organized into about a dozen subsystems. Although this was a fairly large team, it was extremely effective primarily because it allowed the demands of the problem to dictate its size and structure.

The most important thing to remember is that the team and the system architecture are intertwined. They affect, and are affected by, each other.

Chapter Summary

- Software architecture is focused on the *big picture*.
- The structure of the team and the structure of the system are inevitably intertwined.
- Architecture concerns both technical and nontechnical issues.
- Key reasons why architecture determines success include:
  - Longevity: The typical architecture will outlast the team that created it.
  - Stability: Stable architectures provide the foundation for features and profits.
  - Competitive advantage: Great architectures create sustainable competitive advantage.
  - Architectural patterns provide excellent places to begin when creating a new architecture.
- Architecture evolves through features and capabilities. A feature defines something that a product does or should do. A capability refers to the underlying architecture's ability to support a related set of features.

- Architectures, like gardens, require care and feeding.
- Be wary of anyone who claims they are an architect after just one release.

Check This

❑ The dependencies that exist between subsystem components are clearly identified.

❑ Each person on the team is working on a subsystem that he or she finds personally interesting.

❑ Each person on the team is working in a way believed by all to improve productivity.

❑ Our architecture is profitable.

❑ We know if our current release is focusing on issues of evolution or issues of maturation.

❑ We understand the degree of technical debt we've incurred in our system. We can identify such debt (e.g., we have placed special comments in our source code identifying areas to fix).

❑ We are in proper compliance with all in-licensed components (see also Chapter 5).

❑ The architect has articulated the principles that are driving architectural choices.

❑ Our team is about the right size to accomplish our objectives—neither too large nor too small.

Try This

1. One way to summarize my position on software architecture is that I see software architecture as *organic.* This position informs a host of management practices, including such things as spending time in each release caring for and feeding the architecture. What is your position on software architecture? How does this position affect your management practices?

2. Here is an exercise that I've found especially helpful when working with troubled development teams, because it helps me identify potential sources of confusion and/or conflict. Ask members of your team to take a plain sheet of paper and draw the architecture of the system. They have to *draw* it, meaning that they can't just fish out some diagram and print it. The drawing must be done individually, with no talking between team members. When finished, tape each of the drawings to a wall to create an "architecture gallery." What occurs to you, and each member of your team, as you review these diagrams? Do you find congruence? If not, why not?

3. Do you have a visual representation of your architecture posted in an easily viewed space? If not, why not? If yes, when was the last time it was updated?

4. Can you enumerate the capabilities of your current architecture?

5. Check out the definitions of software architecture posted at *http://www.sei.cmu.edu/*. Which of the posted definitions work best for you? Why?

6. What are the specific artifacts, or views, that you have created to describe your architecture? Why have you created them?

Chapter 2
Product Development Primer

Many software developers are at a decided disadvantage in creating winning solutions because they don't understand many basic and important concepts in product management. This chapter outlines crucial concepts and processes in product management, including defining the product manager role. If you're comfortable with these basic principles already you may find it sufficient to skim this chapter. If not, you should read it carefully.

What Is Product Management?

Like software architecture, *product management* has a variety of definitions. One that I've found useful is as follows:

> Broadly speaking, the product manager has two responsibilities. First, the product manager is responsible for planning activities related to the product or product line. Thus, the product manager's job involves analyzing the market, including customers, competitors, and the external environment, and turning this information into marketing objectives and strategies for the product. Second, the product manager must get the organization to support the marketing programs recommended in the plan. [Lehmann and Winer, 2002]

My own definition is a bit simpler: *Product management* is the comprehensive set of activities required to create and sustain winning solutions. It is like software architecture in that it is also about "the big picture." In reality, though, the big picture of product management is an even bigger picture than that of software architecture. Product managers deal with everything from pricing the product to creating data sheets, from defining and educating the sales channel to monitoring the behavior of competitors. The job is no less difficult than that of an architect and in some ways is considerably harder.

Why Product Management Matters

Perhaps I've convinced you that architecture matters. Now a potentially more difficult task is convincing you that product management matters. I'm hopeful that I can do this, because product management is as at least as important as software architecture, if not more so.

Let me start with the blunt approach: Technology alone doesn't win. That you're first, fastest, best, coolest, or "obvious" does not mean that you will win in the market. Product management matters because simply building the technically right product isn't enough. A host of complex and interrelated activities, from establishing pricing models to building useful partnerships, is needed to ensure total product success. If any one of these vital activities are weak, the product is at risk of failure.

Successful product management provides the same benefits as a successful software architecture. Chief among these is profitability, in that successful product management will create truly profitable products and companies. Unlike software, where terminated projects are considered failures, successful product managers routinely subject projects to rigorous examination and terminate those that are no longer likely to meet business objectives. What I find most appealing in this approach is that product managers are proactive in terminating projects, whereas many software project managers and architects tend to be reactive—perfectly willing to continue working on a poor project until someone else kills it—and it doesn't have to be this way. This is a topic I will explore later in this chapter.

Perhaps the most important reason that product management matters, especially from the perspective of the architect and the development team, is that it should represent the voice of the customer. Good product managers engage in many activities, including direct and indirect market research, that put them in a position to guide the development organization. When you ask them what the customer needs, they can answer. And because their answer is rooted in data and experience, you can believe them and act on their advice in building the system. In practice, these data are captured and expressed in such things as business plans and marketing requirements documents (MRDs). However, before the MRD is created or the system is built, the successful product manager will have already completed several steps in a successful product development process. Before considering some of the important documents associated with successful product management, let's review this process.

Product Development Processes: Creating Release 1.0

The product development process is the biggest big-picture perspective on the product. My experience is that software development processes, from waterfall to spiral to XP, are each more effective when considered and conducted in this context. This section presents a conceptual foundation of a successful product development process associated with a first release. In the next section, I will show how this foundation can be used to deal with subsequent releases.

The process presented in Figure 2-1 organizes product development in stages. These stages, and some of the product management and engineering activities associated with each, are presented to the right. I'm focusing only on product management and engineering. Other activities such as finance, legal, quality assurance, and techni-

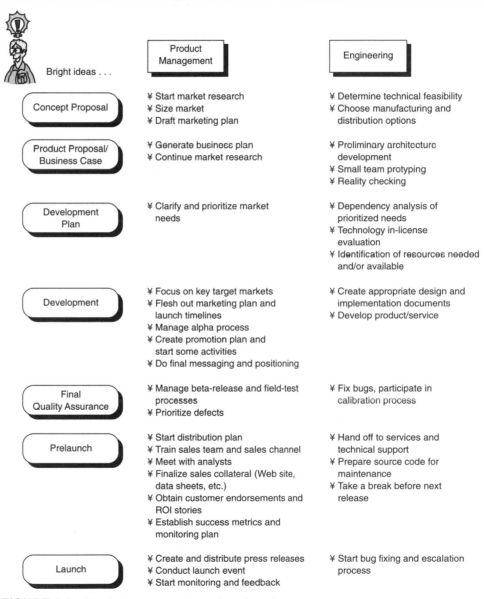

FIGURE 2-1　Product management and engineering processes

cal publications, are clearly important to the overall product development process, but a detailed description of their involvement is beyond the scope of this book.

As you review these steps, keep in mind that the actual sizes of the product management and engineering teams are quite different. A product management team is usually very small compared to the total engineering/development team. I've worked on products where two to four product managers were easily able to keep 30 to 40 developers busy. Some of my friends report even greater variability. One friend told me about a product manager who was able to keep a team of 50 developers satisfied.

Another key difference concerns the distribution of work. In the early phases of the project, product management may be perceived as doing more work than engineering. This is partly because the product management team is producing more tangible results, but mostly because, in a well-run product development process, the early documents created by the product management team are the "high stakes" ones. Many decisions, including those that will affect the product for many years, are being made during the development of these early documents, most notably the business plan. Taking care to create good ones is worth the results.

Bright clever ideas form the foundation of the initial product. The best of these fill us with enough passion to take the considerable leap necessary to create a product. Some companies actually formalize this aspect of the overall process in a subprocess called *ideation*.

Concept Proposal

The purpose of the concept proposal is to establish sufficient motivation for producing the product. Usually created by a small team, the concept proposal includes enough business data to justify the market and enough technical data to justify feasibility. If neither of these conditions is met, the project is gracefully terminated, in a process I describe in greater detail later in this chapter.

Product Proposal/Business Plan

The product proposal/business plan is the *key* document created by the team to justify the product. It outlines a number of important elements so that the business can be certain that the project is justified. It is so important that I will discuss it in depth later. Note that during this phase of product development it is not uncommon for engineering to be doing literally nothing while marketing is creating the business plan.

Development Plan

After approval of the business plan, the two teams begin the highly collaborative development planning. In this phase, the primary responsibility of marketing is to clarify and prioritize market needs, expressing them as desired features of the target product. In turn, the primary job of engineering is to analyze the dependencies within these features, identify necessary architectural capabilities, create some crude estimates of time required to complete various tasks, evaluate technology solutions, and begin to identify needed resources. Marketing should also take primary responsibility for including other teams, as needed, in the development of the product.

The results of this process can range from a formal marketing requirements document (MRD) to an informal set of user stories written on cards and taped to a wall. Indeed, in one system I managed we generated requirements by simply directing questions to a very experienced member of the team, secure in our knowledge that this person would answer each question with unfailing consistency. This was an unorthodox way to obtain and manage requirements, but it worked great. It illustrates that the development team should let the size of the project, the size of the team, and the complexity of the product dictate the formality of the development planning process. Regardless of its ultimate form, the true requirement of a requirement is that it be expressed with a sufficient level of clarity to enable the development team to egage in useful work.

At this point the development team will also create whatever analysis, design, or other predevelopment artifacts they feel are appropriate given their project and their chosen development process. The challenge is, of course, in determining the artifacts needed for success. Sometimes informal processes and artifacts work great, as when a development team sketches the design for a new user interface on a whiteboard using an existing system as a model. At other times formal processes and artifacts are required, as when a development team is working on a hardware device and must create a solution within a narrow set of weight, power consumption, and size constraints. Just about every development team should be conducting some experiments based on the continued advancement of various Web-based collaborative technologies. It's surprising how easy it is to improve communication within geographically distributed teams with just a Web site and a digital camera!

A useful description of design documents, and the value they provide to the team, is found in *Agile Software Development* [Cockburn 2002]. Alistair refers to design documents as the *residue* produced by the development team as they create the system. The goal is to create the minimum amount of residue needed for current and future success. I've found this perspective useful, as it helps me determine if a given design document is worth creating. That said, you must take care in your definition of "development team." My own definition explicitly *includes* technical publications and QA. These teams can both contribute to the development planning process and benefit from their inclusion in it.

Disciplined development organizations usually hold a final review meeting at this point before development begins. The purpose of this review is to assess whether the product can be created within time and cost estimates and to kill the project if it cannot. While it is relatively rare to find organizations killing projects after this stage (most are killed after the concept proposal; many, after the business plan), a well-run product management organization will stop work when it becomes clear that the product cannot be created in a way that will make it a winning solution.

Development

The next phase of the process deals with actually building the system. I find this stage interesting because product management now focuses its attention on what happens *after* the product is released—before it is even built. Engineering, on the other hand, is actually creating the product. There are a wide variety of options, here, including traditional development methods and the newer agile methods, such as XP, SCRUM, and Crystal, but since many authors have written a great deal about development and development processes, I won't go into the details. What I will say is that you should adjust your development process according to a variety of factors, including the size of the team and its geographical distribution and the nature of the product. A complete discussion of how these, and other, variables can affect the team and its processes, can be found in my book, *Journey of the Software Professional.*

Modern development practices mandate that working systems should be delivered in reasonably well-defined pieces that cascade or overlap. Specifically, development *does not* happen "all at once." Instead, it is staggered or overlapped so that working versions of the system can be delivered to QA, technical publications, alpha testers, key customers, and other important stakeholders. One example of overlap is when a working system is given to QA to perform initial testing and to refine final test plans while the development team continues to work on the next set of deliverables.

Final Quality Assurance

The next key phase of the development process is final quality assurance, which comprises a range of activities, each providing a different kind of business value. The foundation is testing—that is, checking that the system created reasonably matches the requirements and providing the product manager with data to help her determine if the system is good enough to ship to the customer. These data include bug trends, bug reports, workarounds for known problems, and so forth, which the product manager uses, along with other data, to make the ultimate business decision: when to ship and to whom. This decision should be made in collaboration with others involved in the development process.

I've been fortunate to work with world-class quality assurance managers. Building on the solid foundation of testing, they understand business strategy and can actively participate in the ship decision. If you're similarly fortunate, learn to include QA's point of view. If not, try to educate your team on the business issues surrounding the product—in the long run you'll get better results.

Quality assurance teams can contribute to development areas beyond testing, such as the following:

- Monitoring and, at times, enforcing development process agreements
- Collecting and publishing testing and nontesting metrics

- Assisting developers in root-cause problem analysis (some problems only appear during testing)
- Helping support and services organizations understand workarounds and/or replicate customer issues
- Managing the source code system and the daily build process, especially when the build process is highly dependent on automation
- Assisting developers in proactively designing the application to make testing easier and/or helping to choose designs that are likely to be more correct
- Participating in the requirements management process, including testing the requirements

Participation in these areas is not concerned with final quality assurance, which is only one part of product development. Rather, they represent the broadening of QA's role and its inclusion in other development processes. Ultimately, QA participation in any of these activities depends on the specific skills and experiences of the QA team.

Since modern development requires QA involvement, you might argue against the need for final quality assurance. This sounds good in theory, but every complex system that I've worked on has required final quality assurance before delivery to a customer. Instead of trying to eliminate final quality assurance through developer-centric automated testing, leverage this testing with final QA. The net result is higher quality.

Beware of QA Automation Blinders

I'm a strong proponent of the agile development methods, especially those such as XP, that place a heavy emphasis on test driven design. In this approach, developers create test cases *before* they write any code. As the code is created it is constantly run against these test cases. By the time you've released the system the typical team will have created several thousand test cases for a moderately complex system.

Unfortunately, some people believe that test driven design and extensive, automated tests make the need for final quality assurance obsolete. This is a dubious claim, and as the complexity of your software system increases so, too, does the need for final quality assurance for several reasons, including the inevitable blinders that QA automation puts on your developers.

To illustrate, one of the products I managed protected software from being illegally copied by binding the software to a given machine through a "hardware fingerprint." The exact composition of the fingerprint is proprietary, but it includes several physical machine parameters that can collectively identify a machine while allowing the end user to modify several of them (e.g., the processor id or the amount of physical memory). Changing just one or two of these won't invalidate the fingerprint, but change enough of them and the software will stop working to prevent piracy.

One of the values used in the fingerprint is the MAC address of the primary Ethernet card. In a Macintosh, this is supposed to be built-in, so my developers created a series of automated tests to ensure the MAC address was always present. They never thought of actually removing the NIC card because they had automation blinders on. Our QA team was able to crash the program in about 10 minutes by simply removing the NIC card and running the automated tests, primarily because they were not wearing automation blinders. More generally, the process of creating and testing the machine fingerprint is characterized by a rather large number of tests that *cannot* be automated. In these cases, final QA is essential because they aren't blinded by automation, and they were willing to take the time to create the necessary physical configurations needed to properly certify the product.

There are other equally important reasons to engage final QA. Multiplatform development requires a careful allocation of resources. What I've found works best is to have the development team create and test the software on the two or three most prevalent or most important platforms. Final QA then confirms the operation of the software on the rest. This approach saves time by saving developers from the inevitable setup and teardown costs associated with loading and testing the program on each platform, and it saves money by allowing the development organization to make a significant investment in a QC lab that can truly represent customer environments.

The importance of security in computer systems is yet another strong motivation for final QA performed by a separate organization. It is very hard to thoroughly test your own systems for such security loopholes as buffer overflows or inappropriately modifying system resources in a way that leaves them vulnerable to an attack. It is far better to have a separate QA organization perform security tests.

Prelaunch

On or near the successful completion of the system, the development process moves into the prelaunch phase. Depending on the estimated time of final quality assurance, prelaunch can happen in parallel with this phase or after. One way to characterize this phase is that the work of the engineering team begins to decrease while that of product management begin to increase. The engineering team prepares to hand its work to services and support, prepares the source code for maintenance and future development, and often takes a short break to catch up on sleep. Product management, on the other hand, is often a whirlwind of activity, doing a variety of things to ensure that the product is successful in the marketplace, including everything from preparing sales collateral to meeting with key analysts to make certain they understand the new product.

Launch

While engineering often celebrates the creation of the "golden master," product management usually waits until a launch event. This may be as simple as the official press release or as complex as a special event managed by a public relations firm. A final, but critical, step in the launch phase is some kind of customer-focused monitoring and feedback. When engineering returns from the party, they should be ready to address issues and escalations coming from the field.

It Isn't Like That

Experienced readers may feel that this interpretation of the product development process has several flaws. Rather than allowing any of these flaws to prevent or distract you from reading further, let me try to address them now.

It Is a Waterfall Process and Those Don't Work

True, the process presented is reminiscent of a "waterfall", but there are several substantial differences. The most important is that the traditional waterfall described the development phase and related primarily to engineering, not product management. The stages associated with it (requirements, analysis, design, implementation, and test) rarely had sufficiently tough evaluation criteria applied to the work products to fix or address them if they were found lacking in some key measure.

Companies that have effective product development practices are most well known for the manner in which the results of each stage are subjected to strictly defined "go/kill" criteria. The overall process is referred to as "stage gate": After each stage, there is a gate, if you do not meet the gate's criteria, the project is killed. These are usually precisely defined financial criteria, which differ dramatically from the very loosely defined criteria for results of a waterfall process.

The careful examination and then termination of a project are what most strongly distinguish a stage gate process from a waterfall process. Software developers often mourn the termination of a project. Product managers who are using a stage gate process celebrate it, because it means that the overall process is working. The proof of this is that well-run product-focused companies may kill a project even during beta testing if it finds, despite prior market research and acceptable development costs, that the product does not meet the needs of the market! Examples abound in the retail sector, where countless thousands of new food products and packaging ideas are introduced into small, target markets and then killed before their launch into larger markets.

It Presents All Stages as If They Were of Equal Importance

This is not my intention. While all of the stages are important, the two most critical stages are concept proposal and product proposal/business plan. To a large extent, the results of these stages drive the rest of the process. It is product management's job to do the hard work associated with these stages to ensure lasting success, which ultimately means creating a sober, credible concept proposal and business plan that demonstrates that the proposed product can become a winning solution.

It Doesn't Detail Any Time

The amount of time associated with each stage is far too variable to make any estimates as to how long any one stage should take.

Where Is the Iteration?

When software developers think of iteration, they tend to think of iterative construction practices, like XP or SCRUM. When product managers think of iteration, they tend to think of a variety of techniques that enable them to sharply define the product before construction begins, such as primary and secondary market research, focus groups, and test marketing on prototypes. The differences and their effects are profound.

The single biggest differentiator of success in new product development is the amount of homework done before construction is initiated. A successful product will have a full and complete business plan, with clear and sharp definitions for the product, its core features, its target market, the planned-for business model, and so forth. Of course, any of these may change during construction based on new data, but before construction begins the product must be defined.

I am *not* advocating a return to waterfall construction practices, as my experience with them is that they don't work. Perhaps the following analogy will help me make my point. Imagine that you are an explorer and you've just crossed a mountain pass and entered a strange new land. You have at your disposal a variety of gear that can help you navigate mountains, valleys, deserts, rain forests, deep lakes, and fast-moving streams. You also have a small, single-person helicopter for reconnaissance. Do you just jump in and start exploring, or do you fire up the helicopter, take a look around, and plot your course?

Good explorers fire up the helicopter and plot their course. They know that to the North lies mountains, to the East is a lake, the West has a desert, the South, a rich and deep forest. Armed with this knowledge, they can plot a course: first South, then West, then East, and then, finally, North. Along the way they can prepare the gear they will need, handle issues associated with the terrain as they are navigating it, and build detailed knowledge through exploration.

The same goes for product managers. The foundational definition of a product could be 48 high-level use cases, organized in 6 groups. None of the use cases are defined in any detailed way, but their collective structure provides a coherent definition of the desired product. Before any single use case or group of use cases is constructed, the product development team (product management and engineering) detail them (generate more detailed requirements, create or update necessary design documents, and so forth) so that they can do a good job creating the system.

It Doesn't Prescribe a Development Process

That's correct: Personally, I prefer to use agile development processes. As a manager, I prefer to use the processes that my team believes will help them succeed. From the perspective of the product manager, overall product development process and decisions are usually more important than the idiosyncratic development process followed by the development team.

It Doesn't Identify the Level of Collaboration Between Groups within Stages

So what? Collaboration between product management and engineering/development is essential to creating winning solutions. There should be *constant* communication among these groups. Figure 2-1 shouldn't have to show this.

The Business Plan

The business plan distinguishes itself from all other development documents as it is the foundation for all the work associated with the product. It does not guide a specific release but an overall family or set of releases.

Product managers have to prepare a business plan that justifies the development of the system. Developers have the right to receive such a plan so that they know their efforts are not in vain. Note that the creation of the business plan usually precedes the creation of the first architecture. In this sense, then, you can expect a business plan associated with the *first* release but not necessarily *every* release.

A well-written business plan is rarely more than 15 to 20 pages and includes the kind of information shown in Table 2-1.

TABLE 2-1 Business Plan Sections

Topic / Section	Description
Executive Overview	Brief (two-paragraph) overview of the plan. A good rule of thumb is that a harried senior executive should be able to read and understand the basic contents of the business plan within five minutes.
Strategic Fit	What is to be accomplished. Show the proposed new products within the current strategy of the company. For product line extensions (or new releases of an existing system) show how the strategy is further enhanced.

TABLE 2-1 Business Plan Sections *(continued)*

Topic / Section	Description
Market Analysis	Who will buy, why they will buy, how they will use this product, and the anticipated size of the market. Describe customers by segments (e.g., researchers, lawyers). Specify target companies (Fortune 500, etc.), and the target market. Market segmentation and market analysis are so important that I will discuss them several times over the course of the book.
Financial Analysis	A simple summary of detailed financial information found later in the plan. It must address, in format and content, the criteria required by the company building the product.
Product Description	Brief description of the product, with an emphasis on target market benefits. If this is a new release, describe the most essential new functions. This is not an MRD, which details requirements, but more of an overview that demonstrates key criteria from the perspective of the marketplace.
Competitive Analysis and Product Differentiation	An overview of the competitive landscape. I find it helpful to categorize competitors and then perform a SWOT* analysis of both the category and the key competitors within it. The end result is a specific statement outlining how your product will compete.
Product Positioning	The relationship of this product to existing products and the target market. Positioning is especially important because it guides what will be conveyed to the target market through various promotional activities (discussed further later in this chapter).
Marketing Strategy	How this product will be promoted and sold. In the initial development of a business plan it is usually sufficient to state if the release is going to be a big, noisy event going to all customers or a low-key, managed event going to a specific subset (as in a patch or maintenance release).
Channel Strategy	How the product reaches customers. This section should detail such things as how the product will be sold (direct or indirect, via the Web, and so forth).
Support Model	How this product will be supported. How the customer will come up to speed on its use.
Impact Analysis	What impact this product will have on other products.
Business Model	The proposed business model, including pricing.
Revenue Forecast	A simple but believable forecast of revenue. Trust your instincts on this, and learn to cut projections in half. Most marketing plans are overly optimistic on revenue and growth.
Cost Analysis	An estimate of engineering, support, and marketing costs. Estimate both nonrecurring and recurring costs.
Critical Risks	Any risks that may prevent you from completing your objective. Include dependencies with other projects, critically needed but not as yet allocated resources, and so forth.
Product Extensions and Futures	Key extensions to this product. Show that it has a future. I recommend using a variety of roadmaps, discussed in Chapter 4 and again in Appendix A.

* A SWOT analysis details the perceived *strengths* of a given competitor, its perceived *weaknesses*, *opportunities* that your company/product can exploit, and *threats* that your competitors can make against you.

Product Development Processes: Creating Release n.n.n

As with software architecture, we spend a lot of time and energy creating the first release. In reality, however, most product development comes in subsequent releases. The primary changes to the product development process presented in the "Product Development Processes" Section are as follows.

- *The concept and product proposal are likely to be skipped.* The value of the product proposal substantially lessens as a product matures. This is because there is less work associated with identifying and targeting a given market and more work associated with identifying how to acquire the next adopter segment (see below) or the next niche within a defined market. Rigorous companies may spend some time writing a product proposal, but this is usually foregone in favor of the MRD.

- *The business plan is, at best, updated to reflect the new release.* The business plan that justified the initial development is often only marginally updated to reflect the new release. This is not a flaw but a reflection of its now higher-level, broader perspective.

- *The MRD becomes the central document of the release.* The MRD, which in the first release captured only those features essential for entering the market, becomes the central document in a subsequent release. To understand why this is so, think of the product in its full context, which can be likened to an ecosystem and includes internal and external stakeholders (developers, QA, marketing communications, partners, customers, and so forth) as well as influencers (trade press, industry analysts, competitors, and so forth). The ecosystem of release 1.0 is likely to be relatively simple, especially for a technology product. The ecosystem of a successful product matures with it, and that associated with release *n.n.n* is usually considerably more complex. Furthermore, the needs of the constituent stakeholders are different, as described further below. The best document to capture these data for release n.n.n. is the MRD, not the business plan.

- *The prelaunch and launch phases vary significantly depending on the release.* Depending on the release, the prelaunch and launch phases may be more important for release *n.n.n* than for release 1.0! Consider Microsoft promoting Windows XP, Apple promoting OSX, or Sun promoting Solaris 2.8. These launches were substantially larger and "more important" than the launch of their predecessors.

Augmenting the Product Development Process

A common concern, and one that I share, is that a sensible product development process will become bogged down in useless detail or busy work. To prevent this, I've found it helpful to augment the development process described with a few key concepts and processes.

Successive Freezing

In the early stages of development I give the responsible team *maximum* flexibility in managing their work products. However, when the time comes for others to make *committed* decisions on these products, they must be *frozen*. As a result, the concept of *successively freezing* various deliverables becomes important. In this approach, various deliverables become frozen over the product lifecycle.

While product managers may examine a wide variety of markets for a proposed idea in the concept phase, they must usually narrow this down to a specific target market in the business plan. For this release, then, the target market is *frozen*. It may then be further stratified into niche markets, with the focus one niche as the target for the launch activities.

On the development side, you may choose to freeze the requirements, then the user interface, then the database schema, then the APIs that exist among subsystems, and finally the code itself. Note that freezing is not designed to prevent change. Instead, the term "frozen" describes a decision that can only change through a relatively formal change-control process, described next.

Change Management Protocols

Change protocols refer to the degree of formality associated with changing a given outcome. The most lenient change protocol is *none*. An example of this is when a developer is free to check out source code, make changes to it, and check it back in to the source management system. A formal change management protocol exists when a proposed change must be approved by a committee.

I've found that many developers become uncomfortable with change management protocols. This is because they often misunderstand their fundamental purpose. The goal *is not* to stifle creativity (as expressed in desired changes to the product) but to ensure that the right people are informed of the change before it is made so that they can properly prepare for it.

Suppose you want to change the layout of the user interface. Before it is frozen, you're free to change it as you see fit. Once frozen, changes need to be managed, if for no other reason than that you have to coordinate changes to the help system, the end user documentation, and the training materials. There might also be changes required in the automated unit tests created by QA and perhaps in updated reference materials for technical support. That's several different groups that must be notified of a potentially simple change.

More generally, the change management process must include those stakeholders affected by the change to make certain that they understand, approve, and can correctly process it. Candidates include technical publications, QA, product management, technical support, and release engineering. In product-centric organizations, change management meetings should be organized and chaired by product management. In other organizations, they should be organized and chaired by the project or program manager running the overall project.

Documentation Balance

One of the most important things that every manager must learn for herself, in her own way, is that there is simply no universal formula for creating the right set of documents needed for a given project. I've created very successful systems using agile methods and a minimum of documentation. I've also had projects fail for lack of key documentation. At times I've taken great care to build precise requirements reminiscent of a waterfall process, with the kind of success that makes you wonder why *everyone* doesn't simply adopt waterfall and be done with it. Finally, I've also produced carefully written and researched documents only to find them producing a system that no one needed or wanted.

Lest you think there is no hope and just randomly pick a process, here are two guidelines that have worked well for me. Early releases should be created using as agile a process as possible. While you and your team may have a lot of experience in the problem domain, you don't have experience with your new product, how your target market and competitors will respond to your offering, or whether or not the business model you've chosen is the best one. Agile processes are often the best way to maximize market feedback. Over time, as the product solidifies and the market matures, you're going to spend more time responding to the needs of the market, including the need for reliability and predictability in deliverables. Thus, development organizations with mature products often find a transition from agile to more formal methods to be appropriate. This transition may sound easy, but it isn't, and many organizations face severe, and sometimes fatal, challenges in making it.

It is vitally important to understand how your team wishes to develop their product. Surprisingly, I've worked with teams that completely reject agile methods because they consider them the domain of "hacks" who don't know how to specify and build reliable software systems. These teams demand MRDs and related documents; they have a process and they follow it. As you can guess, I adjust my own preference for agile processes to meet their needs. Forcing a given team to adopt an approach that they don't believe in, either in their development process or in the language they're using to create the system, is a certain recipe for failure.

Recycle Bin

At several points during the project the team may find that they've bitten off more than they can chew. Rather than throw out potentially useful ideas, I recommend creating a *recycle bin* where they can be stored for future use. A given idea may resurface in a later release or in a future iteration. In a sense, the recycle bin also functions as a *pressure valve*, reducing (at times) the pressure felt by the development team to get every requested feature into the release.

Crucial Product Management Concepts

This section addresses some vitally important concepts in product management and product marketing, some of which will be referenced in future chapters. All of them are useful because they affect, in very serious ways, your system and its architecture.

The Four Ps of Marketing

The activities involved in product management are often summarized as the *Four Ps of Marketing*. You may encounter them when working with product management, so it is useful to understand what they mean.

Product (Offering)

What you're offering to your customer. It could be a product or it could be a service; most likely, it is some combination of the two. Later in this chapter, and in Chapter 3, we'll discuss the product concept in greater depth.

Price (and the Business Model)

Your *business model* is the manner in which you charge customers for your products or services—the way you make money. A *pricing model* defines how much you will charge. Selecting a business model and defining its associated pricing model are among the most challenging areas of product management.

The best business models charge customers in a way that is congruent with the value customers perceive with the product. The best pricing models maximize the revenue for the company without leaving customers feeling that they've paid too much. Charge too little and you're leaving money on the table; charge too much and your product won't grow and you leave yourself vulnerable to a competitor. Pricing can also be counter-intuitive. It is not correlated to technical difficulty. Features that may be difficult to implement, like a sophisticated user interface or a report generator, are not always those that you can charge for. Pricing is not easily correlated to cost. It may cost you a lot of money to license a search engine, an embedded database, or a realtime operating system, but chances are you won't be able to pass these costs directly on to your customer. Instead, they will become buried in your pricing model.

Effective pricing is related to the perceived value of your product. The implications of this are profound and deal more with psychology than technology. A complete discussion of pricing, which may or may not affect your architecture, is beyond the scope of this book. However, business models, which form the foundation of pricing, are intimately associated with your architecture and are discussed extensively in Chapter 4.

Place (Distribution Channel)

The manner in which your product or offering is delivered to your customer. There are several perspectives on the channel for software products. One concerns how the bits are delivered to the customer (e.g., via the Web or perhaps on a DVD). Another perspective concerns who is authorized to offer the product/service to a customer. Consider an enterprise application that can be deployed at a customer's site or through a third-party service provider. In this case, the service provider is acting as a channel for the product. All of these choices affect your system architecture.

Promotion (Advertising and Marketing Communication)

Promotion refers to the full set of activities associated with increasing awareness of your product within your target market. It is often easiest to think of it as just advertising, because advertising is arguably the most exciting promotional activity. When you put aside sheer excitement, however, other promotional activities are often more important.

Total Available Market, Total Addressable Market, and Market Segmentation

The *total available market* is *all* of the customers who could possibly use your good or service. The *total addressable market* is the subset of the total available market that you can reach. An effective marketing program will further divide the total addressable market into well-defined market segments. A *market segment* is a group of customers who share specific characteristics, chief of which is that they must communicate with each other. A very effective marketing program may further divide market segments into *niche markets*, which allow for narrowly targeted promotion and sales activities.

Here is an example of these concepts in action. Let's suppose you have created a Web-based self-service benefits management system that allows employees to manage their 401K, health care, vacation, and other benefits. Your total available market is all of those companies that could possibly use this system (presumably, a large one). These companies will range from extremely large (Fortune 500) to very small (less than $5M in revenue).

The requirements associated with these companies are very different. As a result, you may choose to define one market segment as public companies with between $25M and $50M in annual revenue. This influences all aspects of the marketing mix, including pricing, promotion, distribution, product, and sales models.

Unfortunately, this market segment is probably too large to service in the early releases of the product. Narrowing further, you might define one or more niches within it. One common approach is to divide based on vertical industries: pharmaceuticals, automotive, chemical, technology hardware, technology software, and so forth. Another is to divide based on the strengths of your product relative to your competitors'. Suppose you're creating a new e-mail client that has been extensively usability tested for novice users and that also has extensive anti-spam controls. Chances are good that your competitors are targeting this market and, by virtue of their longevity, claim that they are the most user friendly. By segmenting the market into people who care about spam, you can differentiate yourself from your competitors by promoting your anti-spam features, thereby creating and owning a market niche. Once you've achieved success in this niche, you can expand into others.

The S-Shaped Curve of Adoption

Countless studies have found that the adoption of new products, generally referred to as *innovations*, follows the S-shaped curve shown Figure 2-2. An innovation doesn't just mean a "new" product, but also includes new releases or new versions of existing products. Parts of this curve have been labeled to reflect common characteristics of adopter categories. Understanding these categories can help product management and associated marketing functions change the shape of the curve, which varies tremendously by innovation type. Simply put, some innovations are adopted much more rapidly than others. The differences between categories are not perfectly defined, but they do represent generalizations that accurately characterize the willingness of a given person to adopt an innovation. As will be addressed throughout this book, various adopter categories place quite different demands on your system and its architecture. Understanding adopter category differences will help you meet these demands and accelerate adoption of your solution.

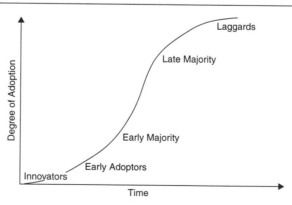

FIGURE 2-2   The S-shaped curve of adoption

Innovators

The very first individuals to adopt an innovation are known as *innovators*. These people are usually more technically curious and enjoy "pushing the boundary" with new products and services. They often have the necessary resources at their disposal to "make" an innovation work. Innovators are tolerant of poor installation and integration features and a lack of training, documentation, and help systems. Unfortunately, early wins with innovators may create a false sense of security that the product is "ready for prime time" when it really isn't. The early majority category is likely to demand that the same system accepted by the innovators have good installation procedures and some integration features and some training, documentation, and help.

Early Adopters

Following the innovators are the early adopters. While they also like pushing the envelope, they are more conservative. Because they are more conservative, they expect a more "complete" product, and are more demanding on every facet of the proposed solution. Meeting these increased demands is worth the effort, as early adopters are key predictors for overall success. If *they* can be convinced of the innovation's merits, chances are good you've got the foundation of a winning solution. If they can't, you probably don't. Closing the gap between innovators and early adopters is referred to as *crossing the chasm*, which is also the title of the influential marketing book written by Geoffrey Moore.

Early Majority

Close on the heels of the early adopters are the early majority. As you might expect, these individuals are considerably more conservative than the innovators and still more conservative that the early adopters. This is not necessarily bad, for this portion of the curve is often when the price/performance associated with the new product becomes most favorable. The earliest of the early majority often find the greatest competitive advantage: Most of the major kinks have been worked out, and they should be getting a fairly reliable product. From the perspective of product management, arguably the most important aspect of the early majority is that they will require references to key early adopters to be assured that the product works. This includes such things as customer success stories and ROI (return on investment) analyses.

Late Majority

The late majority are reluctant to adopt a new product, preferring tried and true mechanisms for dealing with problems. In fact, they may only adopt under significant economic pressure. Unfortunately, adopting this late in the process often results in the late majority receiving far fewer economic advantages than the early majority.

Laggards

Individuals who wait the longest to adopt an innovation are characterized as laggards. In general, they have the lowest social and economic status of all adopter categories. By adopting so late they derive little, if any, economic benefit from the innovation.

These broad categories represent a relationship between an individual and a given innovation. They are not universal labels but convenient tools for understanding the behavior of key market segments. It is important to remember that innovations are adopted primarily because of their perceived effects on current problems. You might quickly adopt a new release of your favorite compiler in the middle of a project, especially if this compiler provides a much-needed bug fix or new feature. In marketing terms, you're an innovator. Alternatively, if the new release fails to address any specific problems, it is far safer and cheaper to stick with the current compiler, which categorizes you as a member of one of the other adopter categories.

The categories define not only adopters but also the maturation process associated with entire markets. As of the writing of this book, the CDMA-based cell phone market is mature, while the 3G-based market is just emerging. Within these markets the adopter categories exist. In subsequent chapters I will refer to both markets and adopter categories in the context of creating and sustaining winning solutions.

The Whole Product

The concept of a "whole product" helps product managers create the full range of solutions required for success in the marketplace. Consider a common product, such as a cell phone. The *generic product* is the cell phone, a device that enables us to conveniently make phone calls. But, as anyone who has one knows, it must be augmented in a variety of ways before it becomes truly useful. For example, if you're unable to receive a call the cell phone service provider almost always provides you with voice mail. This is the *expected product*, which is commonly defined as the smallest configuration of products and services necessary to minimally meet customer expectations.

Moving beyond these minimal expectations is where real value and customer loyalty can be created. An example is a cell phone that allows you to pay online with a credit card or one that has a visible indicator of how many minutes remain on your monthly plan. This is what's known as an *augmented product*, or one that has been designed with a variety of "extras" to provide the maximum value.

These small ideas are just a few of the things I'd like in my cell phone plan. Surely you can think of others. If we enumerated these ideas, we'd have a definition of the true *potential product* that would exist for cell phone users: the full set of creative ideas that continues our product's growth and expands its market.

The four product concepts collectively represent the "whole product." When applied to the world of technology, they reveal some surprising insights. While the generic product might be the application, we expect that it will be relatively easy to install, that it will operate in a manner that is consistent with other applications on our chosen platform, and that it will have basic online reference materials. Augmenting this product with an extensible API or including sophisticated operation and analysis capabilities may make us very happy. All of these capabilities are supported, directly or indirectly, through the choices made in the overall architecture of the system.

Marketing types often use the term *whole product* when they should be using *expected product* or *augmented product*. Unfortunately, this can cause confusion, because the perception of the generic, expected, augmented, or potential product changes over time as technology and markets mature. To make the distinction clear, I use the term *target product* to define what is being created and offered to a given target market. In the early stages of the market, the target product may consist primarily of the generic product, but as the market matures the target product must evolve because the majority of customers are unwilling to accept anything less than the expected or augmented product. The target product is related to a specific release, but the terms are not synonymous. For example, it may include specific choices made regarding business models or support that do not directly relate to the system as it is delivered to your customer.

Technical versus Market Superiority

Product managers love the idea of *superiority* because they can exploit it to create unfair advantages in a given market and thereby dominate it. However, there are various kinds of superiority, not all of which translate into a winning solution. Technical superiority is often easily duplicated, unless protected by patents, trade secrets, or other forms of intellectual property protection. Market superiority can be stronger, consisting of everything from a brand name to a distribution channel. A well-known example of market superiority is Microsoft's OEM contracts, which have resulted in Microsoft operating systems being installed by default in the vast majority of personal computers.

Position and Positioning

Your *position* is a sober, objective, and accurate assessment of how your customers currently categorize or perceive your product. It is their point of view, not yours. It is objective, which means that, if your customers think your product is hard to use, it is.

Positioning is a strategic, managed effort to create and defend a distinctive concept that your customer can care about and remember. Unlike position, which is about the present, positioning is about the future.

Marketing people care about position versus positioning because the goal of positioning is to have potential customers naturally think of your product/service before all others. Consider 7-Up, a lemon-lime soft drink. Common sense might have tried to position it as the freshest lemon-lime soft drink or the most sparkling or the first, the best, or the most lively or the lemon-lime drink for the young at heart. Uncommon sense decided to get 7-Up off that battlefield and to hitch its star to the thriving cola category: "We're not lemon-lime soda, we're the Uncola."

In technical markets positioning can matter more than position, because purchasing decisions are not controlled by rational thought. Instead, most are driven first and foremost by emotions and only later backed up with objective "facts" that support the

The Motivational Impact of Effective Positioning

I've found a very strong correlation between a product development team in trouble and a product with ineffective or nonexistent positioning. Positioning isn't just about creating a future for your customers. To be effective, it must be about creating a compelling future for *everyone*, including the development team.

Whenever I am asked to work with an engineering team I inevitably end up with the product management team (and vice versa!). My experience goes something like this. The development team can fairly quickly create a position, for they know the good and the bad of their product (although struggling teams spend a disproportionate amount of their time focusing on the bad). They can't tell me their positioning either because they don't have one or because it isn't compelling; so I work with product management and help them create a compelling vision of the future.

Once we've done this I've found that it has a tremendous motivational impact on the development team. For perhaps the first time, they know they are going to be creating a future that their customers care about—a future they can live in for quite some time because it is strategic and defensible and not based on a fleeting set of easily duplicated features.

It can be difficult to create a "motivational" positioning from scratch. If you find yourself stuck, try filling in the blanks in this "classic" positioning statement formula to get yourself started.

For	\<target customer\>
Who	\<compelling reason to buy\>
Our product is	\<product category\>
That	\<key benefit\>
Unlike	\<main competitor\>
Our product	\<key differentiation\>

Applying this formula to the fictitious benefits management system described earlier, we might create something like the following: *For hospitals with 250 to 1,000 employees who are finding benefits management costs to be increasing each year, our product is a self-service, Web-based benefits management system, that, unlike traditional mainframe-based benefits systems, provides easy, low-cost, and universal access to all benefits management functions.*

emotions. Consider your own behavior when making a purchase. Do you really go with *Consumer Reports* when it recommends a product or company you've never heard of? Or, like most of us, do you go with the product or company that has positioned itself as the leader?

It follows that positioning is rarely, if ever, feature based. It is far better to own a meaningful and relevant benefit in the customer's mind than to own a temporary advantage in features. Positioning is long term, strategic, defensible, and ownable. Features are short term and can be duplicated. This means that successful positioning can focus on only one concept one that is narrow enough to be compelling and broad enough to allow for the future.

Once positioning has been set, you must continually create and recreate a position that moves you toward this goal. If not, your positioning quickly becomes meaningless and loses all value in the mind of the customer.

Brand

Your brand is the promise you make to a customer—it is why people care. *Everything* you and your company do is reflected in it. This includes partnerships, customer support, the nature and structure of the company's Web site, the quality of the goods and services it provides to customers, and the manner in which it manages profits. To illustrate the importance of brand, consider the differences that come to mind when I compare Mercedes and Hyundai, Coke and Pepsi, or Microsoft and Sun. This is one reason that brand management is a very important part of product and marketing managers' job functions.

Brands are usually represented and communicated through a number of brand elements: terms, symbols, slogans, and names. Brand elements are often protected as intellectual property, notably by trademarks and copyrights. The impact of brand elements on creating a winning solution and their effects of software architecture are discussed in Chapter 9.

The Main Message

Your main message is a short (one- or two-phrase) statement that creatively captures the positioning. It should provide a continually useful bridge between your position and your positioning, reinforcing the positioning while making certain your customer "gets" what you're saying. The main message is important because it drives all creative marketing communication activities, from press releases to advertisements.

The main message should be customer-centric. Unfortunately, the number of times this simple and pretty much obvious advice is not followed is surprising. Too often, messaging for technology products becomes shrouded in technical jargon, which often prevents the message from reaching its intended market. There are times when highly technical messaging does work, but like all good messaging it is what a customer "has ears to hear" that is the true foundation of a good message. Great messages express an important benefit, telling customers why they should care or how the product will solve their headaches. Finally, any specific message that is delivered to customers must be accurate and truly supported by the product.

Chapter Summary

- Product management is the comprehensive set of activities required to create and sustain winning solutions.

- Creating the first version of a software product begins with a concept proposal that justifies the product and ends with a launch plan. These processes are larger and more comprehensive than similar software development processes. The processes for creating subsequent releases are lighter and build upon the materials created during the first release.

- Well-run product development processes are characterized by a stringent "go/kill" decision at every stage. They are augmented and improved by successive freezing, change management protocols, and an idea recycle bin.

- The business plan is the central document that justifies a product's ongoing development.

- The four Ps of marketing are: product (offering), price (and the business model), place (distribution), and promotion (advertising, marketing communications).

- The total available market is all of the customers who could possibly use your good or service.

- The total addressable market is the subset of the total available market that you can reach.

- A market segment is a group of customers who share specific characteristics, chief of which is that they must communicate with each other.

- The adoption of innovations, such as a new product or the new release of an existing product, follows an S-shaped curve. Key adopter categories within this curve are the innovators, the early adopters, the early majority, the late majority, and the laggards.

- The concept of the whole product comprises the generic product, the expected product, the augmented product, and the potential product. The target product is the specific product being offered to a specific market segment.

- *Position* is an objective and accurate assessment of how your customers currently categorize or perceive your product. *Positioning* is a strategic, managed effort to create and defend a distinctive concept that your customer can care about and remember. Your "main message" is a short (one- or two-phrase) statement that creatively captures positioning.

■ Your brand is the promise you make to a customer—It is why people care. *Everything* you and your company do is reflected in its brand.

Check This

❑ We have defined some mechanism for capturing requirements.

❑ Product management represents the "voice of the customer."

❑ There is a way to kill a project or product in our company.

❑ We understand what our competitors are doing. We know what we need to do to win.

❑ We understand for whom we are building our product and to whom we are selling.

❑ We have a useful change management protocol.

Try This

1. Who is playing the role of product manager? When was the last time you ate lunch with this person?

2. Who is playing the role of program manager? When was the last time you ate lunch with this person?

3. It might seem convenient to think that a given person is *always* an innovator or a member of the early majority. Fortunately, this is not true. Each of us has a unique response to an innovation (some new product or service). Sometimes we're innovators, sometimes members of the late majority, and sometimes we don't adopt an innovation *at all* even if we're members of the target market. Name at least one innovation in which you were an innovator, an early adopter, a member of the early majority, a member of the late majority, or a laggard, and did not adopt at all. If you're having trouble with this question, ask yourself, Have I purchased a DVD player? If yes, when? Have I purchased a cell phone? If yes, when? When was the last time I downloaded a file from a peer-to-peer Web site? Have I purchased freeze-dried food in the last 12 months?

4. Get a copy of your current position, positioning, and messaging statements from product management. Critically examine each. Do you think your position statement describes your product with integrity and accuracy? Why or why not? Is your positioning statement credible, true, unique, ownable, simple, relevant, memorable, sustainable? Does it paint a future you'd like to create? Is your message short and direct? Does it creatively link your position and your positioning?

5. The essence of a brand is captured in one word or a short phrase: Mercedes means *prestige* while BMW means *professional driving*. What is your brand? How does it compare to what you think of your product?

Chapter 3

The Difference between Marketecture and Tarchitecture

Chapter 1 presented an overview of software architecture. Chapter 2 followed with a discussion of product management. This chapter returns to architecture and clarifies how the marketing and technical aspects of the system work together to achieve business objectives.

Who Is Responsible for What?

Software systems can be divided architecturally along two broad dimensions. The first is the *marketecture*, or the "marketing architecture." The second is the *tarchitecture*, or the "technical architecture." I refer to the traditional software architect or chief technologist as the *tarchitect* and the product marketing manager, business manager, or program manager responsible for the system as the *marketect*.

The *tarchitecture* is the dominant frame of reference when developers think of a system's architecture. For software systems it encompasses subsystems, interfaces, distribution of processing responsibilities among processing elements, threading models, and so forth. As discussed in Chapter 1, in recent years several authors have documented distinct styles or patterns of tarchitecture. These include client/server, pipeline, embedded systems, and blackboards, to name a few. Some descriptions offer examples of where these systems are most appropriately applied.

Marketecture is the business perspective of the system's architecture. It embodies the complete business model, including the licensing and selling models, value propositions, technical details relevant to the customer, data sheets, competitive differentiation, brand elements, the mental model marketing is attempting to create for the customer, and the system's specific business objectives. Marketecture includes—as a necessary component for shared collaboration between the marketects, tarchitects, and developers—descriptions of functionality that are commonly included in marketing requirements documents (MRDs), use cases, and so forth. Many times the term *whole product* is used to mean marketecture.

The $50,000 Boolean Flag

One "heavy client" client/server architecture I helped create had a marketing requirement for "modular" extension of system functionality. Its primary objective was that each module be separately priced and licensed to customers. The business model was that, for each desired option, customers purchase a module for the server that provided the necessary core functionality. Each client would then install a separately licensed plug-in to access this functionality. In this manner, "modules" resided at both the server and client level. One example was the "extended reporting module"—a set of reports, views, and related database extract code that a customer could license for an additional fee. In terms of our pricing schedule, modules were sold as separate line items.

Instead of creating a true module on the server, we simply built all of the code into the server and enabled/disabled various "modules" with simple Boolean flags. Product management was happy because the group could "install" and "uninstall" the module in a manner consistent with their goals and objectives for the overall business model. Engineering was happy because building one product with Boolean flags is considerably simpler than building two products and dealing with the issues that would inevitably arise regarding the installation, operation, maintenance, and upgrade of multiple components. Internally, this approach became known as the "$50,000 Boolean flag."

The inverse to this approach can also work quite nicely. In this same system, we sold a client-side COM API that was physically created as a separate DLL. This allowed us to create and distribute bug fixes, updates, and so forth, very easily; instead of upgrading a monolithic client (challenging in Microsoft-based architectures), we could simply distribute a new DLL. Marketing didn't sell the API as a separate component, but instead promoted it as an "integrated" part of the client.

Moral? Maintaining a difference between marketecture and tarchitecture gives both teams the flexibility to choose what they think is the best approach to solving a variety of technical and business problems.

Early Forces in Solution Development

A variety of technical and market forces shape a winning solution. These range from the core technologies to the competitive landscape to the maturity target market. What makes these forces so interesting is that they are always changing: Technology changes, the competitive landscape changes, markets mature, and new markets emerge.

Three particularly influential forces in the early stages of development are the *ilities*, the problem domain, and the technology base. As shown in Figure 3-1, driving, and being driven by, these forces are the target market, shown at the upper right, and the development organization, shown at the upper left. Product management is shown in the center to emphasize its collaborative, leadership role in resolving these forces.

The strength of the affinity that the target market and developers have with various forces is represented by single or double arrows. The final solution, including the marketing and technical architectures, lives in the "space" defined by all of the forces that shape its creation.

The *problem domain* is the central force in the development of a winning solution. Any given problem domain, such as *credit card transaction processing*, *automotive power systems*, or *inventory management*, immediately evokes a unique set of rules, nomenclature, procedures, workflows, and the like. Included in my definition of the *problem domain* is the ecosystem in which the solution exists, including customers, suppliers, competitors, and regulatory entities. Understanding the problem domain is a key prerequisite for both the marketect and the tarchitect if they wish build a winning solution. This is why most every development methodology places such a strong emphasis on gathering, validating, and understanding requirements as well as modeling the solution. This is also why effective product development places such an emphasis on the concept proposal and the business plan.

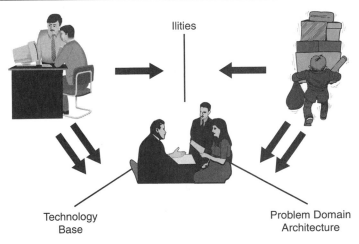

FIGURE 3-1 Forces shaping software architectures

The interplay between the marketect and the tarchitect in this process is quite interesting. Recall from Chapter 2 that the marketect's primary job is clarifying and prioritizing market needs; the tarchitect's primary job is to create a technical solution that will meet these needs. If the marketect is convinced that speed is paramount, as opposed to flexibility or usability, then the tarchitect will make certain choices that emphasize speed. Simply meeting the prioritized requirements, however, is insufficient to produce a successful tarchitecture. For this, the tarchitect must also bring his or her own domain experience to the tarchitectural design.

The requirement of extensive domain knowledge for a tarchitect is so strong that few developers can be promoted to this position until they have considerable experience and skill building systems within the specified domain. My rule of thumb is that, before someone can be considered a tarchitect, he or she must have done one of the following:

- Been a key member of a team that has created, from scratch, at least one major system in the given domain and has experienced the effects of that system through at least two full releases after the initial release (three releases total).

- Been a key member of a team that has made major architectural changes to an existing system and experienced the effects of these changes through at least two full release cycles after the changes were introduced.

You're not an architect in your very first job. You're not an architect after the first release. There is simply no substitute for sticking with a problem long enough to receive and process the feedback generated through customer use of your system. Do this long enough and you may gain sufficient experience to become an architect.

Ilities are the various quality and product attributes ascribed to the architecture. As Bass [98] points out, they fall within two broad dimensions: those discerned by observing the system at runtime and those *not* observed by observing the system at runtime. The former, including such attributes as performance and usability, are directly influenced by the target customer. The latter, such as testability and modifiability, are secondary attributes that govern the future relationship with the target customer. Because these secondary attributes are often informally specified, if they are specified at all, the discipline in tarchitectural design and associated system construction is critically important.

Care must be taken when the marketecture or marketect routinely accepts lesser *ility* attributes than those desired by the development team. When a developer wants to fix a bug or improve performance, but marketing thinks the product can be safely shipped without the fix or that the current performance is acceptable, tempers can flare, especially as you get closer to the projected release date. Keep things cool by creating forums that allow both development and marketing to express their points of view. For example, marketing needs to present arguments that a particular choice is "good enough" for the target customer.

I've found it especially helpful to have customers participate in forums. I vividly remember one customer demanding that we allow her to ship a beta version of our software three months before the scheduled delivery date. Our software was a core

---

Sometimes "The Hard Way" Is the Only Way

Most of the time the only way to learn a domain is through long-term relationships with customers. Among my responsibilities at a major digital content security provider was the creation of a backend server architecture that supported multitier distribution of software. As I learned the capabilities of the system, I also learned some of the lessons key members of the development team had learned over several years of working with major software publishers.

One of the most interesting lessons lay in the management of serial numbers. As it turns out, almost every major software vendor has a unique approach to managing serial numbers through its sales channel. Some create them in real time. Others create serial number blocks that are distributed according to predetermined algorithms to key channel participants. In this approach, the numbers are used not only for identification of shipped software but also for backend reporting and analysis. Other vendors use variants of these approaches.

Supporting every variant requires close interaction between marketects and tarchitects. In the case of this company, it was also vital to involve professional services, since they were the group that made everything "work" for a customer. It was clear to me that the only way the system could have evolved to support all of these demands was through the long-term relationships established with customers that enabled key team members to learn the problem domain.

---

component to her software. Any delays in shipping our software affected her customers. She readily acknowledged that the beta had many issues that needed to be resolved. However, its value was so compelling and her customer's need was so great that we eventually agreed to let her ship the beta subject to some strict terms and conditions regarding its use and a firm commitment to upgrade the released version when we thought it was ready.

Engineering (and especially quality assurance) needs to make certain that the risks associated with *good enough* choices are clearly understood. In the example I just mentioned, engineering provided the customer with a very clear assessment of how the product would fail outright under certain usage scenarios. This didn't change her mind—the beta still shipped—but it did enable her to equip her customer support organization with answers should these problems arisen in the field.

As described in Chapter 1, most development teams must make a variety of technical compromises in order to ship the product on time. Managing these compromises is difficult, as most compromises have their most pronounced negative effect in the release that follows the release in which they were introduced. This is another reason to demand that your tarchitect have the experience of two or more full release cycles. Only experience can help you gauge the potential severity of a technical compromise

Bug Severities, Priorities, and Normalization

One technique that I have found very effective in managing ilities is to classify bugs by severity and priority. Severity refers to the impact of the bug on the customer. Setting it to a value ranging from 1 to 5 works well, where 1 is a crash with no workaround and 5 is an enhancement request. Priority refers to the importance of fixing the problem. A five point priority scale also works well. A 1 is a bug that must be fixed as quickly as possible—such as one that breaks the build or that is required to satisfy an important customer. A 5 means "fix it when you can."

It is relatively easy to create consistency within your QA organization for severities, because they can be objectively verified. Priorities, on the other hand, are subjective. A misspelling in the user interface may get a 4 for severity, but different cultures will ascribe different priorities to fixing it. Americans and Europeans are happy to give these kinds of bugs low priorities. Japanese customers tend not to be as tolerant and give user interface bugs high priorities. Because of their subjective nature, setting priorities consistently across various members of the team can be difficult.

Fortunately, I learned how to improve prioritization consistency from one of the very best QA managers I know, James Bach. When a code freeze occurred, James would hold a bug review meeting that included all of the major stakeholders involved with the release. In this meeting he would review a sample of bugs (or all of them) to set initial priorities. Because all of the major stakeholders were represented, we could learn when and why support might prioritize a bug higher than product management would or why a senior developer would be so concerned if a certain kind of bug appeared. Although the meetings were rather long in the early part of the QA cycle, they had the advantage of "calibrating" the QA team so that they could more effectively prioritize bugs based on their collective perceptions.

These meetings worked well for our organization because we could quickly come together, review the issues, and move on. They don't work for every team, and when they go poorly a lot of time can be wasted. If you try this approach and find it isn't working, consider an alternative approach that my colleague Elisabeth Hendrickson has used: preset quality criteria.

Preset quality criteria act both as exit criteria and as a prioritization guide. Suppose you define them as MUST, SHOULD, and MAY. Any violation of a MUST is an automatic P1 bug, SHOULD violations became P2s, and so forth. You then have to define the various criteria. You might define MUST as follows:

- The system MUST support 100 concurrent users.
- The system MUST retain all data created in a previous version throughout an upgrade.

> - The system MUST present an error dialog only if the dialog contains directions on how the user can fix the problem.
>
> One advantage to this approach is that you get people thinking about priorities (both market and product) long before quality assurance is initiated. Bugs are also managed by exception, with the review committee meeting to handle those that for some reason don't seem to match the preset quality criteria.

and only a long term commitment to the integrity of the product will make absolutely certain such compromises are removed.

The technology base dimension includes the full suite of possible technologies available to the development team. These include the languages and compilers, databases, middleware, messaging, as well as any "uber-tarchitecture" associated with the system—a technical architecture that prescribes the basic structure of many classes of application and that is delivered with an extensive array of development tools to make it easy for developers to create applications within it. Examples of uber-tarchitectures include J2EE, CORBA, Sun ONE and Microsoft .NET (all of which are also marketectures, depending on your point of view).

Choices made within the technology base must support the tarchitecture as motivated by the problem domain. This can be challenging, as developers are people with their own hopes, desires, preferences, and ambitions. Unfortunately, "resumé-driven design," in which developers choose a technology because they think it's cool, is a common malady afflicting many would-be architects and a major contributor to inappropriate architectures. Marketects are also people, and "airplane magazine market research" becomes a poor substitute for the hard and often mundane but necessary market research and decision making that lead to winning solutions.

I have intentionally simplified my discussion of the early forces that shape a winning solution. If you were to ask me about a discrete force not already discussed, such as competitive pressures or requirements imposed by a regulatory agency, I would lump its effect with one associated with the problem domain, the ilities, or the underlying technology. This process is not intended to diminish the effect of this force in your specific situation. To consciously do this would be dangerous and would certainly miss the point. It is imperative that you remain vigilant in identifying the *most important* forces affecting both your marketecture and your tarchitecture.

Creating Results in the Short Run while Working in the Long Run

World-class marketects approach their task from a perspective of time that easily distinguishes them from those less skilled. Instead of listening to what customers want now (easy), they extrapolate multiple streams of data, including current requests, to envision what customers will want 18 to 24 months in the future (hard). To them, the current release is ancient history, and they often use past tense to refer to the features for the next release that are supported in the current tarchitecture as these requirements stabilize—even though this next release may be ten or more months in the future. World-class marketects know that when a feature motivates a new capability or other fundamental change to the tarchitecture they must watch it carefully, for a mistake here may not only hurt their ability to secure future customers but also harm their ability to support existing customers. Envisioning the future on behalf of customers, even when they can't articulate what they want, is the world-class marketect's key distinguishing feature.

Like their marketect counterparts, world-class tarchitects also extrapolate multiple streams of data and envision a technological future that provides superior value to their customers. One of the key reasons certain tarchitectures, such as the IP addressing scheme or the 5ESS phone switch, have provided enduring value is simply that the key tarchitects behind them envisioned a future and built for it.

Projecting the Future

If the marketect and the tarchitect pursue different visions of a future, the total system will fail. You can minimize this risk through a variety of simple diagrams that capture how you want to create your future. I will refer to these diagrams as "maps," even though they do not map what currently exists but what you want to create. These maps are reviewed briefly here and presented in greater detail as patterns in Appendix B.

The first map is the *market map*. It shows the target markets you've identified and the order in which you will create offers for them. (An offering is a bundle of one or more products or services). To make certain you can properly compete for these markets it is helpful to create a *feature/benefits map*, which shows the key features required for each identified market segment and their associated benefits. Variants of these maps are common in product development organizations. A *market events and rhythms map* helps to ensure that the timing of your product releases matches the market timing. Maintained by the marketect, but open to sharing and upgrades by all, these maps are key communication vehicles for the marketecture.

The *tarchitecture map* is the necessary equivalent of the market-related maps. It shows the natural evolution of the tarchitecture in service to the market segments, features, and benefits identified by the marketing team. Essential features that may not be supportable within the existing tarchitecture must be noted as discontinuities so that the changes needed to resolve them can be managed. Alternative, emerging technologies that hold promise for substantially improving the product and/or for opening a new market are shown so that marketects can prepare for these futures.

Examples of discontinuities abound. Consider an application originally designed for a single language. If this language becomes successful, the marketect may include internationalization in her map, but the corresponding entry in the tarchitecture map is often a major discontinuity, especially if the team is not experienced in building such applications. Another example is new business models envisioned by the marketecture. It is doubtful that the original tarchitecture was planned with them in mind, so they should be noted as tarchitectural discontinuities. In a similar vein, known problems with the tarchitecture that grate against developer sensibilities should be identified so that they can be addressed in future revisions.

Although teams can improve their performance by creating any of these maps, the best results are obtained when all are created so that they work together, as shown in Appendix B.

Harnessing Feedback

Marketects typically use the following formal and informal, external and internal feedback loops to ensure that they receive the data they need to make sound decisions:

- Organizing and/or attending user conferences (their own and competitors)
- Reviewing first- and second-line technical or product support logs
- Reviewing feature requests generated by customers
- Interviewing salespeople for features they believe would significantly improve the salability of the product (often referred to as a "win/loss analysis")
- Meeting with key customers or advisory groups
- Meeting with industry or market analysts

Tarchitects employ similar feedback loops to stay abreast of technological trends. Conferences, magazines, mailing lists, home computers, and insatiable curiosity all provide them with data.

Drawing from different data sources results in divergence between the tarchitecture and marketecture maps described in the previous section.

Fortunately, the creation and ongoing maintenance (e.g., quarterly updates) of these maps are the best ways to prevent divergence and to share data. Other helpful techniques include making the raw data that informs these maps available to both marketects and tarchitects. For example, marketects usually obtain primary market data via user conferences or focus groups. Inviting marketects to these events is a great way of reaching consensus on key issues. Marketects, in turn, should be open to reading the key technical articles that are shaping their industry or tarchitecture, and the tarchitect is a key source for such articles. Note that my goal isn't to change the naturally different information-seeking and -processing methods of marketects and tarchitects but to make certain that the subset of data used as a source for key decisions are available to everyone on the project.

What if They Say Something They Shouldn't?

One simple and effective strategy for leveraging primary feedback is to ask your developers to work directly with customers. Several of my clients have been Silicon Valley startups. One created a marketplace for intellectual property licensing and for several years ran a user conference to actively seek feedback from customers on current and proposed product offerings. What made this conference unique was that nearly the entire development staff was present to make presentations, conduct demos, and work with key customers. This direct involvement was a key element of the company's ability to build products that its customers truly wanted.

Of course, you might be thinking, "I'm not going to let my developers talk with customers. What if they say something they shouldn't?" This fear may be real—sometimes developers do say things that they shouldn't—but in practice it isn't that big a risk. If you're really concerned, give your developers the following guidelines:

- Don't make any promises on priorities.
- Don't make any commitments.
- Don't talk negatively about our product or our competitors' products.
- Don't say, "That should be easy." It sets expectations too high and can kill any negotiation to have the customer pay for the modification.
- Don't say, "That's too hard." It can prematurely stop conversation about what the customer really wants and ways to achieve this.
- Listen nonjudgmentally. They are your customers, and they're not stupid. They might be ignorant, but they're not lazy. They might have priorities you don't know about. They're neither your fan nor your adversary.

Generating Clarity

A marketect has among his or her primary objectives and responsibilities the generation of a sufficiently precise understanding of what the development team is charged with building so that the team can actually build it. The specific approach for achieving this varies and is heavily influenced by the structures, processes, and outcomes the *total* development organization has chosen in building the system.

There are a variety of source processes and materials to select from. Marketects can choose simple paper-and-pencil prototypes or more formally defined marketing requirements documents (MRDs). In response, development organizations can create models using UML, entity-relationship models, dataflow diagrams, and so forth. Communication between the teams can take place in regular meetings that formally review progress or in daily meetings that track incremental improvements.

Chief among the variables that determine appropriate structures, processes, and outcomes are the size of the team and the number of external interactions it must support. (See [Hohmann 96] for an in-depth description of these variables). Larger projects require a level of formality and detail that would suffocate smaller ones. Other variables, including team culture, are vitally important.

The marketect has similar objectives and responsibilities but for a very different audience. He must make certain the prospective client is clear on how the system will impact its environment. If the system can be extended, such as in a browser with a plug-in architecture, the API must be made available to the appropriate developers. Data sheets outline the broad requirements, while detailed deployment requirements enable customers to prepare for the introduction of the system within their idiosyncratic IT environment. Performance and scalability whitepapers are common for any software that has a server component.

Managing Cultural Differences in Software Development

In the course of my career I've managed several groups of technical and marketing personnel, including those from Russia, Germany, India, Israel, China, Japan, Korea, Poland, Canada, and Mexico. At times I've had to manage a worldwide team focused on the same deliverable.

There are, of course, several challenges in managing a worldwide development organization, and many of them are logistical. For example, it is nearly impossible to schedule a simple meeting without inconveniencing some members of the team—08:00 U.S. PST is 16:00 in Israel. Some development teams have it even harder—12-hour time differences are common in Silicon Valley. Other examples exist in creating or adopting international standards for naming conventions, coding standards, source code management systems, and so forth. Most of these logistical challenges are relatively easy to overcome given a sufficiently motivated workforce.

A bigger challenge, and one that I've found exhibits no ethnically based pattern, is the relationship that a given group of developers have to their software process. These relationships actually form a culture although not the kind we commonly associate with the word. My own bias is heavily weighted toward processes and practices promoted by the Agile Alliance (*www.agilealliance.org*). However, at times I need to subordinate my own preferences to accommodate the dominant culture of the team I'm managing. Thus, while I firmly believe that in most cases iterative/incremental development practices are most effective, sometimes waterfall models are more appropriate, not because they inherently produce a better result but because the culture of the team *wants* them. Marketects and tarchitects both must pay close attention to these potential cultural differences and choose approaches and processes that work for a given culture.

The marketect is critically dependent on the flow of appropriate information from the tarchitect. An unfortunate, but all too common, situation occurs when last-minute changes must be made to customer-facing documentation and sales collateral because the tarchitect realizes that they contain some grave error resulting from a misunderstanding by the marketect. Even more common is when the tarchitect sheepishly informs the marketect that some key feature won't make the release. Printed material must be created weeks and sometimes even months in advance of a product launch, salespeople must be educated on the product, existing customers must prepare for the upgrade, and so forth. The marketect is partially responsible for making certain all of these happen on time and with accuracy.

Working in Unison

I reject the images perpetuated by Dilbert that marketing departments are buffoons and that engineering departments must bear the pain they incur. Instead, marketects and tarchitects should work together to ensure that the total system achieves its objectives. Lest I be misunderstood, I will try to be much more explicit: There is much for each side to gain from a strong, collaborative relationship. While this sounds good, learning to work in unison takes time and effort. Are the potential benefits worth the effort?

Let's first consider this question from the perspective of the marketect. Over the years I've found that marketects routinely underestimate or fail to understand the true capabilities of the system created by the development team. Working with tarchitects or other developers can expose marketects to unexpected, and often delightful, system capabilities. Think about systems that can be extended via plug-ins or APIs. I was delighted when a member of the professional services team of an enterprise-class software company I worked for elegantly solved a thorny customer problem by hooking up Excel directly to the system through the client-side COM API. We had never intended the API to be used in this manner, but who cares? One of the primary goals of creating extensible systems is that you believe in a future that *you can't envision* (extensibility is explored in greater detail in Chapter 8).

Now consider features that can be offered because of choices the development team made when implementing one or more key requirements. In one project I managed, the development team had to build a functional replacement of an existing server. The old architecture had a way of specifying pre- and postprocessing hooks to server messages. Unfortunately, the old architecture's solution was difficult to use and was not widely adopted, so the development team implemented an elegant solution that was very easy to use. Among other things, they generalized the pre- and postprocessing hook message handlers so that an arbitrary number of hooks could be created and chained together. The generalization was not a requirement, but it created new features that the marketect could tap.

A final set of examples illustrates marketing's ability to exploit development tools for customer gain. I've co-opted and subsequently productized developer-created regression test suites for customers so that the operational health of the system could be assessed by the customer onsite. I've converted log files originally created by developers so they could be used as sources of data for performance analysis tools. I'm not advocating goldplating, which is wasteful. But marketects who fail to understand the capabilities of the system from the perspective of its creators lose a valuable opening for leveraging latent opportunities. By establishing strong relationships with tarchitects, marketects can quickly capitalize on their fertile imaginations.

Reflexively, a tarchitect's creative energy is most enjoyably directed toward solving the real problems of real customers. By maintaining a close relationship with marketects, tarchitects learn of these problems and work to solve them. I'm not referring to the problems that the tarchitect would like to solve, that would be cool to solve, or that would help them learn a new technology. I'm talking about the deep problems that don't lend themselves to an immediate solution and are captured on the maps described earlier. Working on these problems provides a clear outlet for the tarchitect's strategic energy.

The following sections describe activities that have proven effective in fostering a healthy working relationship between the marketect and the tarchitect.

Reaching Agreements

Agreement on the project management principles and resultant practices driving the project. A variety of principles can drive any given project. Project leaders select the specific techniques for managing the project from them. Differences on principles and resulting techniques can cause unnecessary friction between marketects and tarchitects which will be felt throughout the entire project organization.

To illustrate, many software projects are driven by a "good enough" approach to quality assurance, but some, especially those dealing with human safety, require much more rigor. These goals motivate marketects and tarchitects to utilize different principles. These different principles motivate different project management practices. Not better or worse, just different.

Identifying and agreeing to the set of principles that drive the project, from the "style" of documentation (informal versus formal) to the project management tools used (MS Project or sticky notes on a shared wall), are an important step toward marketects and tarchitects working in unison. As described earlier, this agreement is also vital to meeting the cultural requirements of the development team.

Making Data Available

Visibility to maps and features is crucial. None of the approaches I've described for capturing and planning for the future are much good if the data are hidden. Get this information into a forum where everyone can share it. Some teams accomplish this through an intranet or a Lotus Notes database. Other teams are experimenting with Swikis, Twikis, or CoWebs with good results, although my own experience with these tools has been mixed and is heavily influenced by team culture. Other teams simply make lots of posters available to everyone. Visibility, in turn, is built on top of a corporate culture founded on trust and openness. Putting up posters merely to look good won't fool anyone. Making a real commitment to visibility—and dealing with the inevitable issues your project team members will raise—is a powerful tool to ensure marketect and tarchitect cooperation.

Context Diagrams and Target Products

Context diagrams are a great tool for keeping the marketect and the tarchitect in step. A context diagram shows your system in context with other systems or objects with which it interacts. It typically shows your system as a "single box" and other systems/ objects as boxes or stylized icons, with interactions between systems shown using any number of notations. Avoid formal notations in context diagrams and instead focus on simple descriptions that capture the important aspects of the relationships between the items contained within the context diagram. Context diagrams are not a formal picture of the architecture but a "higher level" shot that shows the *system in the context of its normal use*.

Context diagrams are useful for a number of reasons.

- They identify the technologies your customers use so that you can make certain you're creating something that "works" for their environment. This can range from making certain you're delivering your application using a platform that makes the most sense to ensuring that the right standards are used to promote interoperability among various components.

- They identify potential partnerships and market synergies. One of the most important applications of the whole-product concept is identifying partnerships that create a compelling augmented product and defining a map to a potential product.

- They clarify your value proposition. Clearly understanding your value proposition is the foundation of a winning business model.

- They identify the integration and extension options you need to support in the underlying architecture. A good context diagram will help you determine if you need to provide integration and/or extension capabilities at the database, logic, or even user interface levels of your application. They are a guide to the design of useful integration and extension approaches. (See Chapter 8 for more details.)

- They help you understand what deployment and target platform options make the most sense for your target customer. If you're selling to a target market that is generally running all other applications in house, it doesn't make sense to offer your part of the solution as an ASP. If your context diagram indicates that all of your partners use a specific technology to integrate their applications, it is probably best if you use it, too.

The marketect must take primary responsibility for the context diagram, although, of course, other members of the team can and should provide input to it. For example, the tarchitect can identify key standards, salespeople may suggest new entries based on how customers use the product, and so forth.

Chapter Summary

■ The marketect (marketing architect) is responsible for the marketecture (marketing architecture).

■ The tarchitect (technical architect) is responsible for the tarchitecture (technical architecture).

■ Marketecture and tarchitecture are distinct but related.

■ Three forces that are particularly influential in the early stages of solution development are the *ilities*, the problem domain, and the technology base.

■ To become an architect you have to have extensive experience in the problem space and have worked on systems in this space for a relatively long period of time.

■ You should classify bugs along two dimensions: severity and priority. Severity refers to the impact of the bug on the customer. Priority refers to the importance of fixing it.

■ Use the patterns in Appendix B to create a strategic view of your product and its evolution.

■ Winning solutions are much more likely when marketects and tarchitects work together.

■ Context diagrams are an essential tool for creating winning solutions. Learn to use them.

Check This

❑ We have a marketect.

❑ We have a tarchitect.

❑ We have a bug database that classifies each bug according to severity and priority.

❏ We have followed the patterns in the Appendix and have created a market map, a feature/benefit map, a market events and rhythms map, and a tarchitecture map. These are in a place that is easily accessible for every member of the team.

❏ Developers who meet with customers have been properly trained on what they can and cannot say.

❏ The marketect has created a context diagram for our system.

Try This

1. What is the *natural* tarchitecture of your application domain? Do you have the requisite skills and experience to work effectively in this application domain?

2. What are the *specific* responsibilities of marketect? tarchitect?

3. How do the *ilities* match between the engineering/development team and the customer? Are there significant differences?

4. How do you obtain feedback from your customers?

Chapter 4

Business and License Model Symbiosis

Your *business model* is the manner in which you charge customers for your products or services—the way you make money. Associated with every software business model is a license model, which is made up of the terms and conditions (or rights and restrictions) that you grant to a user and/or customer of your software as defined by your business model.

The symbiosis between these models is reflected in how easily we have created shorthand terms that describe them both in the same phrase. "An annual license for 10 concurrent users with the right to receive upgrades and bug fixes" is both a business model based on metered access to the software (by concurrent user) and a license model that defines some of the terms and conditions of its use—the duration, the right to use the software, and the right to receive upgrades and patches. Still, although business and license models are symbiotically related, they are *not* the same thing.

Many software companies practice *Model-T* business and licensing model strategies. They create very few business models (often only one!) and expect each of their target markets to adapt to it. Moreover, they define relatively rigid licensing models, failing to realize that within a business model market segments will pay to obtain certain kinds of rights (like the right to upgrade) or remove certain kinds of restrictions. Rigidly defined business and licensing models may work for a new product in an emerging market, but mature markets need flexibility to capture the maximum revenue and market share from each segment. Just as we want to choose the color of our cars, so customers want choice in how they license their software.

Instead of forcing each target market to adopt a single business or licensing model, it is better to examine each target market to determine the combination that will provide you with the greatest market share and revenue. Doing this well requires that your product marketing organization understand the basics of each model and how these work in a given target market. Given the plethora of possible models, this can be a challenge.

Considering all of the work involved in creating and supporting a business model, you may wonder why software is licensed and not sold (like a pen or a coffee mug). Perhaps the biggest reason is control. If someone sells you the software like a physical good, they lose control over what you can do with it. Thus, someone selling you software can't prevent you from modifying it, reselling it, reverse-engineering it to determine how it works and using that information to make competing products, or copying it and loading it on multiple computers or making it available over a network. A physical object does not suffer from these problems, which is why nearly all software—even the software you're using to create your next program—is distributed via license.

As one of the key embodiments of the marketecture, the business model and its licensing models may have a *tremendous* impact on your tarchitecture, imposing requirements throughout the system. More sobering is the fact that if your business model is the way you make money, creating the right one, licensing it the right way, and supporting it technically are essential to a truly winning solution. Missing any one of these things, for any given target market, means you might lose it all.

This chapter explores business and license models and the effects they can have on software architecture. I'll review how to make certain your business models are properly supported, discuss key license models often associated with business models, and present a few emerging techniques for making certain you're getting the most from your model. When I'm finished, you'll have the background you need to create effective business and licensing models of your own.

Business Model Nirvana

A key objective of the marketect is to ensure that the company is profitably rewarded for the value it provides to its customers. This often requires multiple co-existing business models because customers often perceive different kinds of value with different functions of a software system. In one application I worked on, the main server was licensed to customers based on transaction fees while optional modules needed for large installations were annually licensed. This combination of business models matched how our customer received value from the system and allowed us to sell to a larger total market. Transaction fees have the virtue of scaling with size in that small customers, having few transactions, pay less while larger customers, having many transactions, pay more. Thus, only customers that need them license the optional modules. Careful design of tarchitecture to support these two models was key to creating a winning solution.

Common Software Business Models

The most common software-related business models make money by

- Providing unfettered *access* to or *use* of the application for a defined period of time
- Charging a percentage of the *revenue obtained* or *costs saved* from using the application
- Charging for a *transaction*, a defined and measurable unit of work
- *Metering* access to or use of the application, or something the application processes
- Charging for the *hardware* the application runs on or hardware intimately associated with the application, and not the application itself
- Providing one or more *services* that are intimately related to application operation and/or use

Traditional software publishers or independent software vendors (ISVs) rely heavily on the first four models. The other models may be associated with an ISV or may be based on an open-source licensing model. For example, you can't *sell* Apache, but you can certainly base your business model on installing, configuring, and operating Apache-based servers.

Before you read further, go back to the beginning of this list and replace the word *application* with *feature*. Applications are collections of features, each of which can be offered under a different business and licensing model. Thus, for example, you can provide unfettered access to the base application for an annual license fee but charge a

Will That Be an Application, Suite, Bundle, or Feature?

Companies that offer more than one product often try to create synergies around their various product lines. One way of doing this is to associate a set of products as a suite or studio. To be effective, the products the suite comprises should work together and should address some aspect of a common problem domain. Organizationally, it is best if there is a separate marketect in charge of the suite, whose primary job is to work with the marketects of each suite product to make certain the suite is a good value for customers.

A bundle is a simpler concept than a suite and is usually based on a set of products that may have no special relationship to each other, may not interoperate, and may even be normally targeted at different market segments. There may be a separate marketect in charge of a bundle. Ultimately, the marketect must answer the questions associated with creating a suite or a bundle, or with marketing a feature or an application.

transaction fee for invoking a special feature that produces a defined and measurable unit of work. Defining this mix is a key responsibility of the marketect.

The more sophisticated business models are usually associated with enterprise applications, although this is continually changing as the technology to enforce license models matures. Metering is a good example. Many enterprise applications meter by concurrent user. In consumer applications, you might want to meter by the amount of time the user has been accessing your application, but this requires sophisticated technologies, including a reliable way to capture usage data. As these technologies mature, you will find these business models offered wherever they increase business!

Let's consider each of these business models in greater detail, keeping in mind the following points:

- A complex system may have multiple business models. The "base" system might be transaction-fee based while additional "optional" modules might be annually licensed. The central business model should be congruent with the value received from the customer by the generic and expected product. The augmented product may benefit from different licensing models.

- Business models are often coupled with one or more field-of-use license restrictions, which constrain where, when, and how the software can be used. Common field-of-use restrictions include single computer, a single site (called a *site license*), or one or more geographies (which export restrictions may require).

- Field-of-use restrictions work in conjunction with the core business model to create more total revenue for a company. Consider an annual license that is restricted to a single computer. If the licensee wishes to use the software on another computer, he must obtain an additional license, thereby driving more revenue. Field-of-use restrictions are another aspect of the licensing model, much like the "right to upgrade" or the "right to receive technical support." For consistency in contract language and in enforcing your licensing model, it may help to convert a field-of-use restriction to a right (or *entitlement*)—you have the right to use this software on a designated computer, or you have the right to use this software on any computer in your company.

- All of the business models associate some period of time with their use. This period is defined in the license model. Common time periods include months, quarters, and years.

- The licensing model may also define how and when a customer must make payments as a way of extending a given business model to a new market. For example, a service based on a monthly payment originally created for the small to medium business (SMB) market and requiring a purchase order might have to be augmented with the ability to accept credit cards to reach the small office/ home office (SOHO) market.

Time-Based Access or Usage

In this model, the licensee can use the software for a well-defined period of time, such as when you *purchase* an operating system. What is really happening is that the operating system publisher, or its agent, has granted you the right to use the operating system, typically on one computer, for that time. Other rights and restrictions will be defined in the license model, but the core business model is based on accessing or using the software (you *pay* to license the software so that you can *use* it).

Common time periods for time-based access or usage include the following.

Perpetual

The licensee is granted a license to use the software in perpetuity—that is, forever. Upgrades or updates are not usually included and instead are separately priced. Bug fixes or patches may be included as part of the original fee, or you may be required to pay a maintenance fee (typically ranging from 15 percent to 30 percent of the initial license fee). Be very careful of perpetual licenses, as they often increase total support and maintenance costs (unless you're careful, you may have to support *every* version—*forever!*).

Despite the potential drawbacks of perpetual licenses, they are surprisingly common and often required in many markets. Consumer software; common productivity tools, such as word processors or presentation software; operating systems; and many enterprise applications are based on them. Perpetual licenses may be required if you're providing a system or technology that may be embedded within other systems. Examples range from the runtime libraries provided by programming language vendors (e.g., the C runtime library) to systems that may become components of hardware devices or information appliances.

Annual

The software can be accessed or used for one year from the effective date of the license. The effective date can be defined as the time the license is granted, the time the software is installed, or the time the software is first used. Annual licenses often include software updates or patches. They may or may not include other services, such as technical support or consulting fees, and they are usually renewable. Renewal may be automatic, and it may be priced differently from the original annual license.

The difference between a perpetual license with an annual maintenance fee and an annual license is subtle but important. In the case of a perpetual license, the maintenance fees are added on as a way of enticing the licensee to pay for additional services, such as bug fixes or new releases. In the case of an annual license, if the licensee hasn't paid and continues to use the software, it is in breach of the license. You will ultimately have to decide how you want to enforce license terms and conditions, a topic explored in greater detail later in this chapter. Annual licenses are common in enterprise-class systems.

Although perpetual and annual licenses are the most common predefined time periods, there is nothing that prevents you from defining other periods (e.g., nine months) or a collection of times when the software can be accessed (e.g., Monday through Friday from 8 to 5). The hard part is defining one that works best for your target market and making certain you can appropriately enforce the business model and license terms. After all, which market segment would find a nine-month period or only accessing software Monday through Friday from 8 to 5 sensible?

Here are a few additional time-based usage models.

Rental

A rental is a time-based model in which the time allowed for use is set when the license is granted. In reality, it is just an annual license with a different term (or an annual license is just a rental of one year). Rentals are becoming increasingly popular in certain industries, including software test automation and electronic design automation (EDA). As license management technology matures, I predict that rentals will reach all market segments and that we will be able to rent just about every application available.

The business motivations for rental are compelling. For one, a rental allows you to reach a new market. Suppose, for example, that you rent a high-end, professional video editing system for $50,000 for a single-user annual license. One way to reach the home user market is to create a simpler version of this system, with fewer features. Another way is to offer the system as a rental (say, $100 per hour). For the user who has learned the system at work but wants to use it at home, the rental price might be a real bargain—she already knows how to use the application, so why go with anything else?

Key issues that must be resolved with a rental model include specifying when the rental period begins (when you purchase the license? install the software? start using the software?); determining how the software should respond when the rental is finished (will the program stop working entirely, or will you give the user some kind of grace period so that she can save her work?); and pricing (if you can obtain a perpetual license for a graphic design package for $2,995, what is the cost for a one-hour rental? a one-day rental?).

Subscriptions

At the other end of the spectrum is a subscription, in which customers pay a periodic fee to access the software. A subscription is like a rental or an annual license—all that differs is the terms and rights. For example, a rental may not include the right to receive upgrades or patches. Most subscriptions and annual licenses do include this. A rental and a subscription may include technical support, while in many cases you must purchase an additional contract (which can define varying kinds or levels of support) with an annual license. Because subscriptions are often associated with some backend service, the license models that define them are relatively easy to enforce. Simply cut off access to the backend service!

Pay after Use

An interesting question arises in any time-based usage model: What happens when the user accesses the application after the approved period of time? How you answer this question can make or break your relationship with your customer—and your bank account. At one end of the spectrum is absolute enforcement of a business model with no grace period: When the term is finished, the software becomes inoperable. This very severe choice is simply inappropriate for most target markets. An emerging business model charges the customer *after* he has used the software by keeping track of how long he has used it. This model places a host of complex demands on the tarchitecture (see below), but it does help ensure that the company is receiving every dollar it can from the use of its software.

An analogy is a car rental. You're typically charged for each day you rent the car, with strict definitions as to what constitutes a day. If you go beyond the original contract, the car company continues to charge you (they have your credit card on file, and the rate that you'll be charged is predefined in the contract). This pay-after-use business model will become more popular as the relationship between business models, licensing models, and billing systems matures, and as marketects learn to use these new capabilities to create compelling "pay-after-use" solutions.

Per-User Licenses

A special category of software that uses time-based access or usage licenses is applications designed to work on a single personal computer, workstation, or handheld device. As a group, these licenses are often referred to as *per-user*, and often cost less than $500. Per-user licenses work great when the publisher is licensing one copy to one user but not so well when a publisher is trying to sell 500 or 5,000 licenses to an enterprise.

To address this issue, most major software publishers have created *volume licensing* programs to more effectively reach enterprises (businesses, charitable organizations, academic institutions) that license more than one copy of the same software. Volume licensing programs are not fundamentally new but, instead are sophisticated pricing models based on an access- or usage-based business model. They offer enterprises a way to acquire multiple licenses of a given program, usually at a discount. The more copies licensed, the greater the discount.

In a *transactional volume licensing* program, each product is associated with a certain number of *points*. A high-end, expensive product may be worth five points; a low-end, inexpensive product, one point. As an enterprise creates a purchase order (500 licenses to this software, 230 licenses to that software) a point total is dynamically computed. Applicable discounts are calculated based on the total points as specified by the transaction.

In a *contractual volume licensing* program, the enterprise estimates the number of licenses they will need for a projected period of time and commits to acquiring *at least* these licenses by the time specified in the contract. The commitment to purchase a minimum number of licenses entitles the enterprise to a discount. Bonus discounts may be allowed if additional licenses are acquired, and penalties may be assessed if the customer does not license enough.

Both transactional and contractual licensing programs are highly regulated by the companies that offer them. Consider them whenever you sell multiple "copies" of the same software to one enterprise. Such licenses are more appropriate for applications that can be used in the enterprise context (games are probably not a good choice for a volume licensing program). You may not want to offer a personal finance program as part of a volume licensing deal, largely because the target market will be a single user on a single computer. That said, marketects should be aware of the benefits that a volume licensing program can provide to their customers and their product lines.

OEM

Another category in which time-based access or usage is dominant is in the OEM (original equipment manufacturer) or royalty market. The business model is access to the software. The pricing model is whatever makes sense (in the case of an OEM) or a fairly defined royalty.

Transaction

Transactions are defined and measurable units of work. Business models based on them associate a specific fee with each transaction or a block of transactions. A transaction can be surprisingly simple or maddeningly complex. For example, it can mean *executing* the software. This is common in a business model known as "try and die," in which you can execute the software a predefined number of times—say, five—before it becomes inoperable. I've worked on systems in which a transaction was distributed among multiple servers; the business model was based on charging the customer whose "root" server initiated the transaction.

Fees may be calculated in many different ways. I've worked on systems based on *flat* fees (a fixed cost per transaction), *percentage* fees (a percentage of some other calculated or defined amount), *sliding* fees (the cost per transaction decreases as certain volumes are realized), or *processing* fees, in which the work to perform the transaction is measured and the customer is billed accordingly (e.g., a simple transaction that could be computed with few resources costs less than a complex transaction that required many resources).

There is nothing about a transaction-based model that requires all transactions to be the same size, duration, or amount. Indeed, such differences are the foundation of many business models, and you can use them to create different pricing structures. For example, in the telecommunications industry a phone call is a transaction, the duration of which determines the price.[1]

---

1. I'm intentionally simplifying this example to illustrate a point. In reality, the price of a call is determined by many complex factors, including, but not limited to, tariffs and the time of day of the phone call. The telecommunications industry is a great case study of how both the marketect and a tarchitect must know the subtleties of the legal issues in creating the business model.

Transaction-based business models are found almost exclusively within enterprise software. Creative marketects know how to define a transaction and construct a transaction fee that works best for their target market. It is imperative that the tarchitect understand both the legal and the business-model transaction definition.

Sounds Great, But What Do I Charge?

A business model defines *how* you will charge a customer for your products and/or services but not *how much*. A *pricing model* defines how much. Transaction fees, for example, can be just a few cents to many millions of dollars depending on the nature of the transaction! If your business model is based on access to the software, the associated pricing model could be a one-time payment based on the specific modules or features licensed (a "menu" approach), or it could be a set fee based on the annual revenue of the enterprise.

Pricing a product or service is one of the hardest of the marketect's jobs. Charge too much and you face competition, lower revenue (too few customers can afford your product), and slow growth. Charge too little and you leave money on the table. While a detailed discussion of pricing is beyond the scope of this book, here are some principles that have worked well for me.

- Price should reflect value. If your customer is receiving hundreds of thousands of dollars of quantifiable benefits from your product, you should receive tens of thousands of dollars or more. From the perspective of your customer, price isn't affected by what the product costs but by what it's worth.

- Price should reflect effort. If your application requires a total development team of 120 people, including developers, QA, technical publications, support, product management, marketing, and sales, then you need to charge enough to support them. From the perspective of your employer, if you're not going to charge enough to be profitable, your product will be shut down. And it should be. Either it isn't providing enough value or the value it provides costs too much to create.

- Price should support your positioning. If you're positioning yourself as "premium," your price will be high. If you're positioning yourself as "low cost," your price will be low.

- Price must reflect the competitive landscape. If you're the new entry into an established market, a new business model or a new pricing model may win you business. Or it may simply confuse your customers. If it does, you're probably going to end up switching to a business model that your customers understand. Either way, understanding the business models of your competitors will help you make the right initial choice and will help you quickly correct for a poor one.

- Pricing models should not create confusion among your customers. I realize that this can be difficult, especially when you're creating a system with a lot of options. Find ways to reduce the complexity of the menu approach by offering bundles, or just plain simplify your offerings.
- Pricing models should reflect market maturity. If you're in an emerging market, you may need to try several different pricing models before you choose the one that works best. Be careful with your experiments because later customers will ask earlier customers how much they've paid. Note that you can only do this if you have a method for tracking and evaluating the model performance. This can be a tarchitectural issue, in that you may need your software to report certain information to back-office systems when it is installed or used.
- It is usually harder to raise prices than to lower them for the same product. If you start too low and you need to raise prices, you may have to find a way to split and/or modularize your offering.
- Pricing models should reflect your target market. Selling essentially the same solution at different price points to different markets (e.g., the student or small office version) often makes good sense.

Metering

Metering is a business model based on constraining or consuming a well-defined resource or something that the application processes. A constraint model limits access to the system to a specific set of predefined resources. A consumptive model creates a "pool" of possible resources that are consumed. The consumption can be based on concurrency, as when two or more resources simultaneously access or use the system, or on an absolute value that is consumed as the application is used. When all of the available resources are temporarily or permanently consumed, the software becomes inoperable. Many successful business models blend these concepts based on the target market. Here are some of the ways this is done.

Concurrent Resource Management

This business model is based on metering the number of resources concurrently accessing the system, with the most common resource either a *user* or a *session*. The business model is usually designed to constrain the resource ("a license for up to 10 concurrent users"). Both user and session must be defined, because in many systems a single user can have multiple sessions. The specific definition of a resource almost always has tarchitectural implications; managing concurrent users is quite different from managing concurrent sessions, and both are different from managing concurrent threads or processes.

Like transaction fees, concurrent resource business models have a variety of pricing schemes. You may pay less for more resources, and you may pay a different amount for a different resource. Concurrent resource models are almost exclusively the domain of enterprise software.

Identified Resource Management

In this model, specific resources are identified to the application and are allowed to access the system when they have been properly authenticated. The constraint is the defined resources, the most common of which is a *named user*, that is, a specifically identified user allowed to access the application. Identified resource business models are often combined with concurrent (consumptive) resource business models for performance or business reasons. Thus, you may create a business model based on any 10 out of 35 named users concurrently accessing the system or any 3 out of 5 plug-ins concurrently used to extend the application.

The concept of a user as the concurrent or identified resource is so prevalent that marketects should be alert to the ways in which they can organize their business model around users. One common way is to classify users into groups, or types, and separately define the functions and/or applications that each group can access.

The idea is analogous to how car manufacturers bundle optional/add-on features in a car and sell it as a complete package (the utility model versus the sport model). As a result, it is common in concurrent or named user business models to find defined user types (bronze, silver, or gold, *or* standard or professional) with specifically defined functionality associated with each (e.g., a concurrent gold user can access these features . . .).

The administrative burden of this approach can be overwhelming for corporate IT departments. To ease it, try to leverage existing directory or user management infrastructures, such as any AAA (access authentication authorization) or LDAP (Lightweight Directory Access Protocol) servers that may be installed. These systems are designed to assist IT in capturing and managing these data.

Consumptive Resource Management

In this model, you create a specified *amount* of a resource and consume that amount once when the application is invoked or continually while it is running. Unlike a concurrent model, in which consumption varies based on the specific resources simultaneously accessing the system, a purely consumptive model expends resources that are not returned.

Consider time as a consumptive resource. In this approach, you define a period of time (e.g., 100 hours or 30 days) and provide the user with a license for it. As the software is used, it keeps track of the time, "consuming" the designated value from the licenses. When all of the allotted time has been used the software becomes inoperable. Key issues that must be resolved in this approach include the definition of *time* (actual CPU time, system-elapsed time, or other), the manner in which the software will track resource consumption (locally, remotely, or distributed), and the granularity of the time-based license (milliseconds, seconds, days, weeks, months, and so forth).

More generally, it is possible to define an abstract resource and base your business model on metering it. Suppose you have an application for video publishing with two killer features: the ability to automatically correct background noise and the ability to automatically correct background lighting. You could define that any time the user invokes the background noise correction feature they are consuming one computing unit while any time they invoke the background lighting correction feature they are consuming three computing units. You could then provide a license for 20 computing units that the user could *spend* as she deems appropriate.

Consumptive resource models can underlie subscription-based service models—during each billing period (e.g., monthly), for a set fee, you get a predefined number of resources; when the resources are consumed, you can purchase more or stop using the application, and any not consumed are either carried over to the next billing period (possibly with a maximum limit, like vacation days at many companies) or lost forever. This is similar to the access-based subscriptions, except that you are metering and consuming a resource. The difference may be fine-grained, but it is worth exploring the potential benefits of each type because you may be able to access a new market or increase your market share in a given market with the right one. In addition, both models make unique demands on your tarchitecture, so the tarchitect will *have* to know the difference.

Consumptive models have another critical requirement often overlooked—reporting and replenishment. It must be extremely easy for a user/administrator to predict how much an operation will "cost" *before* she decides to spend, the rate at which *spending* is occurring, and when the rate of spending will exceed the allotment for the month or a resource budget is nearing depletion. Because customers will often overspend, it should be painless to buy more. No one will blame you if they run out of a critical resource on Friday afternoon at 6 P.M. Eastern time, just before a critical big push weekend—especially if you warned them yesterday that it would happen. But they will *never*, *ever* forgive you if they can't buy more until Monday at 9 A.M. Pacific time.

Hardware

Hardware-based business models associate the amount charged for the software with some element of hardware. In some cases the software is *free*, but is so intimately tied to the hardware that the hardware is effectively nonfunctional without it. A more traditional approach, and one that is common in business applications, is to associate the business model with the number of CPUs installed in the system. As with all business models, the motivation for this "Per-CPU licensing" is money.

Say an application has been licensed to run on a single machine. If the performance of the machine can be substantially improved simply by adding additional processors, the licensor (software publisher) stands to lose money because the licensee will just add processors without paying any additional license fees! If this same application is licensed on a per-CPU basis, then adding more processors may improve performance but the licensor will get more money for it.

Hardware based business models can be based on any aspect of the hardware that materially affects the performance of the system and can be enforced as required to meet business needs. Per-CPU or *per expansion card* are the most common, but you can also use memory, disk storage (e.g., redundantly mirrored disk drives might be charged twice), and so forth. I wouldn't recommend basing the model on the number of connected keyboards, but you could if you wanted to.

Services

Service-based business models focus on making money from one or more services, not from the software that provides access to them. My favorite example is America Online. AOL doesn't charge for the software; they charge a monthly subscription fee for access to a wide range of services, including e-mail, chat, and content aggregation.

Service-based business models are often used with open source licenses. Examples here include providing assistance in the installation, configuration, and operation of an application or technology licensed as open source or built on open-source software, creating education programs (think O'Reilly) and custom development or integration services.

Creating a service-based business model through open source software (OSS) licensing is a creative approach; however, as of the writing of this book there are no provably sustainable, long-term successful open-source software service business models. This is not an indictment of OSS! I'm aware that most of the Internet runs on OSS, and many companies have very promising service-based business models related to it. I'm merely acknowledging that the market is immature and so such models have yet to be proven. Therefore, any marketect approaching his or her business through OSS should proceed with caution.

Revenue Obtained/Costs Saved

Another business model that is common in enterprise software is a percentage of revenue obtained or costs saved from using the application. Suppose you've created a new CRM (customer relationship management) system that can increase sales to existing customers by an average of 15 percent. You may consider charging 10 percent of the incremental revenue, provided that the total dollar amount is large enough to justify your costs.

Alternatively, let's say that you've created a new kind of inventory tracking and warehouse management system targeted toward small companies ($5M to $50M in annual revenue). Your data indicates that your software will save these companies anywhere from $50K to $1M. A viable business model may charge 15 percent of the savings, again provided that the total dollar amount is sufficiently large.

In choosing these models you have to have a rock-solid analysis that clearly identifies the additional revenues or savings. If you don't, no degree of technical skill in the development team will help the architecture become successful. The fundamental problem is that the data on which these models are based are extremely subjective and easily manipulated. You might think that your new CRM software generated $100,000 more business for Fred's Fish Fry, but Fred thinks it's the spiffy new marketing campaign that Fred, Jr., created. Result? You're not going to get paid the amount you think you've earned.

Enterprises also appear to be more resistant to models based on cost savings. I once tried to create such a model. Even though we had a very solid ROI, the model didn't work and we switched from costs savings to transaction fees. Percentage of revenue obtained or costs saved are also unpopular because they make *customers* track how much they should pay. It is usually much easier to determine how much a customer should pay in the other business models.

Open Source Does Not Mean Free

Sleepycat Software has married a traditional time-based usage business model with an open source certified licensing model in way that drives widespread adoption while still making money. The way it works is that Sleepycat provides its embedded database system, Berkeley DB, as an open source license. The terms allow you to use Berkeley DB at no charge, *provided* that you give away the complete source code for your application under an open source license as well. This is a great example of the viral element of open source licensing.

Many people who use Sleepycat can do this. Proprietary software vendors aren't able to offer their software under the open source license, so Sleepycat sells them a different license for Berkeley DB that permits them to use it without distributing their own source code. This is where the business model comes into play—the way that Sleepycat makes money is very similar to standard licensing models.

Sleepycat can use this approach because the proprietary vendor must link the database into their application and because Sleepycat owns all of the IP associated with the code. The linking process gives Sleepycat leverage to impose licensing constraints, and the ownership of the IP means that Sleepycat can control license terms as they choose. According to Michael Olson, the CEO of Sleepycat, the marriage is working quite well, as Sleepycat has been a profitable company for several years, and is yet another lesson in the benefits of separating your business and license models.

Rights Associated with Business Models

Marketects choose business models to maximize the benefits to their business. Associated with each of the business models just described is a set of rights and restrictions—things you *can* do or things you *get* and things you *cannot* do or things you *do not get*. I've covered a few of these already, such as the right to use, the right to upgrade, and you can only run this software on one computer.

Your business model should distinguish as many rights and restrictions as possible, because each right is a way of capturing and/or extracting value from your customer and each restriction is a way of protecting your interests. Many business models, for reasons of convenience, competitive advantage, or common practice, often create a *standard* licensing model that blends a variety of rights and restrictions into a single package. Remember, however, that separating them can create greater value.

For example, an annual license to use the software (the business model is time-based access) commonly includes the right to use and the right to receive upgrades but not the right to receive technical support. A subscription to a software-based services model (such as America Online, where the business model is service or metering depending on customer choices) may include all of these rights. This section reviews some of the rights commonly associated with various business models.

Figure 4-1 outlines some the rights and restrictions associated with particular business models. The columns list specific rights or restrictions; the rows are the business models. A check means that this right is commonly allowed by the business model. A number means that the right *may* be allowed by the business model and will be discussed in greater detail. I've added a column that addresses whether or not the fees paid by the licensee are one time or periodic. The timing of fees can affect the choice of model.

The table's focus is the subset of license models most closely correlated with various business models. It does not attempt to capture every possible legal issue that can be defined in a license: exclusivity, warranties, indemnifications, intellectual property rights, confidentiality, or any number of other things that a savvy lawyer can think of. Most of these are not a function of the model but of larger corporate policy that governs every license model, regardless of the business model.

1. Do associate this right with the business model if providing it will give you a competitive advantage, reduce technical or product support costs, or create a stronger tie between you and your customer. Don't if your customers don't care about it or if doing so may cause them more bother or pain that it is worth. For example, in the anti-virus market you have to provide upgrades and bug fixes. In enterprise-class software, upgrades may not be as meaningful because of the large time delays that may exist between release cycles and the often substantial costs associated with integrating the upgrade into the current operational environment.

Business Model	Right to upgrade (to latest version)	Right to receive bug fixes and patches	Right to return	Right to move to a different machine	Right to embed	Right to modify	Right to resell	Support options (e.g., phone, Web, e-mail)	Predefined installation/customization support	One time (1T) or periodic fee (P)
Time-based access				1	1	1	1	1	1	
Perpetual license										1T
Annual license	✓	✓								P
Rental	1	1								1T
Subscription	1	1								P
Pay after use										1T
Transaction	2	2		1	1	1	1	1	1	P
Metering				1	1	1	1	1	1	
Concurrent resource	✓	✓								1T
Identified resource	✓	✓								1T
Consumptive resource	1	1								1T
Hardware	3	3		1	1	1	1	1	1	1T
Service	✓	✓		1	1	1	1	1	1	P

FIGURE 4-1   License rights and business models

2. I'm usually surprised to find that transaction-based business models don't automatically include these rights. In these models, your goal is to drive transactions. Improvements to your software, especially those that can drive transactions, should always be made available to your customers.

3. Do associate these rights if the benefits of point 1 apply and your customers find it relatively easy to apply the upgrade and/or patches. Note that in some hardware-based business models you *don't* want your customers to upgrade to new software. Instead, you want them to purchase entirely new hardware, which is another reason to withhold these rights.

Tarchitectural Support for the Business Model

If your total offering is based on a combination of business models, check for key interactions between the various elements. Review these factors every time the business model changes, because these changes may invalidate prior assumptions and/or choices and motivate one or more changes to the tarchitecture.

General Issues

The following sections describe the general issues that are present for every business model.

Capturing the Necessary Data

Assess your business model to ensure that your system is capturing all of the data required to make it *work*. Here are two primary categories of data capture:

- *Direct*: The system captures and manages all data necessary to support the business model. It is self-contained.
- *Indirect*: The system must be integrated with one or more other systems to create a complete picture of the necessary data.

To illustrate, a transaction or metered business model will either capture all of the necessary data or work with other systems to capture it. A service-based business model often has to be integrated with other systems, such as payment processing or client management systems, to capture the full set of data needed to create a viable business model.

Reporting/Remittance Requirements

Somewhere along the line your accounting department is going to require that information be submitted for billing purposes. Your job is a lot easier if you can define the format, security, and audibility requirements of these reports.

Business Model Enforcement

What happens when the license to use the software is violated? Does it stop working? Should an entry be made in a log file? Is an e-mail sent to a key person? Should a new billing and licensing cycle be automatically initiated?

Focusing *ility* Efforts

In an ideal world, the tarchitect's ility efforts (reliability, stability, scalability, supportability, usability, and so forth) are congruent with the key objectives of the business model. Suppose your business model is based on processing various transactions, such as check clearing and/or processing in financial services or in health care claims processing for large insurance carriers. In these cases, reliably and accurately computing a lot of transactions quickly is critical to your success. Performance *matters*, and *faster really is better*. Who cares if the product is a bit hard to install or upgrade as long as it's the fastest possible? If your tarchitect and the development organization with building the system also care about performance, you're doing great. If not, you may have some problems.

Of course, performance is not the primary criterion of every business model. In a service-based business model, great performance with lousy customer support may not be good enough to succeed. Instead of focusing on performance, your development team may need to focus on service elements such as ease of installation and upgrade. A key goal in a service-based business model is to reduce and/or eliminate phone calls to technical support, so it is best to find a tarchitect and a development team who care about these issues. Tradeoffs are determined by how the software will typically be used—applications used infrequently should be easy to learn, while those part of a daily routine should be fast and easy to use.

Increased Revenues or Decreased Costs

Once you know your business model it is easy to focus tarchitectural efforts on activities that increase revenues. Don't forget the *costs* your tarchitecture imposes on your customer. Any time you can reduce those costs, you have more revenue potential. You can reduce costs by making installation and/or upgrade easier or by improving performance and/or backward compatibility so that your users won't have to purchase expensive new hardware every time they upgrade to a new version.

Copy Protection/Antipiracy Protection

All software is subject to illegal copying and distribution, although certain kinds of software, such as that inside a video game cartridge or cell phone, are more resistant to piracy because of the hardware dependency. Even so, hardware is not a strong deterrent—just check out the number of places where you can find replacement software that can boost the performance of your car! Most software, however, is trivially copied, as proven by the many online services that provide easy access to pirated software. Depending on the amount of money you may lose from piracy (some companies estimate several million in losses) you should consider a copy protection scheme, as described further below.

Verifying Business Model and License Model Parameters

Many of the business and licensing models involve setting one or more parameters. For example, an annual license has a definite end date, a concurrent user license has a specific number of concurrent users, possibly further divided by type, and a consumptive, time-based license has the amount of time available for use. Whenever you set a value that is important to your business model, you have to understand when, how, and where this value is set, who can change it, and how its value can be verified. These are nontrivial matters, discussed later in this chapter under enforcing business and licensing models (see also Chapter 16, on Security).

Time-Based Access or Usage

Time-based access or usage business models make few special demands on the tarchitecture, unless you're going to strictly enforce the business model. If this is the case, you're going to need a way of being able to disable the software when the time allotted for use has expired. Many subscriptions don't actually stop a program from working if you fail to remain current in your payments—you just don't get updates (which has the effect of converting a subscription to a perpetual license).

Transaction

Consider the following when dealing with a transaction-based business model.

Define the Transaction

The definition of a transaction, or the unit of work that is the foundation of the business model, must be clear and unambiguous. Once you've defined the transaction, make certain that the tarchitecture can support it and that it is clearly stated in the software license. This is not easy, but it is essential. As you define the transaction, consider the role that each component is playing with respect to it. In distributed transaction systems, the manner in which an element participates in the transaction must be defined, including which participants are the basis of the business model.

Define the Relationship between the Transaction and the Business Model

I've heard some people say that the first step in starting a phone company is purchasing billing software. While this may not be true, the complexity of the plans offered by cell phones for completed transactions requires sophisticated billing management systems. More generally, it is absolutely essential that you can map the completed transaction to the business model. In the case of the phone company, where the transaction is a phone call, key data include who originated the call, who received it, and how long it took.

Keep Audit Trails

Many transaction-based business models require audit trails that can be used to prove/disprove specific charges. This can be especially vital when attempting to reconcile differences between participants in the transaction. You may also need to cross-reference the transactions created by your system with those created by other systems.

Make Certain that Transactions Are Uniquely Identified

Transactions must be uniquely identified. Be wary of simple database counters, which often won't work in today's distributed environments. Instead of relying on the database vendor, create a truly unique identifier through a reliable algorithm. I've had good luck with the built-in algorithms for creating universally unique identifiers (UUIDs) in UNIX-based systems or the globally unique identifiers (GUIDs) available on MS-Windows systems. Admittedly, these require a lot of space, and represent an extraordinarily large number of unique identifiers. Chances are good you don't need an identifier to be quite that long, and you may be able to safely shorten your unique identifier. Short identifiers that work well are based on alphanumeric codes, like "XR349" or "QPCAZZ." One advantage to these codes is that they are short enough to be used in phone-based self service.

Understand Transaction State, Lifecycle, and Duration

When I'm standing in line at the checkout counter about to make some purchase, my mind often leaps to images of mainframe computers processing hundreds of credit card transactions per second. Of course, there are myriad other kinds of transactions, many of which have complex states, lifecycles, and durations. Managing the duration of the transaction can be particularly complex, especially when a transaction can *live* over a system upgrade. The complete transaction lifecycle must be defined because it impacts your back-office systems that account for transactions.

Suppose, for example, that a transaction can last as long as one year and you bill your customer monthly. Normally, you bill for a transaction when it has completed. However, in this case you could be waiting a long time for money, negatively impacting your cash flow. If you know that 80 percent of transactions complete successfully, you could safely bill when the transaction is started, *provided* that your system can recognize a failed or aborted transaction and your back-office systems can properly adjust and/or otherwise credit your customer's account. Before actually doing this, check with your accounting department to make certain that you're not violating any revenue recognition regulations.

Metering

Metering business models entail many interesting challenges, especially when the metering is based on a concurrent or named user. The following sections address some of the issues that are common to both models.

How Do You Authenticate Users?

Authentication attempts to answer the question "Are you who you say you are?" There are many authentication approaches, from simple user names and passwords to simple-to-use but hard-to-defeat tokens to advanced (and costly) biometric systems. If your business model derives a lot of money from uniquely identifying users, you should consider employing any number schemes beyond simple user names and passwords. More generally, you should work with other, established infrastructure technologies to authenticate users (such as LDAP). Authentication is discussed in greater detail in Chapter 16.

How Many Users?

In a concurrent user system there is some limit to the number of users who can concurrently access it. The manner in which you specify that number is subject to considerable variation. I've worked on systems that span the gamut of managing this value. On the low end, we specified the number of concurrent users as a plain text entry in an INI file—completely insecure but entirely acceptable for our requirements. On the high end, we specified the number of concurrent users in a signed license that was then stored on a hardware device using advanced cryptography. To the best of our knowledge, this approach has yet to be cracked!

How Are You Going to Count Concurrent Users?

While you can, and often should, rely on other parts of the infrastructure to authenticate users, you may not be able to rely on them to count users. This may be a function of your application, or it may be obtained by integrating a license manager into your application.

Are Users Gone or Inactive?

Session management is a key issue in concurrent and named user applications. Once a user is logged in, you can't assume that she will explicitly log out. Something might go wrong: Her client might crash; or she might not remember to log out. The general solution is to associate a timeout parameter that forcibly logs the user off or drops her session after a set period of inactivity.

Unfortunately, setting this value isn't trivial. It must be tuned on the basis of how your application is actually used. Consider an interactive voice system that is accessed by a cell phone. Is a period of inactivity caused by the user pausing to consider his next action or has the line dropped because he drove into a "dead zone"? If the user did drive into a dead zone, how will you reestablish the session so that he doesn't have to re-enter a long string of menu commands? It is important that you provide plenty of configuration parameters on these values so that your administrator can properly tune your application.

Consumptive resource management places severe restrictions on your tarchitecture, primarily because you have to maintain some kind of state. If your customer has purchased "100 hours" of total use, you need to record how long she has actually used the application. One approach is to store these data on a centralized server, which can work if you structure it so you can't be spoofed and you always have a reliable network connection. Another approach is to store usage locally. Be careful, however: It is often trivially easy to reset usage data by erasing previously stored values.

Hardware

The biggest issues with hardware-based models are defining what constitutes the hardware and how you're going to manage it relative to the business model. What, exactly, is a central processing unit (CPU)? In many ways the concept of a CPU is meaningless: Many personal computers and engineering workstations now come with at least two processing units as part of their standard equipment, and some new chip designs have multiple processing units in a single package. Arbitrarily picking one as *central* seems a bit silly. Still, per-CPU business models are common. To support them, you will have to define a CPU and how it will be enforced in your system.

Enforcing Licensing Models

Once you've defined your business and licensing models, and ensured that your tarchitecture can support them, you have to decide how strongly you wish to enforce the licensing model. Typically, *enforcement* means disabling some or all of the application when the license manager determines that the license has been violated. You can avoid creating or using a license manager and rely on the honor system, create your own licensing manager, or license one from a third-party provider.

The Honor System

The honor system is the simplest and easiest way to enforce a license model. You simply expect your customers to honor the terms of the license, which means not changing the license terms, illegally copying the software, changing configuration parameters to obtain more use of the software, and so forth. You're not giving up any rights, as you still have legal protection under contract law if you find your customer cheating. Rather, you are putting nothing into your application to explicitly prevent your customer from cheating.

I suspect that a large percentage of software publishers rely on the honor system. Whether or not this is a good choice should be based on a careful analysis of several factors, including the relationship you have or want to create with your customer, the potential for lost revenue, and your ability to track the use of your software via the honor system. Compare these against the cost of creating, maintaining, and supporting a more advanced licensing system or licensing such a system from a third party. An additional motivation to use the honor system, especially with enterprise software systems, is that it provides account managers with the opportunity to talk with customers each time the license is up for renewal, and to possibly convince them to purchase more software. In consumer software, where you may have tens of thousands to tens of millions of copies, the honor system may not be a good choice. In enterprise-class software, where you may have several dozen to a few hundred customers, it may be a good choice, especially if you maintain a close relationship with your customers through support or service organizations.

Home-Grown License Managers

In this approach the development team creates the infrastructure for license management. Such a solution is not industrial strength, in that it is often relatively easily defeated. However, it has the advantages of being low cost, lightweight, easy to implement, and completely in control of the development organization. Once you've made the choice to enforce the licensing models, the economics of defeated enforcement must be considered to determine if a home-grown solution is sufficient or a professional system is required. If your software costs $700 per license, a home-grown system may be acceptable. If you're software costs $70,000 per license, there is simply too much money to lose with a home-grown license manager, and you're better off switching to a professional solution.

Some kind of home-grown license management is almost always required for session-based licensing schemes, because the development organization needs complete control over the software's response to the system running out of the internal

It Doesn't Have to Be Unbreakable

One enterprise-class system I helped create provided for a combination of named and concurrent users: Any number of users up to the concurrent user limit could log on at the same time, but only users explicitly identified were allowed access. We implemented our own lightweight but extremely effective licensing manager. The number of concurrent and named users were simply stored in an INI file, with user IDs and passwords stored in a database. Changing either of these entries defeated the licensing scheme, in that if you licensed 20 concurrent users but changed this to 100, you cheated my employer out of 80 concurrent user licenses and tens of thousands of dollars in license fees. We didn't expect anyone to actually cheat, and to this day I know of no company that did. The net was that for a reasonable development effort we were able to devise a scheme that "kept honest people honest."

resources it needs to manage sessions. In other words, do you stop the application (extreme, not recommended) or simply refuse the session (common, but the associated issues are application specific).

Third-Party or Professional License Managers

Professional license managers are typically organized in three main components: the license generator, a client (or local license manager), and a server (or remote license manager). The business model and the software being enforced will determine how you use these components.

The License Generator

The license generator generates a valid license for consumption by the client and/or server. Most license managers will generate digitally signed licenses based on public key cryptography that cannot be altered and that can be used to prove that the rights delivered to the license manager are correct. License generators are typically located at the independent software vendor (ISV) or its agent and are integrated with other backend infrastructure systems, such as order fulfillment, which may initiate license generation, and accounting systems, which may use the records maintained by the license generator for billing. Once a license is generated it can be distributed in a variety of ways, including fax, phone, e-mail, or direct connection from the server to the license generator via the internet.

The Client

The client license manager manages the software running on an end user's computer or workstation. At its simplest terms, it either allows or prevents access to a given application or licensed feature. The client can typically be configured to operate in one of two ways. One is as a standalone, in which it manages enforcement without working with the server. This mode of operation is common for single-user, consumer-oriented software run on one machine and works well for time-based access or usage models.

Here is an example. You work for SuperSoft, which markets SuperDraw. You want to distribute a 30-day trial of SuperDraw, which can be thought of as a free rental. When SuperDraw is installed the client-side license manager is also installed to enforce these rights along with the digitally signed trial license (e.g., the trial expires and the software cannot be used after 30 days).

The other mode of operation requires the client license manager to work with a server to enforce license rights. This mode is common in business-oriented software that uses metering, such as named or concurrent users. When the application is invoked, the client license manager checks with the server to determine if access is allowed. Your customer must be connected to a network, and you need to consider application behavior when your customer is not connected.

The Server

The server component interprets digitally signed licenses and provides a variety of enforcement services to client license managers. As just described, the server component is required (in one form or another) for the licensing models that support counting or metering.

Here is an example to illustrate how a server works with a client to enforce license rights. You're licensing a high-end CAD system that wants to sell concurrent user licenses at $8K per user. In this case the software can be installed on any available workstation, but each user consumes a concurrent user. The server works with the client to keep track of each concurrent user and ensure that the license terms are properly enforced. This model may seem like a great model, but remember that you still must handle the unconnected user. The easiest way to handle unconnected users is to simply not support them and instead require connected use.

Although I've talked about enforcement, I haven't addressed how your software interoperates with the client and/or server components of the license management system. *Normal software*, or the software that you create to fulfill your customer needs, has no concept of enforcing a business model. Something must be done to it to prepare it for license management, and the way you do this can vary a lot for home-grown systems. Third-party license managers, on the other hand, generally employ two approaches to integrate the software with the license manager: injection or APIs.

- *Injection:* Given a "normal" application, the "injection" approach analyzes the object code and "injects" into it new code that typically obfuscates and/or encrypts the original code and adds the client license manager to enforce the license. In other words, injection works just like a virus, albeit a beneficial one. Table 4-1 lists some of the advantages and disadvantages of the injection approach.

TABLE 4-1 Advantages and Disadvantages of the Injection Approach

Advantages	Disadvantages
• Requires little or no work by developers • Can result in more secure protection, because the injection approaches obfuscate and/or encrypts code	• Increases size of code • Decreases execution performance • Can only be used with binaries; typically not suitable for interpreted languages

TABLE 4-2 Advantages and Disadvantages of API-based Approaches

Advantages	Disadvantages
• Provides maximum flexibility—you can control exactly how the license model works • Can be used with interpreted languages	• If not used properly can be easy to defeat • Creates lock-in to an existing vendor • Usually takes longer to implement a complete solution • Can lead to a false sense of security

- *API:* In this approach developers write to an API (or SDK) provided by the license manager vendor. The API provides for such things as license registration and enforcement (e.g., it has calls for "checking the validity of the license" or "logging in a concurrent user.") This approach is not strictly required for concurrent licensing, but it makes implementing such schemes vastly easier. APIs can be used with interpreted languages, but most vendors feel that using them in this manner does not provide very strong security. More plainly, it is relatively easy to hack the API approach in Java/C#. Table 4-2 captures the advantages and disadvantages of API-based approaches.

While professional third-party license managers have many virtues, you need to evaluate them very carefully. Consider the issues in the following sections when conducting this evaluation.

Business Model Support

To the best of my knowledge, no licensing manager supports all of the business models listed earlier. For example, I don't know of any that provide direct support for most hardware-based business models (such as per CPU or per-expansion-card). Most work best if you alter your business model to work well with their specific technologies.

Traditional license managers provide a fixed set of models with fill-in parameters. An example is a time-based usage scenario, in which you simply fill in the amount of time. More modern license managers provide a license scripting language, similar to languages like Visual Basic, that allows you to create customized scripts for creative licensing models.

Platform and Operating System Support

Make certain your license manager vendors can provide support for all required platforms and operating systems. When examining their supported platforms, take the time to explore their development roadmap, because, when a new version of an operating system is released, your development efforts are stalled until your license management vendor supports it!

Check Cracker Web Sites to Determine Solution Strength

It is easy to create a simple license manager. It is *very hard* to create an industrial-strength license manager that will consistently thwart crackers, maintain the security of your software, and ensure that you're getting the maximum revenue from your licensing model. If you don't have the skill to assess the strength of the solution, hire a consultant who does.

Check Backend Integration and Volume Capabilities

As stated earlier, the license generator is almost always integrated with backend systems. Examine your potential license manager vendor's ability to integrate its system within *your* environment. While you're doing this, make certain they can also meet your performance, volume, scalability, and stability requirements.

Make Certain Operational Environment Matches Yours

License managers create a whole host of operational issues. For example, customer service representatives may have to regenerate a license, or create a temporary evaluation license on the fly, or cancel a previously generated license. You'll have to make certain that the integrations created between your license generator and other backend components are sufficiently scalable and reliable. Make certain that your license manager vendor can meet your operational requirements. In other words, if your customer service environment is completely Web-based, make certain your license manager vendor can provide all required functionality via a browser.

Check Branding and User Interface Control

When the code enforcing the license detects a violation, chances are good that some kind of error message will be displayed to the user. Assess the degree of control you have over the content and presentation of this error message. You want to make certain that it meets all of your usability requirements, especially internationalization. You don't want to discover that your vendor has twelve dialogs it might bring up in obscure circumstances, and that you can't change any of their contents.

Examine License Content and Format

The format and content of the license should be understandable and should match your business requirements. Anything generated by your system, even if it is not used by the license manager, should be digitally signed. For example, you may wish to put a serial number inside the license to integrate the license generator with other backend systems. Any custom or proprietary data that you store in the license should be signed.

Examine License Distribution Capabilities

Licenses can be distributed in a variety of ways. Make certain the vendor supports the approaches that are most important to you. Internet, e-mail, phone, and fax are the most common license distribution options.

Market Maturity Influences on the Business Model

The maturity of your target market is one of the strongest influences on the selection and management of a given business model. In the early phases of a given market, business models should be chosen so that they can be quickly and easily understood, primarily because you may not be certain of the best way to structure them. You may find that your customers prefer an annual license to a subscription, or that they expect discounts if they purchase in bulk. Moreover, despite the best intentions of the business plan, innovators and early adopters may expect and/or demand special terms.

As the market matures, chances are good that your business model will become increasingly complex in order to serve the idiosyncratic needs of different market segments. I helped one client whose growth had stalled attack a new market segment with the same underlying system simply by defining a new business model. The original one consisted of an annual license. The new one was pay per use. The easy part was modifying the underlying architecture so that both models could be supported. The hard part was creating the appropriate price points so that a given customer could choose the best model without harming the relationships with current customers.

The enforcement of business models also matches the maturity of the target market. In early market stages, enforcement tends to be lax. As the market matures, or in cases where you suspect piracy, the enforcement tightens up. My experience is that marketects and tarchitects take enforcement *far too lightly*. You've worked hard to create your system, and software piracy is a serious problem. Create a business model that identifies the real value provided to your customers, price it competitively, and enforce it accordingly. Just remember that onerous enforcement will lead to dissatisfaction among honest customers, so be careful.

Choosing a Business Model

Choosing a business model is one of the most challenging tasks faced by the marketect, as it incorporates everything that has been discussed in this chapter *and* several factors that are beyond the chapter scope, such as the business and licensing models offered by competitors (which may constrain you to existing market expectations) and corporate and/or environmental factors beyond your control (such as when another division does poorly and you need to find a way to increase short-term revenue). To help you through the potential morass of choosing a business model, consider these questions.

- *What is the target market? What does it value?* A crisp description of the target market and what it values is the first step in creating an appropriate business licensing model. If you're not certain of what it values, consider how it wants to use what you're offering. Once you've determined what your market values, show how your solution provides it.

- *What are your objectives relative to this target market?* In an emerging market you may wish to capture market share, so create simpler models. In a mature market you may wish to protect market share, so create more complex models to provide flexibility.

- *What is your business model?* Pick one of the business models defined above and customize it to meet your needs.

- *What rights do you wish to convey?* Begin by asking your legal department for a "standard" contract, as it will contain a variety of nonnegotiable rights and restrictions. See what you can do about everything that is left.

- *What is the effect of this business model on your software architecture?* Work with the tarchitect to make certain that any business model you propose is appropriately supported.

- *What is the pricing model?* The business model provides the framework for defining how you're going to make money. The pricing model sets the amount the customer will pay. You'll need to consider such things as volume discounts, sales and/or channel incentives, and so forth. Pricing choices may also affect your software architecture, so make them carefully.

As you develop the answers to these questions, you're likely to find that the best way to reach a given target market will require a variety of changes to your current business model, licensing model, and software architecture. You'll have to rank-order the changes in all areas of your product so that you can reach the largest target market. The benefits will be worth it, as creating the right business and licensing model forms the foundation of a winning solution for both you and your customers.

❑ ❑ ❑ ❑ ❑ ❑ ❑ ❑ ❑

Chapter Summary

- Your business model is how you make money.
- Business models are associated with, and to a large extent define, license models.

- Your license model is the terms and conditions you associate with the use of your software.
- The most common software-related business models make money by
  - Providing unfettered *access* to or *use* of the application for a defined period of time
  - Charging a percentage of the *revenue obtained* or *costs saved* from using the application
  - Charging for a *transaction*, that is, a defined and measurable unit of work
  - *Metering* access to or use of the application, or something the application processes
  - Charging for the *hardware* the application runs on, not the application itself
  - Providing one or more *services* that are intimately related to application operation and/or use
- Business models associated with users (such as concurrent user licensing) motivate integration with corporate systems that manage users (such as LDAP servers).
- Make certain you understand every right associated with your business model. Separating rights may provide more opportunities to create revenue.
- License models may be enforced by home-grown or third-party professional license managers.

Check This

- ❑ Each member of the development team can define the business models currently in use or under serious consideration for the future.
- ❑ Our license agreements are congruent with our business model.
- ❑ Our license agreements define the specific set of rights provided to customers.
- ❑ We have chosen an appropriate mechanism for enforcing our business model.
- ❑ The costs of changing tarchitecture to support alternative business models are understood and communicated to marketects.

Try This

1. What is your business model?
2. How well does your architecture support your business model? Why do you claim this?
3. Can you demonstrate support for a new kind of business model? For example, if your current system is sold on an annual license, can you easily add support for some kind of concurrent license, in such a way that you can open a new market for your software?

4. If you're using a license manager, have you allocated enough time in your project plan to properly integrate it into your application?

5. If you are using a license manager, have you examined their development roadmap to make certain it supports your own?

6. Are your target customers likely to be innovators, early majority, majority, late majority, or laggards? How does this characterization affect your business model?

Chapter 5
Technology In-Licensing

You can't build everything new. Every complex software system is part new code and part systems integration with previously written software—even if the software you are integrating with is nothing more than the C runtime library that comes with your favorite compiler. What you're integrating is a product from another company, and as described in Chapter 4, this product comes to you based on a business and license model. The process of licensing this technology and incorporating it into your offerings is called technology in-licensing.

There are many motivations for technologies in-licensing. Licensing technology can be cheaper and faster than building our own. Sometimes licensing isn't a choice but a requirement, as a company may have obtained a key patent on a technology essential to your success. An additional consideration is the skills and experience of key staff. You may not want them spending precious time and energy designing and building components that you can obtain via a license.

Any, or all, of these factors mean that you are likely to be licensing one or more key technologies from another party. As a result, understanding basic concepts associated with in-license agreements and how they affect your tarchitecture is vital for everyone on the team.

> Disclaimer: I'm not a lawyer. Any contract that may affect your system, including any license agreement, should be thoroughly evaluated by a properly trained attorney. That said, an attorney can only do a good job when she understands the business objectives as well as the relationship between the licensed technology and the underlying tarchitecture. Thus, everyone benefits when key members of the team understand the core issues associated with technology in-licensing.

Licensing Risks/Rewards

The introduction outlined some of the motivations for licensing technology. While these motivations are quite real, so too are the associated risks. The following list captures both the motivations and the risks that must be considered in every licensing situation.

Motivation/Reward. You can reduce, manage, or otherwise eliminate complexity and risk by licensing technology from a third party. The technology or provider is an *expert* in a given area that you deem important to success. By licensing their technology you gain the provider's expertise.

Risk. You may be able to shift complexity from your team to the technology provider, but in doing so you increase risk by increasing your reliance on third-party technology. If the technology evolves in a way that fails to match your needs, you could be in serious trouble.

A supplier might change focus, leaving you without an equivalent replacement. You may not even be able to find a plug-compatible supplier. This almost happened to one of my teams when a search engine vendor whose technology we had licensed decided to reposition themselves as a portal vendor. They initially stopped development of their core technology (text indexing and searching). Fortunately, several customers, including us, managed to convince the vendor to maintain its investment in the core technology. Everything worked out, but the situation was very tense for several weeks as we explored several undesirable replacement scenarios.

Finally, make certain that you assess the viability of the technology provider. Given today's volatile corporate market, there is always the risk that a technology provider may go out of business.

Motivation/Reward. In-licensing technology promotes component-based software systems, which can be easily changed (such as replacing one component with another).

Risk. In-licensed technologies can become too intertwined with a solution to make changes to support a different implementation.

For example, suppose you in-license a reporting component. Chances are good that you could only replace it with a different implementation *if* that implementation supported the same level of functionality. If you expose or rely on any vendor-specific functionality you've probably locked yourself to this vendor. If this was a conscious choice, great. If not, you might be stuck.

Motivation/Reward. In-licensing technology makes your system easier to construct because you can focus on creating your unique technology.

Risk. In-licensed components increase configuration complexity. Incompatible business models may make the use of certain kinds of technologies practically impossible. I'll elaborate on this later in this chapter.

Another potential risk deals with the restrictions that may come with various components. (Consider high-end cryptographic libraries, which are often subject to various forms of export restrictions.) Licensing these technologies means that you're subjecting your software to these restrictions. Keep in mind that this is one of the goals of many open source licenses, most notably GNU GPL.

Motivation/Reward. You can obtain *protection* by licensing technology protected by a patent.

Risk. Indemnity, legal exemption from the penalties or liabilities incurred for using the component, is hard to secure. Suppose you license a component from company A because it has a patent on a key technology. This license is not likely to protect you from being sued by company B, who may claim that you're infringing on its rights.

Motivation/Reward. You can reduce *time-to-market* by reusing technology.

Risk. Licensing technology does not always result in faster time to market. At the very least you have to invest time in learning the technology, integrating it into your solution, and verifying that it works correctly for your total solution.

Sometimes it really is faster to build your own technology, from scratch, to meet your needs (consider your choices for creating or licensing a license manager, discussed in Chapter 4).

Motivation/Reward. Vendor-created components are *higher quality* than those you write on your own.

Risk. Many times this just isn't true—in-licensed technology is often lower in quality than what you create from scratch.

Motivation/Reward. Vendor created components are *lighter,* and consume fewer resources, such as memory or processor cycles (presumably because they have been optimized).

Risk. In-licensed technology may be surprising *heavy,* consuming more resources or running more slowly than code you write on your own. Moreover, it is nearly impossible to substantially tune the performance of most in-licensed technologies: You're left with the "switches" the vendor gives you and not much else. You can't recompile someone else's library to turn on multi-threading or modify the code to perform I/O operations more efficiently.

Motivation/Reward. Licensing a component relieves some of the burden associated with technology currency because the vendor will be continually improving this component.

Risk. Vendors don't always update components as fast as needed. Sometimes they drop support for other components that you must still support, such as an OS.

Motivation/Reward. The component is *state of the art,* and using it will *future-proof* your application.

> **Risk.** This sounds like resumé driven design, in which developers seek to use a technology because it is *cool*. If you can't easily justify the use of a given technology based on your real needs, drop it.

Motivation/Reward. Licensing technology is cheaper than building it from scratch.

> **Risk.** The claim that it is cheaper to license a technology is usually based on building an *equivalent* replacement. You may not need an equivalent replacement, which substantially lowers development costs. License fee structures can ruin the economics associated with a good product.

Motivation/Reward. Licensing components will reduce service and support costs because the bugs associated with these components have been handled.

> **Risk.** Providing support for in-licensed technologies is one of the biggest challenges faced in creating a winning solution. While a mature component may have fewer bugs, in-licensing introduces new possibilities for errors.
>
> Suppose you in-license three technologies: A database management system, a search engine, and a report writing tool. When your customer calls you for support, you're going to have to determine the source of the problem and how it should be fixed.
>
> There are several potential sources of problems. It could be a previously undiscovered bug in your code or in any of the in-licensed components. It could be a bug in how you've integrated the component or in how the components interoperate.
>
> When the situation is tense it can become quite easy for each vendor to blame the other. Your customer doesn't care about this infighting; they just want you to fix the problem. Make certain that you can properly support a component before choosing to in-license it.

Fixing Their Code

In one project we decided to license an essential technology from a new start-up. Unfortunately, its libraries had some real problems: The APIs were poorly documented, the technology didn't scale to our needs, the code was written in C++ and riddled with memory leaks, and the technology lacked functions that would greatly enhance our ability to use it.

We could have dropped the technology, but it was felt by all involved, especially product management, that we simply had to have it. Since the underlying algorithms were protected by some very strong patents, we couldn't simply create our own solution. In fact, even if the underlying technology was not protected we probably would not have created our own version, as the technology was based on extremely sophisticated mathematical algorithms, and it would have taken several months for my team to build the knowledge necessary to create this basic technology. Moreover, we had been given direct access to their source code, and developing a duplicate or replacement version would have put us on very precarious legal grounds (if you're going to try this, you need a wide variety of techniques, including clean-room reverse engineering, to protect yourself as much as possible).

The best choice was to work with the vendor to help them modify their technology to meet our needs. I instructed my team to carefully prepare a document that outlined all of the problems with the technology, including the memory leaks. We also documented what we wanted to see in the APIs, prioritized the additional features we wanted, and provided the vendor with sample code that we had written to test their technology. As you can guess, the vendor was stunned by our apparent generosity. They had never expected that we would work so hard to help them be successful. Of course, we were working for our own benefit because we needed this technology. The vendor adopted our suggestions, and I've maintained a strong, positive relationship with them ever since.

Contracts—Where the Action Is

The heart of any technology licensing is the contract that defines the terms and conditions associated with its use. This section outlines some of the basic elements associated with technology contracts and some of the terms and conditions commonly found in them.

Contract Basics

A valid contract requires three things: an offer, acceptance, and consideration.

- An *offer* is a statement by the offeror (a person or a corporation) that indicates a willingness to enter into an agreement on the terms stated.
- *Acceptance* occurs when the entity to whom the offer was addressed (the offeree) indicates a willingness to accept the offeror's proposed agreement.
- *Consideration* is anything of value exchanged by the parties. Technology licensing contracts usually specify monetary forms of consideration as payment terms, discussed in greater detail in the next section.

Pretty boring, yes? The real action is in the license terms, discussed next.

License Terms

Before you can understand how license agreements and if the terms can affect your tarchitecture, you have to have an idea of what kinds of terms exist. This section discusses terms commonly found in technology in-license agreements.

Definitions

A precise, legal description of all important items or terms referenced in the license agreement. Descriptions of technology often go something like this

- *Software* means the object code software proprietary to {licensor} and listed on the pricing schedule.

or this:

- *Software* means the object code software proprietary to {licensor} and listed in Attachment A of this license agreement.

Pay attention to what is listed, because the definitions will often include specific version numbers, supported operating systems, and so forth. If you need something that isn't defined, you may be unable to obtain support and/or upgrades, or you'll have to create another contract to pay your supplier to provide you with the needed or required technology.

Usage or Grant

The manner in which the in-license technology can be used. This section may be one of the longest in the agreement, as it often contains many of the other terms discussed here.

Duration or Term and Other Key Dates

When the agreement begins and ends. By working together, and by negotiating precise agreements about specific dates, the marketect and tarchitect can create a better overall result for their company. To illustrate, suppose that you agree to license a key technology under an annual license fee. You estimate that it will take you four months to integrate the technology, another month to QA the integration, and another two months to roll it out. From your perspective, the best deal will allow development with the new technology to commence once the contract is signed but will delay payment of the initial annual license fee until the technology is actually delivered to customers, the reason being that until the technology is used by a customer it is only a cost to the licensor. From the perspective of the technology provider, payments should begin when the contract is signed because they are not responsible for how long it takes you to integrate the technology and you're getting the benefits of it from the moment it is delivered. Who's right depends on your role in the negotiating process.

Most in-license agreements specify a variety of other important dates beyond the beginning and end of the agreement. If you don't understand these dates you can be headed for a lot of expensive trouble. At a minimum, keep track of the dates listed in Table 5-1.

TABLE 5-1 Dates to Keep Track Of

Date	Why Important
Effective	Date the agreement is considered in effect.
Expiration	Date the agreement is ended. May be specified any number of ways, including an absolute or calculated (such as adding a fixed period of time to the effective date).
Payment	Dates when fees are due, usually listed along with payment terms (e.g., Net 30 or payments shall be made the fifteenth and the last day of each month).
Audit periods	Period during which the licensor can audit how the technology is being used.
Termination notice	Amount of time allowed to terminate the contract. It should be long enough to properly replace the terminated technology. (Many agreements do not specify a long enough period of time.)
Other	A wide variety of additional dates depending on license and contract requirements. The license might require usage reporting according to a well-defined schedule. OEM and partnership agreements may specify quarterly, biannual, or annual technology reviews. Timetables associated with new releases may be listed in the contract, along with penalties should these dates be missed.

The Costly Renewal

One product I worked on had licensed a cross-platform database access library. The license agreement clearly specified an end date. When that date arrived, the product development team had a simple choice: renew the agreement or reengineer the product to remove the library. We chose to reengineer the product, primarily because the vendor wanted to raise the price by several thousand dollars. We also felt that we could improve quality and build a higher-performance implementation using a mixture of freely available technology and a new database access layer. Unfortunately, we couldn't finish the reengineering effort by the specified renewal date, so we had to renew the license agreement at a substantial cost to the company.

A variant of this example is the automatic renewal associated with many contracts. With an automatic renewal, once the contract has been signed it automatically renews unless you explicitly cancel it. It is vitally important that you remain aware of these renewals. Circumstances change, and you may not want to re-up.

Territory

The applicable territory where the in-licensed technology can be used. It is especially important to be careful of geographic restrictions because they can be very hard to honor in our Web-connected world.

Specific Use

Development, quality assurance, technical support, or commercial use of technology as specified by the in-license agreement. It is important to understand what the agreement covers. Note that general terms are sometimes captured in one agreement while specific terms are captured in other, related agreements.

Exclusivity

The degree to which the licensee agrees not to license the technology to anyone else. In general, exclusivity is hard to obtain, although there are ways to get it. For example, suppose that you want to license a key technology but only intend to use it in Europe. It might be possible to obtain exclusivity for the European market. It can also be obtained for higher fees. In most circumstances you don't really need exclusivity, so it isn't something you should worry much about.

Sublicense

The degree to which you (the licensee) can license the technology to a third party. Sublicense rights are usually required for embedded technologies. Suppose, for example, that you license a core technology for use in an information appliance. Chances are very good that you're going to license your solution to your customers, which requires a sublicense right from the technology's vendor. As I will discuss later, sublicense rights often have a substantial impact on your tarchitecture.

Termination

The ways in which one party may terminate the contract. All of the contracts I've seen contain at least one termination clause, and most of them contain several. These clauses allow either party to withdraw from the agreement if there is a breach in performance. Performance breaches are usually specifically stated, such as failure to deliver by a specific date or failure of a system to meet defined processing requirements. Enumerating and describing potential breaches and remedies is one of the more time-consuming aspects of contract negotiation. Withdrawing from a contract because of breach is harder than it seems, because there is usually a process for recovery from the breach (the remedy).

Many technology licensing contracts allow either party to withdraw from the agreement provided that they give the other party sufficient advance warning, ranging from as little as 30 days to as much as one year. Always try to negotiate the longest period of time possible. Replacing an in-licensed technology with another one or with technology developed inhouse always takes longer than planned.

The contract can be terminated if either party goes bankrupt or fails to meet defined financial criteria, if one party elects to drop support for the technology, or if there is a substantial change in control (such as when a competitor acquires a technology provider). Although termination sections can get quite lengthy, it pays to read them carefully.

Renewal

Technology license agreements often contain one or more renewal clauses. These clauses may be automatic, which can actually cause a company to pay too much in fees depending on the evolution of the tarchitecture. Automatic renewal clauses can also create a false sense of security (an automatic renewal does not mean an automic upgrade). In general, I recommend against them as this forces you to evaluate each license agreement to make certain it is still meeting your needs.

Fees or Payment Terms

The foundation of a valid contract is some form of consideration. As discussed in Chapter 4, there are any number of creative licensing and business models, all of which end up in this section of the contract. What is vitally important is that your tarchitecture support the payment terms required. If you are in-licensing a technology based on a transactional business model, *your* tarchitecture needs to support *their* business model. A key point of contention is when the business model required in the license is different from the one you use with your customers. Such differences can often be resolved only through careful negotiations, as discussed in the next section.

Deployment Restrictions

Some license agreements restrict one or more deployment options associated with the technology. For example, the vendor may require one agreement to use the technology for a customer deployment and a different agreement if the licensed technology is to be used as an ASP. Deployment options are discussed in greater detail in Chapter 7.

Other or General Restrictions

In addition to the terms that define what you *can* do, license agreements also carefully define what you *cannot* do. As with the other terms, any of these restrictions can have an impact on your tarchitecture. One example is the very common restriction against any form of reverse engineering or modification of the licensed technology.

The practical effect of this kind of restriction can be fairly surprising. Suppose, for example, that a developer finds a bug in a licensed component. A restriction against reverse engineering may prevent analyzing the technology to identify the bug. Let's say that this restriction doesn't exist, and that you instruct the developer to research the bug. Even if he finds a fix, you may still be out of luck as a restriction against modifications means that you can't apply it. You may only be allowed to supply the fix to the vendor and wait for them to issue a patch or a new release. Since the best thing you can do is influence their development plans, you might be waiting a long time.

Noncompete

Vendors may require that the solution you create not compete with their technology. In other words, you have to create a new offering. This may sound silly, but it prevents people from doing things like licensing a J2EE Web server under the pretense of integrating the technology into a new product without really creating a new product. The net result would be a new solution that competes with the original vendor's solution.

Access to Source Code

Technology agreements often specify that a copy of the source code be placed in escrow and given to the licensee should the licensor breach. In theory, this is great because it makes certain that you can get full and complete access to the technology you need. In practice, however, it is often worthless. Suppose that the vendor does breach and you're given access to the source code. What then? Chances are good that you won't have the necessary skills or staff to manage it.

Marketing Requirements

The agreement may obligate you to issue a press release or allow the licensee or the licensor (or both) the right to use the name or corporate logo of the other on their Web site. Any number of other marketing-related requirements associated with the technology may be laid out, so read these sections carefully. Marketing and branding requirements can mean nasty surprises for your tarchitecture.

When Business Models Collide, Negotiations Ensue

Before you actually license any technology, you have to make certain that your business model is compatible with your provider's business model. If the two are not compatible, you're going to have to negotiate an acceptable compromise. These choices can have a significant impact on the tarchitecture, so everyone needs to be involved.

Suppose, for example, that you're building an enterprise application and you want to base your business model on concurrent users. You want to integrate a search engine, for which your preferred vendor will charge an annual fee. While the business models are different, this situation can be fairly easily resolved. If the annual fee is low enough, you can just pay it. If it is too high, you might be able to negotiate something more acceptable and, again, pay it.

A more complex strategy is to negotiate a license fee based on the projected revenue from your concurrent users, with a *floor* (a guaranteed minimum amount you'll pay) and a *ceiling* (the maximum amount you'll pay). You can pay the floor to gain access to the technology and, at the end of the license term (one year), provide the licensor with a statement that details your actual revenue and the amount of money you owe. This isn't an easy choice because it requires you to disclose potentially sensitive information to your provider (such as the number of concurrent users and your annual revenue). Along the way, your tarchitecture or, more likely, your back-office systems will need to be checked to ensure that you can meet your license payments.

Let's invert the above example and see what happens. In this case, your business model is based on an annual license and your technology provider's business model is based on concurrent users. You can resolve these incompatibilities by creating a

---

Nice Try, But . . .

One product team I managed planned for their system to be built on a major J2EE vendors' application server. The target market was both end users and application service providers who would operate the product on end-users behalf. The default license agreement of the J2EE application vendor explicitly prohibited the right to operate its product in an ASP or service provider environment. Product development stalled until I was able to negotiate a fee schedule that protected the interests of the vendor and was acceptable to our company.

---

mutually agreeable estimate for the number of concurrent users accessing your system for a given annual license, by negotiating with your technology provider to accept an annual license instead of charging by concurrent user, or by offering your provider's technology as an "optional" module and licensing it as a concurrent user option. If you really need this technology and you can see no realistic way to make it an optional module, and if the provider is adamant about maintaining its business model, you may have no other choice but to convert to a concurrent user business model. The point is that you must understand the business models of all your technology suppliers and how they relate to your own.

A special case of business model negotiation is required when you change technology vendors. Let's say that you've created an enterprise application and have licensed a search engine from technology vendor A. Sometime later, for whatever reason, you decide to change to technology vendor B. Along with the fees associated with new systems sold using vendor B's technology, you're going to have to calculate the fees associated with upgrading from vendor A's technology to vendor B's technology. Depending on your licensing agreements, you may or may not be able to charge your customers for the upgrade and/or change. Marketects must model the complete costs associated with changing technology vendors, including the cost of converting the installed base.

Honoring License Agreements

Just about anything you can think of has, or will be, specified in a license agreement. Examples of issues that are commonly covered in license agreements that are likely to affect your tarchitecture include the following.

- *Definition of technical terms:* This is probably the biggest single area of license compliance and one that tarchitects should be familiar with. Do all the definitions reflect the actual product under development? Are the version numbers in the contract correct? What about the defined operating systems and operating environments? Do you have the rights to use the product in the manner envisioned by your business plan? More specifically, can you operate the in-licensed technology in a way that supports all your deployment architectures? Can you fully embed the technology in your product? What is the degree or nature of the embedding? Are there any geographic or export restrictions?

- *APIs:* Can you simply expose any third-party APIs provided in the license agreement? Chances are you can't, and trivially wrapping third-party APIs with your own API won't cut it. Most license agreements require you to *substantially enhance* the functionality of an API before it can be *exposed* (whatever *that* means).

- *Support:* Who fields what support questions? What kind of information must you capture and forward to the third party? License agreements can get very precise about the support information required, affecting both your tarchitecture and other corporate processes.

- *Branding:* Do you have to include visible or direct attribution of the third-party component? Consider the ubiquity of the "Intel Inside" marketing campaign to get a sense of just how important third-party technology suppliers consider such attributions.

Managing In-Licensed Technology

A proven technique for managing in-licensed technology is to create a "wrapper" or "adapter" for it. Instead of programming to the API provided by the vendor, you create an abstraction that you can replace if needed. A common example of this approach in Java is JDBC, which provides a common interface for databases.

Wrappers may make it easier to replace one vendor's technology with another's, but they aren't without their drawbacks. Wrapping frequently introduces a least-common-denominator approach, in which the development team cannot use superior but proprietary technologies. Also, wrapping takes time and must be tested. If the technology is never replaced, or replacement is extremely unlikely, then the additional expense associated with wrapping is not justified. The decision to insulate or protect your tarchitecture from direct access to an in-licensed component must be made with the support and involvement of both the marketect and the tarchitect.

Open Source Licensing

Open-source software presents a wide variety of options for both marketects and tarchitects. Using key open source technologies within your products can provide substantial benefits to you and your customers. This section assumes that you've evaluated a given open-source technology against your technical requirements. It is neither a blanket endorsement nor an indictment of the quality or appropriateness of a given technology but merely states that, for whatever reason, you want to use an open-source technology as part of your overall solution.

The first step is to read the specific license that governs your technology, as all open-source licenses are not created equal. It may seem that the differences are minor, but helping you understand the nuances of these agreements is the kind of work that lawyers love to charge for!

When you're finished reading the license, look for the sections that govern how the licensed technology can be incorporated into other technologies—this is likely to be your most important area of concern. According to the *Open Source Definition, version 1.9* (www.opensource.org), your fears are likely to be unfounded as it is entirely permissible to incorporate a portion of an open-source technology into your product (see also the *GNU Lesser General Public License*), *provided* that you maintain the same rights for the incorporated technology and that you meet the other terms of the specific license.

It is beyond the scope of this book to provide detailed legal advice (remember, I'm not a lawyer), but practically this means that you can often use a variety of open-source technologies to create a new, for-profit work. This is an advantage, and open-source strategies should be considered by both the marketect and the tarchitect.

License Fees

Third-party technologies come with a variety of license fees. A good way to think about these fees is that anything you license represents the business model of some technology provider. As a result, you may have to deal with any of the business models described in the previous chapter or, for that matter, any business model the vendor has identified as being useful. Fortunately, technology providers tend to keep their business models at a reasonable number. The most common approaches, and their likely impact on your tarchitecture, are described next.

Prepaid Fees

In this arrangement you pay an agreed-upon fee for the time-based access or usage of the technology, whether or not you actually use it. Such an arrangement usually results in minimum impact on your tarchitecture, as you are given maximum flexibility in integrating the technology into your system. The fee must be included in the cost estimates provided by the marketect to justify initial development and in the ongoing costs associated with maintaining the system.

Usage-Based Fees

In this arrangement you pay an amount based on some measured usage of the in-licensed technology, often with a minimum payment required to access it (metering). Such an arrangement always has an impact on your tarchitecture because you must ensure your compliance with the license agreement. Specifically, you must make certain that your tarchitecture can capture the metering data. Clearly, it is advantageous for the marketect to negotiate a usage model that is conveniently implemented.

As described earlier, when the fees are variable the in-license technology vendor will often require a minimum payment, referred to as a *floor*. You'll want a *ceiling*, or the maximum amount you'll have to pay—which the vendor will resist. The strength of the technology supplier, the kind of technology being provided, the quality of the relationship, and the overall volume of the expected deal are all factors that play a part in negotiating usage-based fees.

Percentage of Revenue Fees

In this arrangement there are no up-front fees to license the technology; instead, you pay the provider a percentage of the gross or net revenue gained from its use. As with prepaid fees, such an arrangement has little impact on the tarchitecture. It can, however, have a fairly substantial impact on the marketecture, requiring both companies to agree on precise definitions of the fee.

The fee structure specified by the technology vendor will motivate the exact negotiating strategy. However, the following are some universal strategies that I've found useful.

Protection from Product Obsolescence

A marketect needs to know that her technology providers are going to be able to support her needs for as long as necessary. If she intends to support a given platform or operating system, she should make certain that the technology providers are also going to support it.

Protected Pricing

Whatever fee structure is chosen, marketects should try to negotiate such provisions as capped price increases, favored pricing plans (in which no other licensor will be given better terms than the licensee; should such better terms be offered, they will also be automatically applied to the licensee), and volume or usage discounts.

Milestone Payments

One client of mine made a very costly mistake: licensing a key technology from a vendor, paying a very large up-front fee, and subsequently failing to deliver their technology to the market. A better approach is to base fees on key milestones that represent revenue you're going to receive from the use of the technology.

Say that you've decided to license a core technology based on an annual fee (the usage fee). During initial development, when the technology is being incorporated into your product and you're not making any money, the most you should pay is a small access or development fee. The next payment, and typically the largest, should be upon release or launch of your product. The final payment may be due after the product has been in the market for some months.

> ## Negotiate Fees Based on Value
>
> Modularly designed software systems in which each module is separately identified and priced can provide the marketect the greatest advantage in keeping certain in-license fees as low as possible. In one system I created we had licensed in technology from two vendors based on a percentage of revenue. We isolated the usage in specifically created, nonoptional modules and separately priced each one. We then structured the overall price of the system so that the largest cost element was the core system, which consisted of technology that we had created ourselves (thus, no license fees).
>
> This approach served two fundamental purposes. First, it was inherently fair. Because the core system used no in-licensed technology, our vendors had no right to receive fees associated with it. Second, it reduced the percentage of the average selling price subject to license fees and so resulted in greater profits.

Training and Development Costs

You may be able to obtain free or discounted training or educational materials, preferential access to support or development organizations, or special review meetings in which you can meet with key representatives of the technology provider to make certain your needs are being met.

Whatever the licensing arrangement offered by your provider, the actual costs must be given to your marketect for proper financial modeling. Simply put, too many license agreements, or even just one with onerous terms, can seriously erode any profit margins you expect for a product. In extreme cases the wrong fee structure can actually kill a project.

Licensing Economics

Let's say you're a lucky developer who has been asked to explore new technologies for your next system—lucky because you want to learn Java and J2EE as you think it will be a good career move. You download the trial version of SuperSoft's J2Server, a fully compliant J2EE 1.1 container, and use it to build a slick prototype. In fact, the prototype is so useful that your boss is convinced that using Java, a J2EE-based architecture, and especially SuperSoft's J2Server is the obvious choice for your project. Fortunately, your boss wants to make certain that her next release is fully buzzword compliant, so when you suggest this approach she readily agrees.

Believe it or not, you might have just designed yourself into a real jam. Many evaluation and/or trial licenses explicitly prohibit the development of software for commercial uses. Even if you bend the rules and ship the prototype to a customer for evaluation, you *certainly* cannot release your software unless you've secured the necessary rights.

As discussed throughout this chapter, licensing issues must be aligned with your tarchitecture. Saying that you're going base your application on J2Server isn't going to buy you anything if you don't know how SuperSoft is going to charge you for its products. In fact, integrating J2Server could break the economics of your application, something that a good marketect will be able to tell with a basic economic analysis. The following exercise illustrates why.

Let's assume that you're company requires a gross profit margin of 30 percent and that your marketect estimates the average selling price of an annual license at $100K. The current estimated direct and indirect costs associated with this project are $65K, without SuperSoft's licensing fees. So far, so good—your average estimated gross profit is $35K, or 35 percent. Now, let's assume that SuperSoft wants to charge 15% of the gross annual revenue. This means that on a $100K license you will be paying SuperSoft $15K. You can model this as an increase in costs (from $65K to $80K) for each sale, with the net result that your average estimated gross profit just dropped to $20K, or 20 percent. Something needs to change.

The example is intentionally simple, but it illustrates how vitally important it is that the *total* projected and/or actual costs of technology in-licenses be incorporated into the product and business plan. Without them, you're not likely to create a winning solution.

Chapter Summary

- Every system has some in-licensed technology.

- Effective technology in-licensing requires a full understanding by both the marketect and the tarchitect of its risks and the rewards. This understanding creates a stronger negotiating position and leads to more advantageous terms.

- Every technology in-licensing contract comes with terms that directly or indirectly affect both the marketecture and the tarchitecture. The marketect and the tarchitect must read and understand these contracts so that they can properly manage the in-licensed technology and honor all necessary license terms and conditions.

- It is best to align all of the business models that make up the total solution. Usually this is accomplished through several rounds of negotiation.

- There are a variety of techniques to manage in-licensed technology. The most fundamental is to insulate your tarchitecture from it. Theoretically, this is easy. Practically, it is usually very hard.

■ You must understand the fee structures and associated costs of the license agreements.

■ Technologies based on open-source licenses are increasingly attractive.

Check This

❏ We have a valid contract for every licensed component or technology.

❏ We understand the key terms and conditions associated with each in-license. We have looked at all causes for breaching the contract and are certain that we won't breach because of ignorance.

❏ We have assessed the impact of replacing a licensed component or technology.

❏ We have created compatible business models.

Try This

1. What in-licenses do you have?

2. What are their key terms? important dates? rights?

3. Do you have substitutes/alternatives to the licensed technology? Can these substitutes/alternatives be used to improve your operating and/or negotiating strength?

4. Are you properly supporting all aspects of the business models required by your technology in-licenses in your tarchitecture?

Chapter 6
Portability

Marketects and tarchitects alike often pursue portability with a fiery passion. What fuels this fire? Customer need? *Me-too* feature management ("Our competitor supports this feature, so clearly we have to")? The desire to prove technical virtuosity? By exploring the business issues associated with portability you can determine how hot to build your fire.

The Perceived Advantages of Portability

Here are some of the claimed advantages of portability. Do they hold up?

- *Claim: By supporting multiple platforms, we can address a new market segment.* This is compelling since addressing more market segments with essentially the same product is a good thing. Be careful, though. Effective marketing practices teach us that the key to long-term success is *successful* market segmentation. If you're basing your market segmentation on the kind of operating system or hardware platform your customers are using, you may be choosing the wrong approach. Effective segmentation is based on the problems faced by common customers. Focusing on business problems, such as asset management or improving call center efficiency, usually dominates choices of technology platforms.

- *Claim: By supporting multiple platforms, we demonstrate that we can meet our customers idiosyncratic needs.* This marketecture claim has a tarchitecture corollary. By supporting multiple platforms (or standards) we can demonstrate technical skill. Sadly, technical skill rarely wins customers. Solving their needs does. Portability can detract from this, especially when customers who choose a platform for specific features find that your product does not support them because they are not *cross-platform* portable. I refer to this as the *portability paradox*. Customers choose a platform for its unique features and perceived benefits, but most portable applications are explicitly designed to avoid platform-specific features!

My experience indicates that the real motivations for portability aren't that impressive. Here are some that I've stumbled across.

- *Real motivation: Developers think writing portable software is cool.* It can be a lot of fun to write something that is portable. Portability can stretch your limits as an engineer, and creating an architecture that achieves key objectives (such as performance or stability) across multiple operating environments is an impressive accomplishment. On the other hand, it can be a real pain and no fun at all to create a portable application. Subtle differences in operating systems, even operating systems from the same vendor, often means that things that work in one version break in another. Sometimes there is simply no way to offer the same capabilities in different operating environments, which means that you have to compromise either your product objectives or your technical approach or both. Many developers find it tiresome learning about multiple operating environments.

- *Real motivation: One or two early, key, customers demanded different solutions.* Unless a product is managed with considerable discipline, it is easy to do "anything" to secure early, key, customers, sometimes including porting the application to a different platform. This is usually a mistake. When a marketect finds customers who demand different solutions in the early stages of the product he should continue to search for a better customer (where *better* is defined as "within the target market") and not direct the development team to port the code too quickly. Experience has shown that this is arguably the biggest motivation.

The Business Case for Portability

The collective experience of hundreds of projects demonstrates that writing cross-platform, portable code is well within the skill level of most development organizations. But just because you can write such code, should you? The only valid reason for creating portable solutions is that doing so will ultimately result in a more profitable product.

The revenue side of this equation is based on whether or not you'll obtain a sufficiently large market and charge enough to be profitable. Marketects are often good at identifying these revenue drivers. Unfortunately, they often forget some of the key cost factors. Consider the following.

- *The costs of training the developers, QA, and support people in developing within, testing, and supporting each platform.*

- *The costs of purchasing, configuring, and supporting the hardware and software for each supported platform.* Each group has different needs with respect to these activities. Developers are most productive when you give them fast hardware—often the fastest possible. QA and support need a range of hardware choices to adequately reflect the performance options that match target customer segments. Someone has to support all of this hardware. If your IT department isn't up to the task, someone in development, QA, or support will have to do it. This often creates a hidden cost.

- *The testing time for developers and QA to make sure that the product works properly on each platform.* As a general rule, the larger and more complex the matrix of pain (the complete set of your supported platforms) the longer it will take to release your product. This isn't necessarily a cost, but instead can be lost revenue.

- *The complexity of managing multiple release cycles.* Suppose that you choose to support Solaris, HP-UX, and Linux. This means that you must track three operating systems. When Sun Microsystems releases a new version of Solaris, customers will want to know when you are going to support it. Each time you choose to support another platform you relinquish a bit more control over your release cycle.

These costs can only be justified by a sufficiently large target market. One company I worked with supported Solaris–Oracle and Windows–SQLServer. Approximately 90 percent of their installed base ran Windows-SQLServer, accounting for more than 80 percent of total corporate revenue. The cost to support a cross-platform product was not recovered and the company actually *lost* money on a spurious marketing claim.

The following conditions should be met before building cross-platform solutions.

- Your market analysis identifies sufficient revenue to justify the incremental total product development and support costs associated with each platform.

- You have included the total cost associated with developing, testing, and supporting all of the supported platforms. This means the necessary hardware and the skills necessary to maintain and configure these machines.

- You have sufficient development resources to allow you to create, test, and support multiple platforms.

- You understand the relative impact the various platforms you must support have on your development efforts and can manage it. For example, if you're going to support Solaris and Windows you have to account for their differing release schedules.

A good rule of thumb is that it is easier to justify a portable *technology* than a portable *application*. By technology, I mean a solution designed to be a component of a larger solution. Examples include relational databases and communication libraries

Portability Is *Always* about the Money

I've managed both ends of the portability spectrum. We explicitly designed a new kind of enterprise-class system for an emerging market that was not portable but was designed to run only on Microsoft products—MS Windows NT/2000 and SQLServer—using Microsoft development tools. Our first challenge was selling the system to Sun Microsystems. As you can guess, the initial response was "No thanks, we don't want a system based on Microsoft technology " (although the original wording associated with the rejection was a *bit* stronger). Sun wanted us to port the system to Java/J2EE running on Solaris and Oracle. We also received a no from Pfizer on the grounds that our Microsoft-based solution didn't fit their corporate Solaris–Oracle requirements.

It was difficult to handle these early rejections because we knew that Sun and Pfizer would be good customers and we were a young and hungry startup. But a simple cost analysis showed that we couldn't afford to port the application with the available resources. When we asked Sun for the necessary development funds, they said no. I don't blame them, for we estimated that the job would cost several million dollars.

Although the situation seemed bleak, everyone supported the decision to maintain a platform-specific focus—an amazing show of discipline, especially given our hunger for revenue. Nonetheless, we kept improving our technology and growing our customer list. After each release, we would talk again with Sun and Pfizer. Eventually, something amazing happened: The system had reached the point where its feature set was so compelling that the two companies simply couldn't live without it. Furthermore, their competitors were adopting the system, which provided them with additional incentive to license it. And they did—first Pfizer and later Sun. The key lesson I learned is that building a good solution on a single platform is more important than building a mediocre solution on many.

At the other end of the portability spectrum, I managed server software that ran on Microsoft, Sun, and Linux operating systems and client software that ran on Windows and Macintosh. Unlike the previous example, these were not complete applications (solutions) but core technologies embedded in our customers' environments as part of a larger solution. In this case, the technology requirements justified a portable solution. On the server side, the revenue distribution was almost evenly split between customers running Windows and UNIX. On the client side, our biggest customers, including Adobe, Symantec, Macromedia, Corel, and Roxio, required both Windows and Macintosh. Indeed, they continually asked us to port our technology to additional platforms. This confirms that listening to your customers and making certain portable solutions will be profitable solutions is your best approach.

offered to large target markets. The classic example of Oracle in the book *Crossing the Chasm* [Moore 1999] shows how a portable technology helped a company win significant market share.

Applications, which are rarely designed to be a component of a larger solution, can often achieve a large and profitable enough market share within a given operating environment so that portability doesn't make sense. Countless applications from profitable companies run only one operating system (e.g., Sun Solaris, MS Windows, IBM 360). These companies, for a variety of reasons, have decided to focus on a target environment.

Rules of thumb are just that: rules of thumb. There are also numerous counter-examples of platform-specific technologies and portable applications. Examples of portable applications include any number of mid-range server or desktop applications. Concrete examples are some of the mid-range graphics tools that run on both Macintosh and Windows platforms. For the average user, these tools are acceptable. For the professional, they aren't, and professionals turn to high-end, platform-specific tools that are tuned to leverage all of the capabilities of a given platform. There are also many examples of platform-specific technologies, such as network accelerators that run only on Solaris, or serial port expansion cards that run only on Wintel platforms. The issues are complex, but all of them boil down to well-defined target markets that ultimately determine how the development team should create the application.

Creating Portable Applications

Let's assume that there is sufficient economic justification for writing a portable application. The following sections describe some techniques I've found helpful in making this happen.

Use an Interpreted Language

From Lisp to Smalltalk, Java, and Perl, interpreted languages have an immediate portability advantage over compiled languages because the interpreter provides a much-needed layer of insulation from the underlying operating system. Of course, this doesn't mean that interpreters are foolproof, because differences in operating systems often find their ways into them. In fact, resource handling, threading, file system manipulations, network libraries, and user interfaces all present challenges to the portability of interpreted languages. Still, as a general rule such languages make sense if you're planning on building a portable system (provided, of course, that you have made certain that your language has an interpreter on every platform you intend to support).

If you're using a compiled language, you have to be sure that a compiler exists on every target platform. In addition, you need to educate the development team on the specific idioms that enhance portability within that language. If you're using C or C++, these techniques include using carefully designed source code management and build systems that select the proper file for a given target platform as well as conditionally include specific source code based on the language. Conditionally compiled code is more challenging than normal code because it is harder to write and maintain than its platform-specific counterparts, but the overall process is quite manageable. I know, because I've done it. You can too.

Use Standards-Based Persistent Storage

By persistent storage, I mean the ability to store and retrieve data on persistent media, such as a hard drive. For simple data use XML stored within whatever file abstraction is provided by the target platform. For complex, structured data use a relational database accessed through an intermediary layer like OBDC, Java's JDBC, or Perl's ODB. Although ANSI SQL is far less portable than it should be, try to use it. Limit the use of vendor-specific embedded procedures, such as Transact SQL.

Make Business Logic Portable

The area of your system that should be the most portable is your business logic. As detailed in Chapter 8, a well-architected system isolates business logic. This code should be easliy portable to other environments. If it isn't, further investigation is warranted to ensure that the development staff is not making poor implementation choices.

Closer to the User Means Less Portability

The backend infrastructure holds the areas of greatest portability. Moving from the server or backend toward the user, portability tends to decrease. Indeed, despite a variety of vendor claims to the contrary, the user interface is the area of lowest portability, because of substantial device differences in color schemes, fonts, display resolutions, and so forth. These realities, which don't appear likely to change, suggest a very practical approach in which the greatest investments in portability are in backend or infrastructure (e.g., invest in server-side portability before client-side portability).

Use XML for Standardized, Interoperable Communications between Subsystems

In complex distributed systems that run on different platforms, you will eventually have to resolve the issue of subsystem interoperation. Fortunately, you won't have work too hard, for the bright and talented people who invented the core technologies powering Web services, including XML, SOAP, WSDL, and XSLT, have already done all the heavy lifting. Use XML to support interoperable communications between subsystems—you'll be happy you did!

When an application is centralized on a single platform, or when you require extremely high performance, you might want to consider a non-XML solution. Converting in-memory data into XML and back consumes a fair amount of resources and is not the best choice for every situation. Do this very carefully, as my own experience shows that XML is, in general, the most flexible solution, even though it is slower.

Avoid Hiding The Power of a Specific Platform in the Name of Portability

Consider database portability. While the major vendors claim to support ANSI SQL, they all provide vendor-specific variants tailored to different operations. Oracle's commands for manipulating hierarchies are too powerful to ignore for many applications. SQLServer 2000 commands for manipulating XML are just too fast to ignore. Challenge the notion that portability must mean taking the "lowest common denominator." Structure your tarchitecture to take advantage of the power of specific platforms.

The Matrix of *Pain*

Let's assume that you've made the decision to support more than one platform. Perhaps the market is fragmented and supporting multiple platforms is the only way you can create sufficient revenue. Perhaps your target market simply demands multiple platforms. This is common in enterprise software when a customer standardizes on one platform for its IT infrastructure. Or perhaps your development organization has chosen a very low cost and highly portable implementation, such as a Web solution written in Perl that interfaces to MySQL, making the actual cost to support an additional platform extremely low.

One of the most important things that can be done to minimize the *pain* of portability is to make certain that development and QA understand the relative priorities of the market. Without clear priorities, *everyone* is going to waste precious time developing and testing the wrong parts of the system or not sufficiently testing the parts that matter the most to customers. The best technique for prioritizing is to create market-driven configuration matrices for use by development and QA (the matrix of *pain*). They are a variant of the *all pairs* technique used by QA for organizing test cases. The marketect should drive this process, with participation from development, QA, services, sales, and support.

Suppose that you're building a Web-based system and you want to support the following:

- Five operating systems on two platforms (Solaris 2.7 and 2.8, MS Windows NT 3.5.1 and 4.0, and XP Server)
- Two Web servers (IIS and Apache, omitting versions for simplification)
- Two browsers (Netscape and Internet Explorer)
- Four databases (Oracle 8i and 9i, SQLServer 7.0 and 2000).

The total number of possible combinations for development and testing is thus {OS × Web server × Browser × DB } = { 5 × 2 × 2 × 4 } = 80, which, I'll take as a given, is too many for your QA staff. (If your QA staff is large enough to handle all 80 combinations it's too large.) Your QA manager estimates that his team of three people can handle perhaps 7 to 9 configurations. Your development manager follows the QA manager's lead, under the agreement that development will work on the primary configuration and QA will certify all others. As is common in cross-platform development, the strongest constraints come from QA, not development. Thus, you have to trim 80 possible configurations down to 7 to 9, in way that ensures that your most important configurations are covered.

Step 1: Remove Configurations

A simple reading of the list of supported components demonstrates that many don't make sense. No company that I know of runs SQLServer 2000 on Solaris 2.8! In addition, the marketect may explicitly choose not to support a possible configuration. For example, she may know that Oracle 8i is only supported on Solaris 2.6 because an important customer has not yet migrated to Solaris 2.7. Discussions with this customer indicate that when it migrates to Solaris 2.7 it will still use Oracle 8i until the system has proven itself stable, when it will migrate to Oracle 9i.

Table 6-1 identifies impossible configurations. It shows an interesting effect. Because you need *one* of each of the elements to create a complete configuration, the

TABLE 6-1   Impossible Configurations

	Operating System				
	Solaris		MS Windows		
	2.6	2.7	NT 3.5.1	NT 4.0	XP Server
Apache	PC	PC	PC	PC	PC
IIS	NA	NA	PC	PC	PC
Netscape	PC	PC	PC	PC	PC
IE	NA	NA	PC	PC	PC
Oracle 8i	PC	PC	NS	PC	PC
Oracle 9i	NS	PC	NS	PC	PC
SQLServer 7	NA	NA	PC	PC	PC
SQLServer 2000	NA	NA	NS	PC	PC
Total Configurations (39):	1	2	4	16	16

PC = Possible configuration;
NS = Not supported;
NA = Not applicable

total number of configurations is dramatically reduced. There is only *one* supported configuration for Solaris 2.6: Apache, Netscape, and Oracle 8i, and only *two* for Solaris 2.7.

Step 2: Rank-Order Configurations

Although 39 is smaller than 80, this matrix is still not sufficiently prioritized. The next step in making it manageable is to work with other groups to prioritize every possible/ supported configuration. In the process you will gain insight into a variety of things, including which configurations

- Are actually installed in the field, by actual or perceived frequency of installation
- Are used by the largest, most profitable, or otherwise "most important" customers
- Are going to be most heavily promoted by marketing in the upcoming release (these *have* to work)
- Are most easily or capably supported by the support organization
- Are most likely to provide you with the coverage you need to test full functionality

A variety of techniques achieve a suitable prioritization. I've spent the bulk of my career working in enterprise-class software, and for most of the products I worked on we were able to prioritize the most important configurations pretty quickly (usually in one afternoon). Once you're finished, consider color-coding individual cells red, yellow, and blue for "must test," "should test," and "would like to test but we know we probably won't get to it" to convert your matrix into an easily referenced visual aide.

For larger, more complex software or for developers or managers who insist on numbers, presumably because they believe that numbers will lead to a better decision, assign to each major area a number between 0 and 1 so that all the areas add up to 1. These numbers represent consensually created priorities. Suppose that in discussing the matrix it becomes apparent that no known customers actually use Netscape or Oracle 8i on Windows XP Server, nor are any expected to. This results in a further reduction of configurations to be tested, as shown in Table 6-2.

Step 3: Make the Final Cut

You still have more work to do, as 29 configurations are clearly too many. You have to finalize this matrix and get the configurations down to a manageable number. Be forewarned: This will take at least two passes. As you begin this process, see if you can find additional information on the distribution of customer configurations, organized as a Pareto chart. This will prove invaluable as you make your final choices.

TABLE 6-2 Configurations to be Tested

| | Operating System | | | | |
| | Solaris | | MS Windows | | |
	2.6	2.7	NT 3.5.1	NT 4.0	XP Server
Apache	1	1	0.2	0.5	0.3
IIS			0.8	0.5	0.7
Netscape	1	1	0.2	0.2	0
IE			1	0.8	1
Oracle 8i	1	0.5		0.1	0
Oracle 9i		0.5		0.3	0.3
SQLServer 7			1	0.5	0.2
SQLServer 2000				0.1	0.5
Totals (29):	1	2	4	16	6

In the first pass, consider the impact of the installed base. Suppose that only 20 percent of it uses Solaris but accounts for 53 percent of overall revenue. In other words, you're going to be testing all three Solaris configurations! This leaves you with four to six possible configurations for MS Windows.

Your product and technical maps (see Appendix B) tell you that NT 3.5.1 is going to be phased out after this release and that only a few customers are using it. Based on this information, everyone agrees that one configuration—NT 3.5.1 with IIS, IE, and SQLServer 7—will be okay.

You know you need to test Apache and Netscape. Furthermore, you believe that most customers are going to be on NT 4.0 for quite some time and so you want QA to concentrate its efforts here.

With your knowledge of the architecture you believe that the database access layer uses the same SQL commands for Oracle and SQLServer on any given operating system. Just to be sure, you ask your tarchitect or development manager to run a quick binary comparison on the source code. Yes, the SQL is the same. This doesn't mean that the databases will operate in the same manner but just that if you certify your code on one of them, such as Oracle 8i, you have reasonable evidence that it should work on the other. This knowledge produces Table 6-3. Note that all major configurations are tested at least once.

Unfortunately, you have 14 configurations, which is at least five more than your estimates allow. Removing IIS from NT 4.0 removes four more configurations. The final set is listed in Table 6-4, which is more than you think you can test in the allotted time. From here, you'll have to find additional ways to either test the product as you wish or further reduce the number of configurations. The most likely way to make the cut is by obtaining more hardware, either internally or from your customers, or by a

TABLE 6-3 Simplifying Configurations

| | Operating System | | | | |
| | Solaris | | MS Windows | | |
	2.6	2.7	NT 3.5.1	NT 4.0	XP Server
Apache	✓	✓		✓	
IIS			✓	✓	✓
Netscape	✓	✓		✓	
IE			✓	✓	✓
Oracle 8i	✓	✓		✓	
Oracle 9i		✓			✓
SQLServer 7			✓	✓	
SQLServer 2000					✓
Totals (14):	1	2	1	8	2

TABLE 6-4 Final Configuration Set

| | Operating System | | | | |
| | Solaris | | MS Windows | | |
	2.6	2.7	NT 3.5.1	NT 4.0	XP Server
Apache	✓	✓		✓	
IIS			✓		✓
Netscape	✓	✓		✓	
IE			✓	✓	✓
Oracle 8i	✓	✓		✓	
Oracle 9i		✓			✓
SQLServer 7			✓	✓	
SQLServer 2000					✓
Totals (10):	1	2	1	4	2

beta program in which your beta customers handle testing configurations that QA won't.

I have intentionally simplified this example. In a real Web-based system, you would probably support more versions of the browser (4 to 8) and more versions of the Web server (2 to 4), and you would probably specify other important variables, such as proxies and firewalls. You also need to add an entry for each version of the application that might exist on the same platform in order to check for any negative interactions between them. These would dramatically increase the potential number of configurations. In one multiplatform, multilingual, Internet-based client application, we had more than 4,000 possible configurations. We were able to reduce this to about 200 tested configurations—with a lot of work.

This approach to prioritizing works for smaller numbers of configurations, but it starts to break down when there are a lot of configuration elements or a lot of possible values for each element. When this happens, you need a more automated approach for organizing your initial set of configurations and then prioritizing them based on the market parameters I mentioned earlier. This is referred to as the *all pairs* technique, and it ensures that all pairings of parameters are covered in the test cases without covering all combinations. James Bach has posted a free tool to calculate test cases using the all pairs technique at *www.satisfice.com*. I want to stress that the output of all pairs should be reviewed to ensure that the market issues presented earlier are covered. Specifically, when you get into a "don't care" condition, prioritize based on marketing needs.

Understanding the matrix of pain makes it crystal clear that *every time* you add another platform you increase the total workload associated with your system.

Beware the Promises You Make

Be vigilant about managing contracts and stating what you support. I once inherited a contract that had us supporting "Macintosh OS 8.1 and later." This committed our marketing team to a future that we didn't want to embrace. More drastically, it created a nearly impossible task for my development team! Practice vigilance when creating portable software with respect to contracts. At the very least, make certain that the versions and platforms you support are very clearly identified. You may also want to specify individual support policies for various platforms, such as limiting the amount of time in which you will provide support for an older platform.

Chapter Summary

- Portability advocates make many claims to support their desires. Common claims include
  - Addressing a new target market
  - Supporting existing customers, who may prefer a different platform but have accepted the current one

- The real reasons you may have, or may be creating, a portable application are often not as grandiose. They may include
  - Developers thinking it is easy and/or cool
  - One or two early innovators or early adopters demanding different solutions

  Carefully check whatever claims your portability champion is making.

- The only valid business case for creating portable applications is that you'll profit by doing so. Marketects are often good at modeling the revenue, but not necessarily the costs, of creating portable applications.

- Creating portable applications is harder than you think. And it will take longer than you want.

- It is usually easier to justify a portable *technology* than a portable *application*.

- There are a variety of proven ways to create portable applications. Learn them.

- Your "matrix of pain" is the complete set of configurations that must be tested in a given release. To create a manageable matrix of pain
  - Remove configurations that don't make sense or are explicitly not supported
  - Rank-order the remaining configurations
  - Review the result and make the final cut

- Always be explicit about the configurations you support. Be *very* cautious about committing to support new configurations.

Check This

- ❑ Each platform that we support has sufficient development, quality assurance, technical support, and sales resources.
- ❑ We have allocated sufficient time to test on each supported platform.
- ❑ We have made entries in our tarchitecture map that capture the significant releases of our platform vendors.
- ❑ We have created a market-driven configuration matrix to help guide our testing efforts.

Try This

1. What platforms do you support? Why?
2. What is the market share of each platform? the cost/benefit of each platform?
3. What might happen if you dropped support for a platform? added support for a platform?

Chapter 7
Deployment Architecture

Enterprise-class software systems have seen many phases of evolution. Centralized mainframe systems evolved into client/server systems, client/server systems evolved into distributed systems, and distributed systems, still in their infancy, are now being recast as reconfigurable Web services. Each of these deployment architectures spawned many variants. Emerging Web architectures extend these ideas and add new ones, bringing alleged new benefits for users and keeping both marketects and tarchitects busy. Not surprisingly, we are also carrying each of these major architectural styles into the future, as much for the unique advantages they offer as for the legacy systems they've left behind.

The wide variety of deployment architectures for enterprise-class software is starting to more strongly influence deployment architectures for common packaged software applications ("shrink wrapped" applications that usually cost less than $500). We're now seeing traditional applications offered as services. As bandwidth continues to increase and hardware devices become more sophisticated, the number of deployment choices increases.

I use the term *deployment architecture* to describe the manner in which a customer deploys a system. This is related to the UML definition of deployment architecture but my focus is more on the strategic implications of a deployment choice and less on the lower-level decisions such as how to allocate work in a multiprocessor computer system. Emerging Web technologies and business models present tarchitects and marketects with considerable creative flexibility. This chapter will help you sort through some of the business and technical issues associated with choosing a deployment architecture so that your customer will see your choice as a winning solution.

Deployment Choices

Common choices for software deployment architectures are discussed in the following sections.

Customer Site

This type of deployment is the most traditional and the most common. The software is installed at the customer's site and is configured, operated, and maintained by the customer. For common packaged software for the consumer market, such as I'm using to write this book, it means I've purchased, installed, and configured it on my laptop. Enterprise-class software, such as corporate finance system, warehouse management, and customer relationship management (CRM), is almost always controlled by the corporate IT department.

Enterprise-class software is usually installed and configured through a consulting assignment. The system vendor may provide professional services to the customer or subcontract them to a major consulting firm (such as EDS, Bearing Point, or Accenture). The duration of the assignment is often a function of the system's effect on existing corporate processes, any or all of which may have to be substantially modified before, during, and often after the installation.

Application Service Provider

An application service provider (ASP) operates an application for the customer, offering a limited set of services, and rarely a complete solution. For example, the ASP may provide 24/7 system monitoring, routine backups, and automatic access to additional internet bandwidth, but not application technical support. The specific services provided by the ASP must be negotiated.

ASPs are slightly more common for business applications, although that is changing. For example, many early ASPs offered large enterprise applications to smaller customers. Newer ASPs offer consumer applications, such as estate or tax planning software, as a service.

I'm not making a distinction between a software publisher that offers its application as an ASP and a software publisher that licenses its application to a third party that then offers it as an ASP. These distinctions, while important for the publisher and the third-party provider, are largely irrelevant for the purposes of this chapter.

Managed Service Provider

A managed service provider (MSP) extends the concept of an ASP by offering an array of services in addition to the operation of the application. In marketing terms, an

ASP competes at the level of the generic/expected product while an MSP competes at the level of the expected/augmented product. The exact services offered vary, but usually they include extensive monitoring and backup, and possibly call center support, commerce operations/management, and security/firewall management. Early MSPs targeted the business market. Some recent ones target very specific consumer markets, such as corporate e-mail hosting or digital photo appliances.

MSPs focused on very well-defined specialized hardware market niches will continue to emerge. For example, in the financial services industry some very large MSPs offer online banking services to millions of consumers. Of course, you don't know this because the MSP has allowed the bank offering these services full branding control.

In both ASP and MSP, relationships it is common for service level agreements (SLAs) to precisely define acceptable performance parameters. Also, when the application is a traditional software system, at least some customer data is stored at the service provider. This has important tactical and strategic implications for security and operations that extend far beyond the service actually being offered.

Transactional (Web Service)

A transaction deployment is one that computes an answer in a single, whole transaction, often through Web service protocols. It commonly provides services to individual users, such as when you ask for a map on the Internet. In certain cases end user data may be stored at the service provider, but this is rarely corporate data. This style of system is not yet common in enterprise software, but recent efforts to build complex systems around collections of transactional Web services may dramatically increase its use. Web-service based application architectures will eventually become common for every type of application. This does not mean that they will "win," because they are not appropriate to every market segment. It does mean that we are going to be faced with increasingly sophisticated choices.

The four broad categories just outlined capture the basic deployment options. Savvy marketects have created subtle variants to gain a competitive or positioning edge. For example, some service providers classify themselves as "Internet business service provider" (IBSPs), focusing on a single element of a complex solution (e.g., loan portfolio management for banks). Others define themselves as enterprise application providers (EAPs) and focus on a single kind of enterprise-class system, in the hope that they can leverage that experience across their entire customer base. In the framework presented above, IBSPs and EAPs would be classified as either managed service providers or application service providers, depending on the specific services they offer.

> ### The Hybrid Deployment Architecture
>
> I've been presenting deployment architectures as relatively exclusive choices: either ASPs or MSPs. In fact, there is no technical requirement that the deployment architecture be all one way or another. As is true with other aspects of tarchitecture, it is often best to let your customer and the problem guide you in your choice.
>
> One of the more successful tarchitectures I helped create was a true hybrid. In this case, customers needed realtime access to more than five terabytes of data and required certain kinds of private transactional data. The solution was straightforward: Put some parts of the design, such as the transactional data, at the customer's site; put other parts, such as the five terabytes of data, at a service provider. Making this hybrid architecture work was a bit of a challenge, but the benefits to our customers were worth our efforts.

Customer Influences on Deployment Architectures

Choosing a deployment architecture that meets your customer's expectations is an important part of a winning solution. Consider the following customer concerns when making this choice.

Control and Integration

Customers vary in their perceived need to *control* the software system. As a reasonably sophisticated end user of software, I want to control what extensions or changes I make to my system. Thus, I don't want a managed service for my laptop because I want to be able to add or remove software as I see fit. But I don't want to control everything! I just want my high speed internet connection firewall to "work" without spending a lot of time configuring or adjusting it.

Customers of enterprise-class software have similar demands for control, expressed in a number of ways. They may want to control the system's operational infrastructure. Specifically, they may believe that the control afforded by a system operating onsite is absolutely crucial for mission-critical applications ("I know *exactly* who is going to answer the pager if the system breaks and how long it will take them to fix it"). Conversely, they may be happy to give control to a service provider based on their perception that the service provider can provide high-quality, uninterrupted service.

Another issue associated with control is the long-term retention and management of data. Service providers who approach this topic carefully may be able to argue that they can do a better job than the customer. Alternatively, the customer may already have sophisticated policies, and may simply feel more confident in their own ability to manage data.

It is imperative that the marketect understand the control issues that are most important to the target ASP or MSP customer. Failing to do so will prevent you from creating a winning solution. Conversely, understanding the deeper concerns that your target customer has regarding deployment will enable you to handle them with skill.

As *integration* needs increase so does the likelihood that the system will be deployed at the customer site. This can range for integration between common desktop applications to linking your CRM system with your inventory management and fulfillment system.

Data Security/Privacy and Peak Loads

The nature of the data manipulated by the system influences customer perceptions of an appropriate deployment architecture. Hospital payroll data, for example, may not be viewed as sensitively as patient records. As a result, the hospital may opt for a managed service solution for payroll processing but license a patient record management system from a reputable vendor and run it internally. A professional services firm, on the other hand, may have a strong need for privacy with respect to payroll data and require that it be managed inhouse. In the case of my home firewall, there is no data to manage, so there is no need for data security. Nonetheless, I purchased a hardware-based firewall because I didn't want to pay a monthly service fee to my ISP. You need to understand your customer's relationship to the data managed by your application, as developers can easily make poor choices based on faulty assumptions. I will talk more about data later in this chapter.

Depending on the application, it can be more cost-effective to place the application at an ASP/MSP whose equipment and/or communications bandwidth can handle peak loads that are not cost-effective to handle with your own dedicated equipment.

Costs and Vendor Confidence

There are times when an xSP (meaning either an ASP or an MSP) can offer a sophisticated, expensive application at a fraction of what it would cost the customer to license and deploy it onsite. Sometimes this is because the xSP can sublicense an application in way that provides access to smaller businesses. Other times it's because the customer doesn't have to invest in the total infrastructure needed to make the solution work.

How does your customer perceive you? Are you a stereotypical Internet startup with programmers sleeping on cots, or are you an EDS- or IBM-style systems integration firm where formal dress is still common? Put another way, would you trust your company's most sensitive data to an Internet startup that can't properly manage its internal servers' passwords? Answering these questions will help you understand why a customer may be somewhat reluctant to entrust the operation of its mission-critical system to your company's engineers.

Earlier I mentioned that failed ASPs have made customers wary about trusting their data and operations to outside parties. Be aware that your promotional materials may have to move beyond simply touting the benefits of your solution to providing access to detailed financial statements in an effort to demonstrate that you have long-term viability in the marketplace. This is often referred to as a *viability test,* and unless you can demonstrate that your company will be viable for the next few years, you may not win the deal.

As stated earlier, another aspect of confidence concerns the manner in which you archive and retain your customer's data. As your total solution evolves, you will inevitably change the kind of data you're storing. Reassuring customers that they can always get at old data is important to your complete solution design.

Customer Skills and Experiences and Geographic Distribution

Your application and its deployment architecture will dictate the skills and experience required by your customer's staff. If the application has relatively simple operational requirements, this isn't really a factor. It is when the application exhibits complex operational requirements that the choices become interesting.

The easiest deployment choice, from the perspective of the vendor, is to make your customer responsible for all system operation. They have to care for and feed the application—monitoring it, backing it up, administering it, and so forth. All of these are skills that must be learned.

If you elect to offer the application as an xSP or license an xSP to offer the application on your behalf, you or your xSP partner will have to assume the responsibility to meet the needs of your customer. Be careful, as customers often place greater demands on xSPs than on their own MIS staff. One or the other of you will have to hire a staff with enough experience and skills to create the necessary data center. You can subcontract this, and many companies do, but you still need someone with the necessary experience to manage the subcontractor.

It is important to consider the operational culture associated with the deployment architecture. If your company started as a highly dynamic, "let's just get it done" entrepreneurial venture, you may find it hard to switch to the more formal demands of data center operation. In an entrepreneurial company, for example, data center security is often lax; in an xSP, data centers require tight operational control.

It can often be easier for a customer to provide an application to geographically dispersed employees or workgroups when an xSP manages it.

As you consider how customers influence your choices, keep in mind that your target customer will provide you with the strongest requirements for a deployment architecture. Earlier in the book I talked about the dangers of resumé-driven design, in which designers make technical choices in order to pad their resumés. I've witnessed the same phenomenon in choosing a deployment architecture. Investor-driven design swept through Silicon Valley in the late 1990s as many startups were capitalizing on the growing popularity of xSPs. Many of these xSPs subsequently failed, for reasons that included an inability to understand their customer's true motivations for a deployment architecture. Unfortunately, some failures were truly catastrophic. Many customers

---

Please Disregard Those Credit Cards

One of my clients running a managed service had a rather embarrassing episode when the director of managed services operations distributed a spreadsheet that detailed the growth in customer transaction revenues. Unfortunately, he forgot to delete the worksheet that contained the complete customer contact information, including credit card numbers! As you can guess, much more appropriate operational controls were put in place after this incident. As the vendor, you should make certain this kind of mistake never happens. As a potential customer of an ASP or MSP, you have the right to demand a careful review and audit of all operational procedures.

---

irretrievably lost crucial corporate data when these companies went under. Such losses have made corporations justifiably wary about storing key data at a service provider.

For this reason, and others, it is essential that the marketect choosing a deployment architecture work to understand not just customer requirements but corporate objectives as well.

When the Risk Really Is Too Great

One client of mine had created a traditional, enterprise-class system for manipulating extremely sensitive data that represented hundreds of millions of dollars worth of intellectual property. The initial customer-site deployment model was a success because customers were allowed complete control over its every aspect. Unfortunately, it came with a rather high price tag, and my client felt that they had to offer an ASP model to broaden their market. Unfortunately, they failed to understand that the factors described above are not isolated from each other. Instead, each is considered and weighed against another in the context of a winning solution.

In this specific example, the extreme sensitivity of the data meant that my client would have to build a substantial infrastructure and ensure that the data center was operated under exceptionally stringent conditions. However, they had neither the organizational nor operational maturity to undertake this task. In addition, many of the target customers were global companies who required 24/7 access and support. Preliminary research also indicated that customers didn't want an ASP—they wanted an MSP. Sadly, my client chose not to invest in the additional infrastructure to create an MSP until the new model had proven successful.

I urged my client to avoid offering the ASP and to create a truly winning solution. To my dismay, they went ahead with their plans and introduced the new model. It failed, and the company eventually went bankrupt.

Corporate Influences on Deployment Architecture

The marketect must consider more than customer requirements when choosing a deployment architecture. Sustainable winning solutions require the marketect to understand the capabilities, desires, needs, and short- and long-term strategies of the corporation offering the solution. Here are some of the strongest corporate influences on deployment architectures.

Sales Cycle

The sales cycle refers to the length of time and number of steps it takes a corporation to make a sale. In general, it is correlated to the price and complexity of the software. Consumer software, with low price points, simpler implementation and integration requirements, and very few decision makers (usually one or two) has a relatively short sales cycle. Enterprise-class software, with substantially higher price points, complex implementation and integration requirements, and many decision makers (usually a committee with or without approval authority) usually has a longer one. When a corporation is considering a multimillion dollar purchase, they're going to think about it carefully. I've been involved with sales that took two years or more.

In general, most consumer software is still deployed on a PC (a customer site deployment), so I won't discuss its relationship to the sales cycle further. Business software is a different matter. If you seek a shorter sales cycle, consider deploying your software as an xSP or licensing it to one that is properly qualified. The sales cycle is usually shorter and the implementation cycle should be. This is important, as once customers have made the commitment to your product they're going to want it up and running as quickly as possible. Watch out, though. Choosing this option without understanding customer influences is not going to create a winning solution.

Experience with xSPs indicates an even more complex situation than I've just described. There are times when a customer wants to use an xSP as a quick starter solution and then migrate it to their site (for an on-site deployment). I've also had to manage reverse migrations, in which customer-site deployments were migrated to a service provider primarily because of the service provider's superior infrastructure. While this kind of deployment migration is extremely rare at the moment, I expect that it will become more common in the future.

Infrastructure Investment

When an application provider considers offering their solution as an xSP or Web service, they must carefully consider the investment needed to create a long-term, viable offering. Companies with a service-based applications model routinely underestimate the often significant investment that is required to create a reliable infrastructure capable of handling projected demands.

You don't have to create a solid infrastructure, but then you risk poor customer service. Investment calculations must include technical resources (such as hardware and infrastructure) and nontechnical resources (experienced data center staff, support staff, and so forth). Unless your corporation has the necessary capital and willpower to invest in a solid infrastructure, I recommend against an xSP or Web service.

Cash Flow

Like sales cycle and infrastructure investment, cash flow must be carefully modeled. Suppose, for example, that an MSP offers a complex enterprise application to customers on a rental basis, with no minimum contract. If they are paying an annual license (common), they have a single payment due at the beginning of their year of service. If their customers are paying a rental, it may not be enough for the MSP to pay for the next annual license. Ultimately, xSPs must take a careful, sober approach to managing the cash reserves needed for successful long-term operations.

Flexibility

An installed base of customers who use your software on their premises can limit your ability to rapidly innovate and improve it. Customers who have invested time and money in a given release are usually reluctant to modify it. As a result, chances are good that if you go with customer-site deployment you will be supporting several releases in the field simultaneously.

This is one of the most appealing aspects of offering your solution as an xSP or Web service. By maintaining complete control, you gain considerable flexibility in such things as upgrade schedules. In an emerging market, where rapid release cycles are often required for growth, you have the luxury of upgrading as often as necessary. Patches can be quickly obtained and installed by development. Of course, appropriate care must be taken whenever you modify your own operational environment, but installing a new release in an operational environment that you control is usually much easier that coordinating upgrades across dozens, hundreds, or thousands of customers.

Geographic Distribution

If you're trying to sell an application to a global company, they have the right to expect that the deployment will provide them with the necessary support and service. When they choose a customer-site deployment, they can control the level of service provided by their inhouse MIS staff, including such things as the language used to answer the phone. When considering an xSP, they may require that it provide local customer support throughout the world.

A global company may also make unforeseen technical demands on the total solution. If an application is deployed inhouse, the customer is responsible for installing and maintaining it as appropriate, subject to the license terms. If, on the other hand, you're providing the application as an xSP, you may have to install it in multiple locations around the world to guarantee such things as performance and availability. Communications networks are fast and increasing in speed every day, but for the most part locally maintained applications and data are faster.

Service, Not Price

Early xSPs competed on price. Most of them have not survived. Second- and third-generation xSPs have begun to compete on service—convenience, reliability, support and so forth. They have a chance to make it in the long run, provided they maintain their service focus.

Choosing a Software Deployment Architecture

Figure 7-1 illustrates the rough relationships that exist between customers, corporate influences, and deployment architectures. It also captures the effects that one dimension often has on the others. For example, if your enterprise-class customer has a high need for integration with existing or legacy systems, wants more control over system operations, and is dealing with highly sensitive data, chances are good that they will favor a system that can be deployed at their site under the control of their MIS staff. Relaxing these constraints makes other deployment choices viable and in many cases even preferable.

I've intentionally simplified many of the variables that are associated with deployment architecture in the figure. For example, even if the customer has a high preference for deploying the system on site, they may still choose an ASP/MSP if the skills of their operational staff are insufficient or if the application's peak demands will exceed inhouse capabilities. The variables in black—control, integration, and data—all share the same effect on the choice of deployment architecture (when high, deploy at the customer site). The variables in gray are on an opposite scale—when high, deploy as an ASP, MSP, or Web service.

The upper-right corner of Figure 7-1 captures some of the corporate influences previously described. The figure also shows the migrations between various deployment options as light gray lines.

Deployment Architectures and the Distribution of Work

No matter what deployment architecture you choose, someone is going to have to install, maintain, administer, and support it. These basic service and support functions can't be ignored. In a customer-site deployment, or when integrating with a Web service,

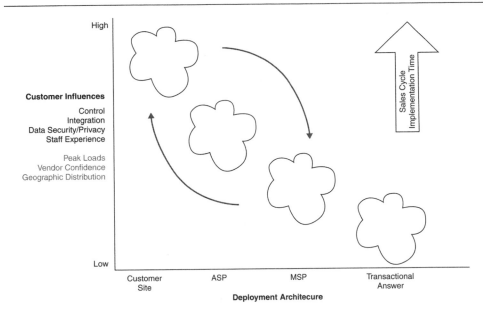

FIGURE 7-1   Choosing a deployment architecture

the customer is responsible for the bulk of the workload. In an ASP, these responsibilities are shared. In an MSP and transactional service, they are the service providers. The various deployment choices shift the locus of control among the entities, as shown in Figure 7-2.

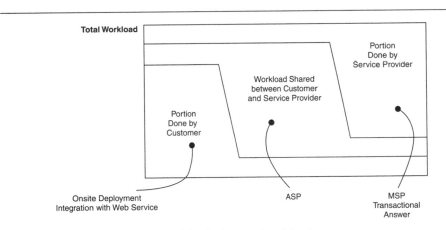

FIGURE 7-2   Distribution of work in deployment architectures

The Information Appliance

A completely different kind of deployment architecture, and one that can be operated almost equally well at a customer site, as an ASP, or as an MSP, is the information appliance—a specialized device that provides one or more specific functions designed to create a better total solution for a well-defined target market. Examples of information appliances include

- Linksys EtherFast DSL Firewall/4-port hub. I have installed this in my home to provide me with a simple firewall and 4-port LAN.
- Aladdin Knowledge Systems, Inc., eSafe appliance. This provides anti-virus and malicious mobile code protection for enterprises.
- TiVo and Replay digital video recorders. These provide a single device for managing television viewing.

Several trends motivate the growth of information appliances. One of the biggest is the continued adoption of the Linux operating system, which is reliable, free from expensive licensing models, and easily customized and embedded. While there are other excellent choices for appliance operating systems, most of them come with a license fee, which directly increases total cost but provides little additional value to users.

One point in favor of proprietary operating systems is any tools they have created to support a specific market niche, making them better than similar tools available on Linux. In other words, there is no simple way to make the choice; you will have to compare a full set of issues, among them license fees, development tools and related infrastructure, and development team experience. What is undeniable is that Linux is the platform of choice for a growing number of information appliance vendors.

Another important trend is the need to simplify complex solutions. Appliance vendors usually place a premium on simplicity. Just install the appliance and set a few simple parameters. Many times you don't have or need things like keyboards, monitors, or even expansion slots. The absence of such items simultaneously drives down costs and simplifies use.

Information appliances are not appropriate for every kind of software, particularly any system that creates or manages data or that requires substantial customization or programmatic integration, or that just runs better on existing hardware. That said, the move toward Linux and other open source software will continue, as will our desire to reduce complexity for our customers. Thus, we will see the continued growth of single and multi-function information appliances.

Deployment Choice Influences on Software Architecture

A given deployment choice may exhibit any of the following influences on your software architecture.

Flexible, Parameterized, or No Integration Options

A system deployed at a customer's site has the greatest demand for flexible integration options. A system deployed as an ASP or MSP may require flexible integration, but the xSP vendor is often not motivated to provide it because of its extremely high costs. In fact, the more standard the xSP can make the offering, the better. Standardized offerings are simpler to create, simpler to manage, and more profitable to operate. Any deployment choice can be offered with no integration options, which is surprisingly appropriate when you're creating a system with very well defined functions and relatively simple boundaries.

Upgrade Policies

Different deployment architectures make different upgrade demands. For systems deployed at a customer site upgrades must be carefully planned to be minimally disruptive. This can be especially challenging if the customer has crucially important data or has extensively integrated the production system with a large amount of their own programming. For this reason, enterprise-class systems deployed onsite are rarely upgraded more than once every nine months. In contrast, I know of one worldclass MSP that safely modifies their production system approximately every 10 to 12 weeks, rapidly introducing new features to their customers in an emerging market. They are able to do this because early in the development of the system they made substantial changes to make upgrading easier. Upgrades are discussed more thoroughly in Chapter 12.

Data Protection and Access

Application data maintenance must be appropriate based on the application, the users, and the data's sensitivity/importance. When the system is deployed at a customer site all responsibility for handling these issues, especially as they relate to corporate data, is the customer's. As mentioned earlier, the converse is also true: Storing customer data at, or as, an xSP requires that the xSP or your engineering, product development and operations staffs follow strictly defined guidelines that deal with proper data handling. Would you let your company manage your confidential information?

Migration Options

I expect an increase in the number of solutions that can be deployed either as ASPs/MSPs or on a customer-site. Furthermore, I suspect that these solutions will ultimately need to support migrations as previously described in this chapter. The possible effects of migration should be considered in the overall design of your architecture.

The Future of Consumer Software

Web services enthusiasts paint a picture of the future in which savvy, Web-connected users won't license software for use on their home computer, but instead, will connect to a Web service via a persistent, reliable, high-speed Internet connection and license the software on a rental or subscription basis. Fortunately, the deployment architectures presented here, which are currently most applicable to enterprise-class software, will guide you in navigating this brave new Web services world.

Like enterprises, users will make their deployment choices based on the quality of the *solution*, not on the technology powering it. For people like me, who rely on their laptop during international travel, the thought of using software only via an Internet connection seems a bit crazy—perhaps in the future, but certainly not now. However, for many, accessing software via a trusted vendor through the Internet is very appealing. I'd like to see certain data, such as financial records, properly maintained for the rest of my life. Other data, such as my digital photos, I *want* to be shared, making a Web services model a natural fit. Because of these forces, and others that will emerge, I envision a complex environment for consumer software like that for enterprise-class software, creating very interesting choices and tradeoffs for marketects, tarchitects, and their customers.

Chapter Summary

- Your deployment architecture is the manner in which the system is deployed for use by a customer. Common choices include
  - Customer site
  - Application service provider (ASP)
  - Managed services provider (MSP)
  - Variant of a service provider (xSP)
  - Web services

  Hybrid models, in which part of the system is deployed at a customer site and part at a service provider will become increasingly common.
- Customer influences that motivate the selection of a deployment architecture include
  - Control desired
  - Integration with other systems
  - Data security/privacy
  - The ability to handle peak loads

- Initial and ongoing costs
- Customer confidence in you
- Skills and experience of the system's operational staff

■ Corporate influences on the selection of a deployment architecture include
- Desired and actual sales cycle
- Infrastructure investment
- Financial model, most notably cash flow
- Desire to move quickly and efficiently in managing your customer base
- Geographic distribution of your company relative to your customers

■ The choice of a deployment architecture does not change the total of work associated with a successfully managed system. It may change the distribution of this work.

■ Information appliances are a growing category for deployment architectures in a wide variety of environments. Open-source licensing models, which can lower total costs of ownership, are in part fueling this growth.

Check This

❑ Our deployment architecture matches our target market's need for
- Control
- Integration
- Data security/privacy

❑ We have sufficient performance models and are sure that our deployment architecture can handle all anticipated workloads (see Chapter 10).

❑ We have instituted appropriate operational policies.

❑ We have accounted for the following in our choice of deployment architecture:
- Sales model and sales cycle
- Required infrastructure investment

❑ We have defined the amount of work we expect the customer to perform.

Try This

1. Using Figure 7-3, identify how your software is deployed and the key forces behind this choice.

2. What would you have to do to change your solution from its current deployment to a new one? Would doing so enable you to expand your current market or allow you to reach a new one?

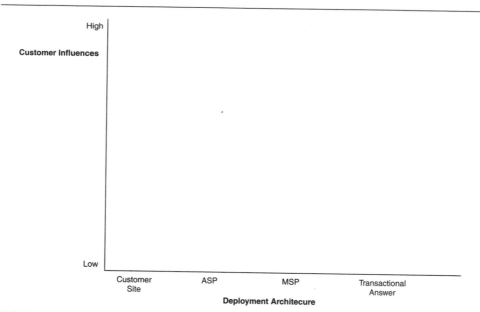

FIGURE 7-3   Identifying your software deployment

Chapter 8
Integration and Extension

As described in Chapter 3, integration is the degree to which your system can or must work with other systems, usually programmatically, to produce the expected product. Extension refers to the degree with which your system can be extended to produce an augmented product. In this chapter I will discuss the motivations for creating architectures that can be integrated and extended with relative ease and the business ramifications of doing so.

Customer Control—The Driving Force

The motivations for integration and extension are similar: In complex systems, both provide the ability to create a superior product. In some circumstances, integration and extension shift work from you to your customer. Paradoxically, this can increase customer satisfaction, much like our satisfaction with an ATM machine even though we're assuming responsibilities formerly taken by tellers. Part of the reason is that we're in control, which most of us like even when it means more work.

Motivations for Integration/Extension

Some of the strongest motivations for creating systems that can be integrated and/or extended with other systems including the ones discussed in the following sections.

You Can't Predict, But You Can Plan

In today's complex environment it is impossible to predict precisely how your customer will want your system to behave in every context. By providing customers with one or more ways to integrate or extend the system, you won't have predicted the future but you will have planned for it. Plug-in architectures, such as those in Adobe Photoshop or Web browsers, allow components to be added in well-defined ways. They are an excellent example of adding functionality that enhances an existing system.

Customers Hate To Hear, "We Can't Do That"

When you can't extend a system, you can't respond to customer needs. Ultimately, this means you'll have to eventually say no to a customer request, which, not surprisingly, customers hate to hear. A good strategy for integrating and/or extending your system will help you convert "No" to "Yes, we can do that. It might take a bit of work, but here's what we propose."

The Larger Solution Comprises Multiple Smaller Solutions

Many enterprise-class business systems are not designed to work in isolation. Instead, they work with a supply chain to solve a larger problem. One example is a Web storefront or online ordering system, which cannot work without integration. In such implementations several systems must be integrated to produce the expected product, including a catalog system, a storefront engine, a content engine, a payment processing engine, and backend order tracking and accounting systems. If you've participated in the creation any of these systems you already know that an easily integrated architecture is essential to success.

You Want Information Not In Your Own System

There are times when the only way to produce an interesting report or analysis is to integrate the data contained in one system with the data contained in another. A common example of this is when you integrate clickstream data from Web servers with customer purchase transactions.

You Want To Increase Switching Costs

Switching costs refer to what your customer will pay should they stop using your system and start using another. These costs include a number of things, such as re-integrating your solution into a competitor's. Extension and integration options don't increase switching costs until they are used by your customer. At that point switching costs dramatically increase because your customer not only has to replace your system but also has to replace all of the integrations and extensions they created on top of it. The more proprietary the extension and integration options, the greater the cost to switch.

You Want to Create A Product Ecosystem

Regardless of your company's success in creating, marketing, and selling your product, you can often achieve greater benefits by sharing your success with other companies. I think of this as creating a product ecosystem, in which various entities interoperate to achieve one or more mutually beneficial goals. A classic example of an ecosystem is the set of companies that create plug-ins for Adobe Photoshop. These

---

Some Assembly Required

The Aladdin Privilege Software Commerce Platform (PSCP) includes a storefront engine that software publishers use to sell their goods directly to customers via a Web site or indirectly through a multitier distribution channel that consists of distributors and resellers. Integration with other systems is required in either approach.

In the direct approach, the storefront engine must be integrated with credit-card payment and other transaction-processing systems, catalog systems (product descriptions and price quotes), fraud detection systems, and so forth. In the indirect approach, the storefront engine must be integrated into a network of servers linked together to support transactions. In both cases, the system must be integrated with other systems in order to function properly.

---

plug-ins extend the product in well-defined ways, usually providing specific functions required by niche markets. Key participants in this ecosystem benefit, including Adobe, the company creating the plug-in, and, most important, the customer.

It's Common Sense

A good tarchitect will just about always add some form of API to his system to make it easier to test via a solid automated regression test framework. A good marketect will seek to leverage this technical investment—after all, who knows what the future may bring, and all that may be needed to add this feature to the product is some documentation.

Regardless of your motivation, it is essential that the development effort embrace the notion of an API as a *commitment* to your customer. A customer, partner, or other entity, such as a system integrator or value added reseller (VAR) that chooses your APIs is tightly bound to your product and your company. This commitment is for the long haul.

Layered Business Architectures: Logical Structures

In one of the most common system architectures for business applications, subsystems are logically and physically arranged in layers (see Figure 8-1). These architectures, which form the foundation for frameworks such as J2EE, provide an excellent case study of integration and extension. In this section I will briefly review layering the architecture. In the next, I will discuss extending the architecture.

The User Interface Layer

The *user interface* layer presents information to the user and manages the user's interactions with this information. It is usually graphical—either as a heavy client that runs

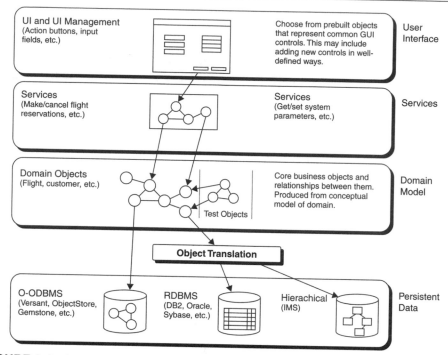

FIGURE 8-1   Layered system architecture

as an application or a thin or light client that runs in a browser. Other increasingly common forms, include voice and handheld. The user interface layer often must shoulder the bulk of the work in internationalized applications, which are always more difficult than they seem. Some of the worst user interface problems I've had to resolve dealt with internationalization.

The most essential thing to keep in mind when constructing the user interface is that it not contain any application or business logic. This kind of logic belongs in other layers. In thinking about where to place application logic, ask yourself the following question: "What parts of my system would have to change if I replaced the current user interface with an entirely new one, such as replacing a geographical user interface with an automated voice response system?" If the answer includes changing substantial portions of your application code (e.g., edit or validation checking), chances are good that your user interface layer contains logic that should be in the services or domain layer.

Many enterprise applications split the user interface between two layers—one that deals with the actual presentation of information and one that mediates the "micro workflow" between a given user interface and the services layer. For example, suppose you're creating an application to manage flight reservations. If the specific user interface is a browser, you may be able to acquire all of the necessary data in one screen. If it is a phone, you may need to coordinate multiple dialogs. Because these operations are based on a specific kind of user interface, they belong in the user interface layer. The "micro workflow" layer may be responsible for reformatting any domain-specific data for the interface.

I strongly recommend a simple "command-line" interface, which is easy and fast for developers to use, facilitates many forms of automated testing, and is trivially scriptable using a language such as Tcl or Perl. It can also be easily implemented on top of the other layer's model via a simple API.

The Services Layer

The *services* layer provides various application-defined services to the user interface and other applications. These services may be simple, such as obtaining the current system date and time, or complex, such as changing or canceling a flight reservation in an airline reservation system. Complex services are often implemented as transactions, with complete transactional semantics (e.g., rollback). Thinking in terms of services is one of the most important steps if you're thinking about exposing some or all of your application functionality in a Web service.

There can be a close correlation between services and use cases. At times, a whole use case may be represented as a single service, at other times, individual steps within one may be. CRUD operations (create, reference, update, and delete) are often represented as services as well.

The Domain Model Layer

The *domain model* or *domain layer* represents the fundamental business concepts and rules of your application domain. I consider it an optional layer in enterprise applications, only required when business rules are too complex to be represented in simple services or when object structures are more efficiently represented by in-memory representations.

When the domain model is needed, it often emerges as the core of the application. In other words, instead of thinking of your architecture in layers, think of it as an onion. The center is the domain model, and other layers are built, or grown, depending on your development method, around it. It needs to be correct.

I admit, this visualization suffers a bit because it doesn't consider persistent data. More dangerously, it could imply that the domain model is more important than the persistent data model, when in fact in most applications these two elements of your tarchitecture are equal. However, the onion analogy reinforces that the domain model is the core of a good application.

Decoupling the domain layer from the user interface and transaction management layers provides substantial flexibility in system development. We might replace the screen presented to a service agent with an interactive voice response system or a Web page without changing the underlying application logic (provided they have reasonable interfaces and appropriate service objects to make this replacement—more on this later). It also contributes to cohesion: Each layer of the architecture is responsible for a specific set of related operations.

I do not mean to imply that the domain model *must* be constructed before the user interface is designed. While it is often helpful to design the user interface after the preliminary domain model, I have worked on several successful projects in which the user interface was prototyped first, using paper-and-pencil ("lo-fidelity") techniques. Once the user model was validated, the development of the domain model was relatively straightforward. During implementation the domain model was implemented first, and the user interface followed quickly thereafter based on the previously agreed to public interface the domain model provided.

The Persistent Data Layer

Most business applications rely on a database management system to manage the persistent storage of objects. In enterprise applications the most common approach is to use a relational database and to create a separate layer to manage the mapping between objects or service buyers within the domain and objects within the relational database.

This is not as easy as it may sound. Complex object structures, objects comprising data from multiple sources, objects with complex security restrictions (such as operations that can only be performed by certain classes of users), or transactions that involve large numbers of objects all contribute to the challenge of efficiently mapping domain objects to relational databases.

For these reasons, there are times when it makes sense to structure the domain model so that it can work easily and efficiently with the underlying database schema. Indeed, if the schema is unusually complex, or if the performance requirements are particularly severe, it may make sense to forego the domain model entirely and simply connect the services layer to the schema. This may seem counter-intuitive, especially if you've been trained in object-based design methods. However, the reality of many enterprise applications is that creating a rich domain model and then relying on an object-to-relational mapping to store and retrieve objects just isn't worth it. A better approach is to define an appropriate set of services that connect to the database through SQL statements and the occasional stored procedure and/or trigger.

Another interesting way that you can relax the formal structure of a layered architecture is by moving business logic into the database. Architectural purists will tell you that this isn't a good thing, and they're right. Moving business logic into the database usually means writing stored procedures and/or triggers, which aren't portable. It also can mean that the persistent data layer team is not using SQL effectively.

Still, there are times when it is practically appropriate to carefully move business logic into the database. The first concerns performance. If your design involves iterating over a bunch of records, you're wasting valuable resources by moving data from the database and into another tier. Such logic, especially for very large databases, may be better off in the database. A second motivation is when you're working with data that has very sophisticated constraints, such as when you want to conditionally delete records. A final motivation is when you want to absolutely, positively guarantee that one or more actions are taken no matter how data is manipulated. This is especially important when you allow integration of your system at the database layer. By definition, this approach bypasses whatever business logic has been built into the services or domain layers, making such integrations riskier. By moving critical business logic into the database, you can always make certain it is executed.

Variations on a Theme

As a *generic* architecture, Figure 8-1 is a starting point for the design of loosely coupled, highly cohesive systems with the flexibility to handle complex problems. Of course, it is a simplification and abstraction: Distributed computing, legacy systems integration, and/or structural relationships or choices made to support specialized databases or hardware can change the picture.

Creating Layered Business Architectures

Successful projects rarely build all layers of the architecture at the same time. Most of them build it through a process I refer to as *spiking*. A *spike* is a user-visible piece of functionality (usually described by a use case or an XP-style story) that has been completely implemented through all appropriate subsystems or layers of the tarchitecture. It is suitable for alpha (and sometimes) beta testing and is stable enough for the end-user documentation team to begin online help and related end-user documentation features. The key attribute of a spike is that it "drives" some specific aspect of functionality through all relevant subsystems (I use the term "nail" to represent a connection made between two subsystems).

Spikes are an approach to incremental development. I'm not the first person to advocate them, and I'm certain I won't be the last. That said, I've found that they are a good metaphor for the work of the team. Imagine, if you will, that a single subsystem is a four-by-six board. Your architecture can then be thought of as a series of these boards stacked one on top of the other. A nail joins two boards but a spike drives through all of them. One of my development managers recently pointed out that spiking is both a process and an event—a process because driving the spike through many layers can be hard work and new to many development teams; when finished, it's celebrated as an event.

While the first spike proves the basics of the architecture and is the foundation for sound risk management practices, there is still room to adjust the boards to make certain the system is lining up as intended. As more spikes are added, the system becomes more stable. The spikes also come more quickly as the team becomes skilled in driving them through all of the layers. The overall organization also benefits, as the specific functionality of the system is developed over time.

If you have had some trouble adopting an iterative development process, consider spiking. However, even teams that have adopted spiking or another iterative approach can have trouble determining where to begin the development efforts. If you get stuck, try starting with either the services layer or the user interface, as shown in the top half of Figure 8-2.

The top half of Figure 8-2 illustrates the approach of starting with the services layer, preferably with a lo-fidelity (paper-based) user interface prototype to set expectations of how the services may be used by the user interface. With clear and concise interfaces for the services, the user interface team can begin to hoist their functionality on top of them. Note that in many projects the services don't have to be completely implemented before the user interface team begins using them. Many times a service that returns dummy data is more helpful than a service connected to a live data source, because you can move faster with dummy data. In this example, the system is relatively simple, and has no need for a complex domain model. Thus, as services are coded, they are connected to the database and the whole system grows organically through spikes.

I place considerable emphasis on defining services because getting service interfaces right makes it is far easier to get the rest of the tarchitecture right. Getting them wrong puts the project at risk, because eventually it will have to be fixed. More importantly, if you're practicing an iterative development model, chances are good that you're going to base the implementation of additional services after existing services. More simply, after a few services are built, future services tend to be built using the same general style. Agile development methods, such as SCRUM, XP, or agile modeling, are especially useful in these first few spikes, because they are designed to provide explicit feedback loops.

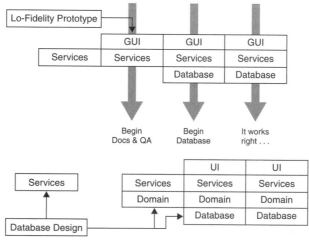

FIGURE 8-2   Spiking the architecture

There are many other ways to build a layered architecture. Another option, shown in the bottom half of Figure 8-2, occurs when the team must deal with substantial amounts of existing data or when the persistent storage requirements are extremely demanding. In this case, it is safer to start with the design of the database and let it inform the design of the services and domain layers. There is a strong correlation between complex persistent storage requirements and complex domain models. Later in the project the user interface is hoisted on top of the services layer.

If there are sufficient resources, multiple layers can be addressed in parallel. The key to this approach is to establish early on the core subsystems of the architecture. This is best accomplished by agreeing on subsystem interfaces early in the development of the project and using continuous daily or weekly builds to ensure that subsystems remain in sync.

If you're going to attempt parallel development, make certain the development team agrees on which layer will be driving the other layers. Something has to come first, and a good rule of thumb is that it should be either the services or the domain layer. This doesn't mean that you'll get everything right—just that you'll have an agreed upon way to get started.

Suppose, for example, that in a complex application you agree that the domain model will drive development. As domain objects and complex business rules are implemented, they are exposed through services and connected to a persistent store. During the development of a given use case it is quite possible that the user interface development team will discover that an important attribute was missed during analysis. Rather than adding this attribute (and its associated semantics) only to the user

Spike Every Layer

The approaches I've described above are simplifications of real world projects. Every team building a layer architecture must take into account their unique environment and address their idiosyncratic circumstances. In practice, this means that a spike plan must be crafted for each project in such a way that key needs are addressed and key risks are managed. What is essential is that spikes are organized so that the team is "pushing" functionality through all layers of their system. While I've had great success using spikes, the times that they've failed me is when the development team didn't include all of the layers of the application.

In one client/server system, we had some problems when the server team created a spike plan that didn't include the client. We created our server—a model of a three layer architecture (service, domain, and database) and forgot that the client needed to interface with this architecture. When we hoisted the user interface of the client on top of this model we identified several problems that would have been easily resolved had we spiked *all* of the layers.

interface, the user interface team should negotiate with other teams, starting with the domain team to add it (and its associated semantics) to the appropriate domain objects. The domain team, should, in turn, negotiate with the database team to ensure that the appropriate changes are made to the persistent storage model.

Unfortunately, there can be an unpleasant wait for all layers to catch up with each other. I have found that a two-stage process works best. First, the domain layer makes the necessary changes, allows the services layer to change to support the user inter-face, and simulates changes to the database model through an "in-memory" database. This allows the user interface team to proceed and allows the domain team to verify the changes to the application. While this is happening the database team is making their changes. When finished, the domain is connected to the database layer, and the entire application works. No matter what, you should spike the architecture as often as possible to reduce risk.

Integration and Extension at the Business Logic Layers

There are many technical approaches to creating systems that can be integrated and/or extended. This section draws from my experience creating the necessary architectural infrastructure for enterprise class software systems. The techniques are easily adapted to other kinds of application architectures. Refer to Figure 8-3 as you read this section and the next one.

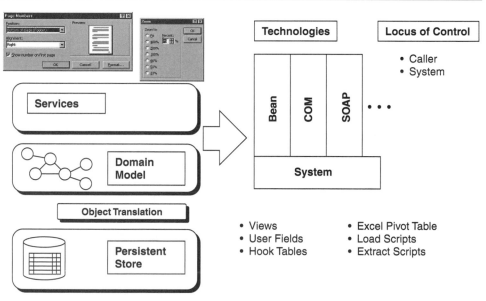

FIGURE 8-3   Integration and extension techniques

Technologies and Locus of Control

Before talking about integration or extension approaches, it is important to distinguish between the technologies that are used to create these features and the locus of control when performing the integration of extension.

The technology part is easy. A well designed services architecture and/or design model should be able to support whatever technology is required by your target market. In practice, this means that you will be supporting multiple kinds of integration technologies. More modern technologies, such as Enterprise Java Beans or Web services, may need to sit alongside more traditional technologies, such as COM or plain old C libraries. You may even be required to support the same functionality with slightly different implementation semantics, as when you are required to support multiple standards that each address the same functionality but have not been unified (such as the cryptographic standards PKCS11 and the Microsoft CAPI).

The locus of control question is a bit more challenging. In general, either the caller is in control or the system is in control. When the caller is in control, they are most likely treating your application as a service that creates and produces a result. The call may be blocking or non-blocking, and you may or may not provide status. Ultimately, though, the caller is in control.

When the system is in control you're almost always using either a registration or callback model in which the caller registers some aspect of functionality to the system. The system then invokes this functionality at predefined events. Ultimately, the system is in control (or should be). These two approaches are discussed in greater detail in the next sections.

Integration through APIs

Application programming interfaces (APIs) expose one or more aspects of functionality to developers of other systems. They are based on the idea that the other developer is creating an application that is the primary locus of control; your system becomes a set of services accessed through any means appropriate—for example, a library, such as C or C++ library; a component, such as a COM, JavaBean, or Enterprise JavaBean (EJB); a Web service; and/or a message-oriented interface. The use of APIs is primarily associated with the desire to integrate your application into some other application.

If you have constructed your application according to the principles espoused earlier, it is usually easy to create APIs that allow customers access to your system's functionality. The most direct approach is to expose the services layer first, possibly exposing other layers as required. This is far superior to allowing your customer direct access to your database, which bypasses all of the business logic associated with your application.

Consider the following items as you create APIs:

Platform Preferences

While C-based interfaces may be the universal choice, every platform has some variant that works best. For example, if you're creating an application under MS Windows, you will almost certainly want to provide a COM-based interface. Other customers may require a J2EE approach and demand EJBs that can be integrated into their application.

Market Segment Preferences

In addition to the pressures exerted on an API by the platform, different market segments may also exhibit preferences for one approach or another. If you're working with innovators, chances are good that they will want to use the most innovative approaches for integrating and/or extending your system. As of the writing of this book, this means providing Web services. In the future, who knows? Other market segments may request different approaches. You may need to support them all.

Partner Preferences

In Chapter 2 I discussed the importance of the context diagram for identifying possible partners in creating an augmented product. Your partners will have their own preferences for integration. Understanding them will help you create the integration and extension approaches most likely to gain their favor.

Naming Conventions

If you have ever been frustrated by a vendor providing a nonsensical API, you should have all of the motivation you need to create one that is sensibly named and sensibly structured. Try to remember that making it *easy* to use your APIs is in *your* best interests.

Security and Session Data

Many business applications manage stateful data, often based on the concept of a user who is logged in and working with the application (a session). State or session data may be maintained in any number of ways. For example, in Web applications a session is often managed by embedding a session identifier in each transaction posted to the server once the user has logged in, either as part of the URL or as part of the data in the Web page. If you're using a heavy client (e.g., a Windows client application) you can manage state or session data directly in the client or share it between the client and the server.

Developing APIs for applications that rely on session data is harder than developing them for applications that don't. You have to provide your customers with a means to specify and manage session-related parameters, such as timeouts and security protocols. Depending on how your application works with other applications, you may need a way to identify another application through a user ID so that rights can be managed. You may also need facilities for managing session data as functions are invoked. If your server manages session data through an opaque session identifier, for example, you have to tell your customers not to modify this handle.

Exposing Only What Customers Need

Be careful about liberally exposing all of the APIs in your system. Every one you expose increases the work in creating and sustaining your product. It is also unlikely

Timing Is Everything

Your documentation (discussed later in this chapter) must make certain that session management semantics are clearly presented to your customer. I remember helping a customer track down one particularly troublesome bug—that wasn't a bug at all—in a multi-user, Web-based application. Each logged-in user represented a session. Because sessions consumed valuable server resources and because each one counted against one concurrent user, we associated a session timeout parameter that could be set to forcibly log a user off in cases of inactivity or error.

The underlying application allowed system administrators to associate various application functions with specific user IDs. Thus, "user ID 1" could perform a different set of operations than "user ID 2." Our API was constructed to follow this convention. Specifically, applications wishing to use the functions provided by the server were forced to log in to it just like a human user. This enabled the system administrator to control the set of functions that an external application was allowed to use.

Our customer had set the session timeout parameter to expire sessions after 20 minutes of inactivity, but then they wrote an application that expected a session to last an arbitrary amount of time! Since normal and "programmatic" users were accessing the same transaction model, both were held to the same session management restrictions. To solve the immediate problem the customer modified the application to log in again if their session expired. They were unhappy with this solution, so we eventually accommodated them by allowing session timeout data to be set on a per-user basis. The customer then modified the session timeout parameter associated with the user ID representing their external application, and everything worked just as they wished.

that every exposed function provides the same value to your customer; not everything is needed. In a complex system, different operations exhibit different performance profiles and make different demands on underlying system resources. Some APIs may invoke complex functions that take a long time to execute and should only be used with proper training. You don't want your customer to accidentally bring the system to a grinding halt through improper API use.

Tarchitects should work carefully with marketects to define the smallest set of APIs that makes sense for the target market. Because there may be many constituents to satisfy, consider defining sets: one (or more) for internal use and one for integration/extension, possibly governed through security access controls. I know of one large application development team that created *three* APIs: one for the team's internal use, one for use by other application development teams within the same company, and one for external customers. The APIs differed in functionality and performance based on such things as error checking and calling semantics.

APIs Stabilized over Multiple Releases

It can be difficult to predict the APIs needed in the first few releases of a product, and it is rare that you get it right the first time. Be forewarned that it may take several releases to stabilize the right APIs for a given target market.

Clearly Understood Options

Your application may provide for certain features that are simply not available in the API. Stating what can—and *cannot*—be done with an API makes it considerably easier for a customer or system integration consultant to determine the best way to approach a complex problem.

Extension through Registration

Registration is a process whereby the capabilities of your application are extended in one or more ways by developers who register a component or callback function with your system. Unlike integration through APIs, your system remains the locus of control, calling the registered component at predefined events. Registration is related to the Observer design pattern or the publish–subscribe models of message queuing systems but is not the same thing. When using registration, your application actually hands over control to the registered component. In the latter, your application notifies other components of events but may not hand over control. A great example of registration-based extension is your Web browser, whose functionality can be extended through well-defined plugins. When the right mime type is encountered, application control is transferred to the appropriately registered plugin. Registration-based APIs include callbacks, listeners, plugins (such as a Web browser), and event notification mechanisms. Consider the following when providing for registration-based solutions.

Define the Registration Model

Provide developers with detailed technical information on the language(s) that can be used to create registerable components, when and how these components are registered, how to update registered components, and so forth. Some applications require that plug-ins be in a specific directory and follow a platform-specific binary model. Other applications require that all components register themselves through a configuration file. Some allow you to change registered components while the application is running; others require you to restart the application to acquire new or updated components. You have a wide variety of choices—just make certain you're clear on those you have chosen.

Define the Event Model

The specific events available to the developer, when they occur, the format of the notification mechanism, and the information provided in a callback must all be made available to developers.

Define Execution Control Semantics

Execution control semantics refer to such things as blocking or nonblocking calls, thread and/or process management, and any important timing requirements associated with external components. Some applications transfer control to a plug-in to process a request within the same process space. Others invoke a separate process, then hand over control to the plug-in. Still others invoke the registered component as a simple function and block, awaiting the results.

Define Resource Management Policies

All decisions regarding resource management, from provisioning to management and recovery, must be defined. Consider all resources that may affect your application or that may be required for a successful integration, including, but not limited to, memory, file handles, processing power, and bandwidth.

Define Error/Exception Protocols

Errors and exceptions in one application often must be propagated through your API to another application. You may also have to define conversion semantics; that is, what might be an "error" in one application may be an "exception" in another.

Integration and Extension of Persistent Data

In the vast majority of cases, you don't want your customer directly accessing or changing your schema or the data it contains. It is simply too risky. Direct access bypasses the validation rules that usually lie within the services or domain layer, causing corrupt or inaccurate data. Transaction-processing rules that require the simultaneous update or coordination of multiple systems are only likely to be executed if they are invoked through the proper services. Upgrade scripts that work just fine in QA can break at a customer's site if the schema has been modified.

All of that said, there are times when a customer wants access to persistent data—and there are times you want to give it to them. They may want to write their own reports or extract data for use in other systems, and it may just be easier and faster to let them do this on their own without your intervention. Or they may need to extend the system with additional data that meets their needs now rather than wait for a release that may be months away. Of course, your marketect may also push to allow customers direct access to persistent data as this makes switching costs exorbitantly high.

Since chances are good that you're going to have to provide some access to your persistent data; the following sections describe a few techniques that should help.

Views

Providing a layer of indirection between components is one of the broadest and most time-tested principles of good design. With reduced coupling, well-placed layers of indirection enhance flexibility.

Putting Business Logic in the Database

One of the most generally accepted principles of enterprise application architecture is to put business logic within the services layer and/or the domain model layer of the architecture. However, while this is a good principle, it isn't an absolute rule that should be dogmatically followed. Many times a well-defined stored procedure or database trigger is a far simpler and substantially more efficient solution. Moreover, you may find that the only way to safely offer integration options to your customer is to put certain kinds of logic in the database: I would rather rely on the database to invoke a stored procedure than rely on a customer to remember to call the right API!

Views are logical databases constructed on top of physical schemas. They provide a layer of indirection between how the data is used in a schema and how it is defined. The value of a view is that it gives you some flexibility in changing the underlying schema without breaking applications or components that rely on a specific schema implementation. It is useful in a variety of situations, such as when you want to give your customer a schema optimized for reporting purposes. The first, and many times most important, way to provide access to persistent data is always through a view.

User Fields

Many times you know that a user will want to add some of their own data to a schema but you don't want to provide a lot of tools or infrastructure to support this, because creating these tools and associated infrastructure is likely to cost a lot of time and money to develop. A simple approach to providing for extensible data is to define extra fields in key tables that can be customized by a user. Simply throw in a few extra ints, dates, and strings, and provide a way to edit them in your user interface. The result often produces user interfaces with labels like: "User Date 1" or "Customer String". This simple approach can be surprisingly effective!

Unfortunately, it has plenty of drawbacks. Database purists feel nauseous when they find systems based on user fields because the database has not been properly modeled. You can't run reports on these data because there are no semantically meaningful fields for query manipulation—`select column_42 from TBL_USERDATA where column_41 > 100` is not very understandable. Different users may interpret the data in different ways, further compounding the errors ("I thought I was supposed to put the date of the last purchase in the *second* field, not the *fourth* field"). This can be mitigated by providing system administrators with tools to edit the field labels (instead of "User Date 1" the field might say "Date of Last Purchase"), but this does not solve the problem. The lack of data modeling means that data is highly suspect, as it is stored without the application of any business rules such as basic edit checks.

You'll have to judge whether or not the relatively trivial ease with which user columns can be added to the database are appropriate for your application.

Hook Tables

Suppose you have created an inventory-tracking and warehouse management system. Each operation on an item, such as adding it to the inventory and storing it in the warehouse, is represented by a discrete transaction. Your customer, while pleased with the core functionality of the application, has defined additional data they want associated with certain transactions, and they want to store them in the same database as that used by your application to simplify various operational tasks, such as backing up the system. As with every other request, your customer wants these data added to the system *now*. They don't want to wait until the next release!

Hook tables are one way to solve this problem. They give your customer a way of extending the persistent storage mechanism that can be preserved over upgrades. The proper use of hook tables requires coordination among multiple layers in your architecture, so be careful with them.

Begin creating hook tables by identifying those aspects of the schema the customer wishes to extend. Next identify the events that are associated with the most basic operations on these data: create, update, and delete. Include operations that are initiated or handled by any layer in your architecture, including stored procedures. Take care, as you need to identify *every* such operation.

Now, create the hook tables. A hook table's primary key is equivalent to the primary key of a table in your current schema; it has been designed to allow customers to add new columns. The primary key should be generated by your application using a GUID or an MD5 hash of a GUID. Avoid using auto-increment fields, such as automatically incremented integers, for this key, as such fields make database upgrading difficult.

Create, update, and delete modifications to the primary table arc captured as events, and a registration or plug-in architecture is created to allow customers to write code that responds to thcm. Thus, when some action results in a new record being added to your database, a notification event is received by customer code. Upon receiving this notification, your customer can perform whatever processing they deem appropriate—creating, updating, and/or deleting the data they have added to the schema under their control.

In general, event notification comes after all of the work has been done by your application. In a typical creation sequence using a plug-in architecture, your application performs all of the work necessary to create a record and does the insertion in both the main application table (with all of its associated data) and the hook table. The hook table insertion is easy, as all it contains is the primary key of the main table. The list of plug-ins associated with the hook table is called, with the newly created primary key passed as a parameter.

More sophisticated structures allow pre- and postprocessing transactions to be associated with the hook table to an arbitrary depth. Preprocessing can be important when a customer wishes to perform work on data that is about to be deleted and is commonly required when you're coordinating transactions that span multiple databases.

Hook tables are not designed to work in every possible situation you may encounter, mostly because they have a number of limitations. Relational integrity can be difficult to enforce, especially if your customer extends the hook table in surprising ways. Because hook tables might also introduce unacceptable delays in transaction-processing systems they should be kept small. You also have to modify your upgrade scripts so that they are aware of the hook tables.

Spreadsheet Pivot Tables

Quite often a customer asks for dynamic reporting capabilities that may be difficult to support in your current architecture. Before trying to create such capabilities, see if your customer is using or has access to any of the powerful spreadsheet programs that provide interactive data analysis. I've had good results with Microsoft Excel, so I'll use it as my example.

Excel provides a feature called a pivot table that allows hierarchically structured data to be dynamically manipulated by users. With a pivot table, users can quickly sort, summarize, subtotal, and otherwise "play" with the data, and they can arrange it in a variety of formats. My experience is that once introduced to pivot tables users quickly learn to manipulate them to suit their own needs.

Pivot tables are based on extracts of your application data. Once these data have been exported they are no longer under your control. Security, privacy, and accuracy are thus just some of the concerns that accompany any use of extended data, and pivot tables are no exception. Pivot tables are often associated with ETL scripts, discussed in the next section.

Extract, Transform, and Load Scripts

Extract, transform, and load (ETL) scripts refer to a variety of utility programs designed to make it easier to manipulate structured data stored within databases. Extract scripts read data from one or more sources, extracting a desired subset and storing it in a suitable intermediate format. Transform scripts apply one or more transformations on the extracted data, doing everything from converting the data to a standard format to combining them with other data to produce new results. Finally, load scripts take the results of the transform scripts and write them to a target, usually another database optimized for a different purpose than the source database.

If your application is in use long enough, chances are good that customers are going to want to extract and/or load data directly to the schema, bypassing the domain layer. There are several reasons to do this, including the fact that the programmatic model provided by the API is likely to be too inefficient to manage transformations on large data sets. A special case of ETL scripts concerns upgrades, when you need to

> ## Charging for ETL Scripts
>
> Recall from Chapter 2 that the key to effective pricing is relating pricing to the value perceived by your customer. Prepackaged ETL scripts are an excellent example of this. In one application we created several of them to help our customers write customized reports. I estimated that these scripts, which were fully tested and documented, cost us about $50K to create, and would cost a customer even more to create. We were able to charge about $25K for them, which quickly became one of our most profitable modules. Another advantage was that these scripts further tied the customer to our application.

migrate from one version of the persistent storage model to another. Although it may be tempting to let your customers do this work, there are distinct tarchitectural and marketectural advantages to doing it yourself.

From a tarchitectural perspective, providing specifically tuned ETL scripts helps ensure that your customers obtain the right data, that transformations are performed appropriately, and that load operations don't break and/or violate the existing schema structure. An alert marketect can also take advantage of productized ETL scripts. As part of the released product, these scripts will be tested and documented, considerably enhancing the overall product value.

Tell Them What's Going On

Even though I generally recommend against giving your customers direct access to your schema, I also recommend that you provide them with complete information about it so that they can gain a proper understanding of your system's operation. This means technical publications that detail the data dictionary, data, table, and naming conventions, important semantics regarding the values of any special columns, and so forth. Such documents become invaluable, usually motivating customers to work within the guidelines you have established for system integration. The lack of usable, accurate technical documentation is the real source of many integration problems.

Business Ramifications

Providing ways for the system to be integrated has a number of business ramifications for both the marketect and the tarchitect. Handle all of them and you increase your chances for success. Miss any of them and you may seriously cripple your product's viability.

Professional Services

The various technical options for integrating a system can create a bewildering array of choices for a customer. Too often, customers are left unsure of the best way to integrate a system within their environment or they fear that the integration process will take too long, cost too much, and ultimately result in failure. Some of this fear is justified, as many large-scale integration projects don't realize key corporate objectives. To address these issues, vendors of systems designed to be integrated or extended should establish a professional services organization to help customers achieve their integration goals, answer their questions, and reduce the time necessary to integrate a system within the customers environment.

The marketect should help create the professional services, outlining their offerings, business, and licensing models, and providing assistance in setting and pricing models. The degree of control can vary. I've worked in organizations where my product managers had complete responsibility for establishing professional services. In other companies, professional services itself was responsible for prices and creating some offerings, in close collaboration with product management. My strong preference is that product management set the standard service offerings because this forces them to understand the needs of their target market. The most essential work of the marketect is in mediating requests from professional services to development.

The marketect also plays a key role in determining how professional services are organized. The two basic choices are inhouse and a partnership with an external firm. In practice, these choices are mixed according to the size of the company and the complexity of the integration. Smaller firms have small professional services organizations and rely heavily on partners; larger firms can afford to bring more of this inhouse. This is a decision of strategic importance, and the marketect should provide data that help senior executives make the best one. My own experience is that smaller companies do a very poor job of enlisting the aide of larger consulting partners, to their detriment.

Development (or engineering) plays a strong, but indirect, role in assisting customers, not working directly with them, but instead with professional services, making certain that they understand the product and its capabilities. A key service that development can provide is the creation of sample programs that demonstrate how to use APIs. I've found it especially beneficial if one or more members of the development team, including the tarchitect, help professional services create some of the initial customer solutions. The feedback on the structure, utility, and usability of the APIs is invaluable, and both professional services and developers welcome the opportunity to work on *real* customer problems instead of artificial examples.

The tarchitect assists the marketect in selecting external professional services partners. Like any other developer, the tarchitect should assess a potential partner's skills, examine their portfolio of successful projects, and interview the potential partner's key customers to assess their overall satisfaction with the quality of work.

Training Programs

Training programs are required for the successful use of just about any system. The trick to creating a winning solution is making certain that the training program matches the specific requirements of the target user. End users, for example, are typically given a base of training materials that show them how to use the application for common purposes. As systems increase in sophistication, so do the required training materials. Training is an excellent investment, because well designed training programs improve customer satisfaction and reduce support costs.

The primary role of the marketect in creating end user training is to coordinate the efforts of technical publications, quality assurance, and development to ensure that the training materials are created and are technically correct. A tarchitect committed to usability can play a surprisingly influential role in this process, ensuring that the training materials are not only accurate but truly represent, capture, and convey "best practices."

The basic training provided to end users must be substantially augmented for systems designed to be extended and/or integrated. Returning to the Adobe Photoshop example, training programs must clearly detail how a developer is to write a plug-in. For enterprise-class systems they can be surprisingly extensive, including several days of introductory to advanced training in dedicated classrooms.

When designing training solutions for the target market, the marketect must take into account all of the system's stakeholders. In one enterprise class system I worked on, we designed training programs for

- Developers who wanted to integrate the system with other systems
- System administrators who wanted to ensure that the system was configured for optimal performance

How Do I Add a Document?

One of the most frustrating experiences I ever had was when I was working for a company that used Lotus Notes. When I joined the company, I received a total of three minutes of Notes training. Specifically, I was taught how to log in, read, and send e-mail.

Over the next several months I watched other people in the organization use Lotus Notes in ways that seemed mystical to me. While they were successfully using Notes' collaboration and file management tools, I was struggling to manage my calendar. It took me several months of trial and error to achieve a modicum of skill.

You might wonder if I used the built-in help and tutorial materials to learn more about the system. I tried this, but to no avail. In my opinion, these materials were useless. I've been left with a very poor impression of Lotus Notes, which is sad because my problems could have been easily corrected by a motivated marketect working in partnership with a similarly motivated tarchitect.

- Solution partners who were integrating their software into our software
- Consulting partners who used our system to provide enhanced consulting services to our mutual clients

This list is not exhaustive and can include programs to service different constituents depending on the specific system. What is important is that complex systems rarely stand alone, that many different people within a company *touch* these systems, and that their ability to use the system can be improved through the right training.

I've found that training materials often suffer from a number of flaws, several of which can be mitigated or even removed by involving the tarchitect. One flaw is that APIs and example programs are often incorrect: In extreme cases, examples don't compile, and they fail to represent best practices. Also, they fail to expose the full set of features associated with the product, which is especially serious, because it exposes your product to serious competitive threats (smart competitors will see these flaws and use them to their advantage). A slightly less serious, but related, flaw, is that the examples provided don't have sufficient context for developers using the APIs to build a good mental model of the system. The result is that it takes developers far longer to effectively use your system's APIs.

Certification

The next logical step beyond training is certification. This is a rare step and one that is required only for systems with sufficiently large market shares. Certification is almost exclusively the domain of the marketect. In deciding whether or not to create a certification program, I recommend considering the following factors.

Product Ecosystem

Certification makes sense in product ecosystems characterized by many third parties who provide services to customers and by customers who want to know that their service providers have achieved some level of proficiency in their offerings. One example is hardware markets, like storage area networks (SANs) that are typically sold and distributed through value-added resellers (VARs). Another is IT/system integration and management markets, where certifications such as the Microsoft certified systems engineer (MCSE) have value.

Competitive Edge

Certification must provide a personal competitive edge that will motivate employees to invest their time, energy, and money in acquiring it.

Currency

Well-designed certification programs include ongoing educational requirements. In general, the more specialized the knowledge, the shorter its half-life. If you're not willing to invest the time to create an ongoing program, don't start one.

Professional Recognition

A well-designed certification program involves professional recognition. In practice, this means that certification must be hard enough to attain that you have to work for it. If anyone can obtain the certification, why bother?

Independent Certification

Although many companies benefit by designing and managing their own certification programs, it is often better if a program is designed and managed by an independent organization. This usually reduces overall design and implementation costs and has the chance to include marketplace acceptance. For example, the Computerized Information System Security Professional (CISSP) certification, created and managed by an independent third party, is a demanding program that requires detailed knowledge of a wide variety of vendor-neutral concepts as well as specific knowledge of various vendor's products. Working with the CISSP, a security vendor could ensure that their products are properly covered without incurring the expenses associated with a comprehensive training program.

Academic Credentials

Some certification programs can be used toward a university degree. This is, of course, an added advantage.

User Community

A healthy and active user community provides a number of benefits to the marketect and the tarchitect. For the marketect, user communities provide primary data on desired features, product uses, and product futures. For the tarchitect, understanding the user community means understanding how people are *really* using your application. For example, I am always amazed at how creatively people can use an API if given the chance!

User communities don't magically *happen*. They need to be nurtured. The marketect, especially, should seek to foster a healthy and active user community. Here are some activities that can help in this endeavor.

Community Web Site

Establish a corporately supported community Web site where customers can share tips and techniques regarding all aspects of your system. If you provide an API, have sections where they can post questions, receive official and unofficial answers, share sample programs, and so forth.

Educational Materials

Distribute unsupported educational and sample programs with your core product so that customers can learn how to create such applications on their own. These programs should be created or certified by your development or professional services

Thanks, But I Think I'll Build My Own User Interface

My team had labored mightily to build a great user interface—not a good one but a *great* one, a testament to usability. When we learned of a power user who loved our system and wanted to share some of his ideas for improving it, we jumped at the chance.

After a long day of travel, we arrived at his cramped office. He was a senior research scientist working for a major chemical company, and amid the many stacks of paper on his desk was a workstation. With an excited wave of his hand, he motioned us over to review his use of our system. Imagine our surprise when we watched him type a few values into Excel, hit a button, and then manipulate the results in a pivot table. What happened to our beautiful user interface? "Oh, it was nice, but it didn't really meet my needs. Fortunately, you guys built a really cool COM API, so I just programmed what I wanted in Excel. Isn't it great?" Yes, it was.

organization (or both). Make certain that this kind of reference and/or sample code is high quality—you don't want your customers to emulate poor practices. The programs themselves don't have to be tested to the same level of detail as the released software, but it should use the system in a corporately approved manner.

Mailing List

A very low-cost way to stay in touch with your customers is an e-mail mailing list. Such a list is a marketing program and should be managed by your outbound marketing department. However, the contents of each e-mail should be driven by the marketect in consultation with development, QA, support, and professional services.

User Conferences

It is vitally important to have one or more user conferences. Depending on the size of your user base, this can be a single annual event or multiple conferences throughout the year around the world. Organizing an effective user conference is a very specialized skill, and, like your mailing list, its objectives and structure should be driven by the marketect. However, the conference itself should be managed and run by your outbound marketing department.

License Agreements

The marketect needs to review proposed license agreements to make certain that the legal team does not put in language unnecessarily restricting use of the API. Such language is usually added with good intentions, but the end result can put the customer in a tough position. At the same time, as discussed in Chapter 5, license agreements for

No License for Testing

Simplistic license agreements often inadvertently prevent customers from utilizing systems as intended by marketects and tarchitects. In one enterprise-class system I worked on, the original terms of the license agreement restricted the use of our system on only one hardware configuration, however, it did allow them full and free access to our API. The problem was that the agreement did not meet the legitimate needs of the customer to install the system on development and staging (or "model office") configurations to create and test their integrations and extensions before installing them on production hardware.

One way around this problem is to make certain that your legal team understands your objectives for use of the API. If you've designed a system to be integrated and/or extended, your customers are going to need development and testing licenses. Some vendors charge for these; others provide them as part of the basic license. (I recommend against charging because that will inhibit customers from integrating and extending their systems.) Regardless of whether or not you choose to charge for them, you need to make certain that they are clearly defined.

in-licensed technology must be examined to make sure rights to in-licensed technologies are clearly defined.

Managing APIs over Multiple Releases

Earlier in this chapter I noted that publishing an API, or any other technique for extending and integrating your system, is an important public commitment to the people relying on it. The level of commitment to an external API for customers is *very* different from that developers may have to an API they are creating for other members of the development team. It is relatively easy to negotiate changes to an API within a team—healthy teams do this frequently during development. However, it is very difficult to negotiate changes to an external, published API, especially when hundreds or thousands of customers have created applications that rely on it. I've read how Web services will change all of this, but I don't believe it. An external, published API represents a serious commitment to your customers. You can't change it on a whim.

Like other aspects of your system, however, the techniques you use to provide extension and integration, including APIs, will change over time. Early versions of the system may not expose the right kinds of services or may not expose the right services using the proper underlying technology. The trick is to carefully manage the evolution of APIs so that the customers relying on this integration/extension technique will have time to plan for and accommodate any changes.

Techniques

Here are some approaches to consider in managing APIs.

Give Plenty of Warning

Customers should know about extension and integration changes as soon as possible. A good rule of thumb is to announce changes planned for release n_{+1} in release n. To help in the transition from the old to the new API, provide tools to identify the old ones and, when possible, automatically convert the old ones to new ones.

Provide One Release of Overlap

Once the new APIs are released in version n, the old APIs should not be fully deprecated until release n_{+1}. In other words, an API must be removed in no less than two full releases of the product.

Provide Backward Compatibility Layers

Once the API is no longer officially supported you may find it helpful to offer an "unsupported" backward compatibility API (or layer), provided that the underlying functionality of the product hasn't changed. This API is often implemented as an optional module that can be installed as needed by users. Be careful with this approach, as it may create a false sense of security among your users that portions of the API will always be there.

Provide Automated Tools That Identify or Convert Calls To Deprecated APIs

Provide tools that can automatically identify and/or convert calls to deprecated APIs and convert them to the new platform. These tools benefit your application by making it that much easier to move to the upgraded version.

Chapter Summary

- Integration is the process of programmatically linking your system with others.
- Extension is the process of adding new functionality to your system through well-defined approaches, such as plug-in architectures.
- Integration and extension enable your customers to create the product they seek. As a bonus, it creates tighter customer relationships and decreases the likelihood that a customer will leave you for a competitor.
- The layered architectural pattern, which organizes various system functions in logical and physical layers, provides several excellent choices for integration

and extension in enterprise-class software systems. The primary layers of a layered architecture are

- User interface
- Services
- Domain model
- Persistent data

Sublayers may exist within these layers, and other layers may be created to handle specialized requirements.

■ Whatever the structure of your architecture, build it in *spikes*—that is, user-visible functionality *driven* through all layers or subsystems.

■ There are several ways to provide integration and extension points at the services and domain model layers. For example,

- Programmatic techniques, such as exposing an API
- Registration techniques, such as creating a plug-in architecture (like a Web browser)

■ Integration and extension of persistent data can be accomplished through

- Views
- Hook tables
- Spreadsheet pivot tables
- Extract, transform, and load (ETL) scripts

■ The business ramifications of applications that can be extended and/or integrated include

- A professional services organization to guide your customers in these activities
- Training programs to ensure that your customers understand how to do this on their own
- Certification programs to create an ecosystem associated with your application
- A community of users around your application
- License agreements that explicitly support integration and extension

■ Any customer-facing method for integrating and/or extending your application must be carefully managed. You're making a public commitment to stability. Honor it.

Check This

❑ For each way the system can be extended or integrated, we have the necessary supporting materials to ensure that our customers can create the desired extensions or integrations.

❑ We have used the context diagram to define how our application might be integrated with other applications.

❑ We have established naming conventions to create a consistent API.

❑ The performance and resource implications of each call to our API are well documented.

Try This

1. To what degree can your system be integrated with other systems? How do you know that your techniques work for your target market?

2. To what degree can your system be extended? How do you know that your techniques work for your target market?

3. What kind of certification program have you established?

4. What kinds of third-party consultants have worked with your application? What information are you providing to them? How are you using their knowledge and experience to improve your application?

5. What steps have you taken to foster a user community?

Chapter 9
Brand and Brand Elements

Product, service, or corporate brands, and their related elements, have a substantial impact on your solution. Recall from Chapter 2 that branding is *vital* to your total success. You can create a great technology, and even a good solution, but a *winning* solution will be reflected and supported by a winning brand.

Brand elements, which are often woven throughout the product and become, often surprisingly, part of the architecture, need to be managed. Among other things, you need to select which elements will become part of your solution, how these relate to the brand elements of other products, when and how to change them, and how your partners may modify them. In this chapter I will explore brand and brand element management and their influence on creating and sustaining a winning solution.

Brand Elements

The brand elements most likely to impact your product are names, slogans, graphic symbols, designs, other customer-facing or customer-visible elements, and even URLs. Elements can be registered for legal protection as trademarks by the U.S. Patent and Trademark Office (USPTO). Registered trademarks have special restrictions on their usage—a topic explored later in this section.

Names

The brand elements often having the biggest effect on your system are the various names associated with your product and your company. Here are some of the areas in which names can affect your tarchitecture.

Physical Location of System Components

Most deployment models, including service provider models such as an ASP or MSP, result in one or more software components being installed on the customer's or user's computer. These range from simple browser plug-ins to the full executable and its supporting files, including DLLs, sample data, documentation, and help files. Once you have identified the platform-recommended location for the software, chances are you will still have to create a subdirectory or subfolder for storing your application components. I recommend the combination of your company name/product name/ subcomponent name or, in rare cases, just the product name/subcomponent name.

This approach has several advantages. It gives you additional branding information for your company and product, and it supports expansion in multiple ways: You can conveniently add subcomponents to a given product or add products. Even if you sell just a single product, you're likely to create additional modules, over time, and you're going to need a place to store them.

If you support multiple versions of your application or product on the same system, it may be convenient to incorporate version numbers in directory names, although this may become irrelevant as operating systems increasingly support the management of component and component versions. Regardless of operating system support, carefully consider your choice because multiple versions on the same system increase testing complexity (remember the matrix of pain?) and often increase version support costs. See Chapters 12 and 15 for more information on supporting multiple versions of the same product.

This approach does not remove all risks associated with identifying the right physical location to store or install a product. A company, product, or subcomponent name, or a concatenation of the three, may be longer than the allowed length of a subdirectory or subfolder name. Any of these may contain special characters not allowed by the supporting operating system. While rare when using fully qualified names, there is always the possibility of name collision. Special symbols that may be associated with the product in printed material, such as ©, ®, or ™, are probably not allowed. Despite the potential challenges, your company name/product name/module subcomponent is the best place to start when determining the physical location of your product.

Names of Key Components

Complex products often have many sellable components, and in addition to the overall product, marketects must name them as well. It is best if the marketect or another person trained in marketing does the naming. This is an important, strategic decision, and you want to make certain that it is made by individuals with the proper training and background. Some companies allow developers to name products. I don't approve, because developer-created names are often confusing.

As for customer-visible technical components and/or features, I encourage marketects to include developers in this naming because the goal is often "technically" accurate names that convey exactly what is going on. These names can be exciting, and a good marketect can use their straightforward, direct, and descriptive nature to quickly

Developers Should Name Variables, Not Products

Product names are *extremely* important, especially in the consumer market. Product and marketing managers spend a lot of time trying to create good ones, and they should. A well-named product has a significantly greater chance for success than a poorly named one. Like a good class, variable, or function name, a good product name has many desirable attributes: It is short, it describes or highlights one or more positive attributes, it is a good fit for the company, it can be legally protected via a trademark, it has a freely available URL, it is unique, and it can be easily pronounced and spelled by members of the target market. This is just to name a few!

Here are some of my favorite high-technology product names and why I like them:

- *Palm.* Can you think of a better name for a hand-held computer?
- *Latitude.* It sounds like a computer made for people on the go, and it is.
- *Photoshop.* A software workshop for image manipulation.
- *Easy CD Creator.* The product lives up to its name—a double win!

I'll admit that product names are often less important in the enterprise market than in the consumer market in which other brand elements dominate. There are many reasons for this, chief of which is that customers of enterprise software often refer to the company more than the product: *Siebel* Sales, *Oracle* Financials, *SAP* R3, *Tibco* ActiveExchange. There are a few exceptions, such as *OpenView* (from HP), or *CICS*, *DB2*, and *VTAM* (from IBM). In some sense, product name versus company name is a bit of a toss-up when it comes to enterprise software—as long as one of them is good and drives your branding strategy, you're probably OK.

The desirable attributes of a product name are sufficiently different from those of technical names that it is almost always better to ask your marketing experts to do the naming. I've inherited a few projects in which product names were created by developers. In a few cases this was okay, as customers found these names acceptable and the names addressed a sufficient number of attributes. Most other times, a name had to be changed because it was too "geeky," the company couldn't secure a trademark, it was too close to a competitor's name, or it conveyed a poor brand (such as when a name seemed cool to a developer but a customer viewed it negatively). As discussed later in this chapter, changing the name of a product is an expensive operation that can often can be avoided simply by letting someone skilled in product marketing select the name to begin with.

To illustrate just how important it is to review names, one of my developers actually named a database upgrade program after himself! We missed the name in our review, and the program was actually shipped to customers. Quite an embarrassment.

educate a potential customer on key features and also differentiate the product from the competition. Creative technical names may also be easier to protect.

Tarchitects and developers should realize that developer-created component names, which probably had a strong correlation to the tarchitecture in its first few releases, are much less likely to maintain this strong correlation over subsequent releases. If a developer-created name catches on, you're going to want to keep it. At the same time, chances are good that the team will want to modify the underlying implementation and possibly even the tarchitecture over time. The result is that the "technical" name and its underlying implementation will diverge.

Instead of fighting this divergence, accept it. Names associated with the marketecture evolve more slowly than the tarchitecture and its implementation. The usually substantial cost of changing a component name is not justified just because you want to maintain a strong correlation between the marketecture and the tarchitecture.

I realize that these are somewhat paradoxical arguments. Fortunately, the marketect is the final arbiter and selector of customer-visible names. By working with developers, a skilled marketect can usually select the best names possible.

Names May Or May Not Be Internationalized

One element of internationalization that needs marketectural and tarchitectural consideration is that the actual name of the product may be different in different target markets. Installing the product in a U.S.-centric directory structure may cause confusion among your user population in countries where English is not dominant. In addition, many product names that make good sense in English must be translated into different names in other languages. Any good marketing book can provide horror stories about good product names created in one culture that were *horrible* in another. Ultimately, you have to check all names before blindly assuming that locally created names will work on a global scale. If you suspect that this might be a problem, make certain that you're storing brand elements in appropriate resource files or are using some other technique to extend your internationalization architecture into brand elements.

Configuration and Log Files May Contain Brand Elements

Product and company names can affect the location, name, content, and structure of configuration and log files.

Error, Diagnostic, and Information Messages May Contain Brand Elements

Messages presented must often refer to the marketing names for key components or functional areas of the product. If they don't, your user and technical support organizations can be confused on how to identify and resolve problems in the field.

Names Are Volatile, Especially in the First Release

The first release of any project is where names are most volatile. This volatility can have negative effects on, for example, the source code management system. I recommend that developers refer to the product through a code name for the first release, such as the name of a fruit or a mythological creature. You don't want to create entries in your source code management system that closely reflect a product name that may change two or three times before the release date. Because names may change during any release, continue using this code name for as long as the product is in development.

Graphics, Slogans, and Other Brand Elements

It seems obvious, but sometimes development organizations forget that graphical user interfaces (GUIs) will be affected by *graphics and iconic* brand elements. Similarly, *voice-based user interfaces* will be affected by *slogans* and other brand elements. While many of these effects are not tarchitectural, they should be addressed by the development team. Pay attention to the following areas.

Icons and Splash Screens

Product management should approve every icon and/or graphic presented to the user, as they are all brand elements. I worked on two projects where the product didn't have a logo until we realized that some kind of icon on the desktop was necessary. In the first project, I was fortunate to have a developer who was also a skilled graphic artist. He created a logo that marketing approved, and it later became the approved trademark. On the other project, we had to add time to our schedule for an outside design firm to create the necessary icons and splash screens, have marketing approve the design, and ensure that the icon was sized correctly and used the right colors. As you might guess, we missed our initially projected delivery date.

Brand Colors

Companies often specify everything they can about their brand, including specific colors, presentation templates, and document templates that are either associated with the brand or must be used with the product. Tarchitects should check in with marketects to determine the effects that any of these brand elements may have on the architecture.

Voice Branding

An emerging area of brand management is voice-based user interfaces. Picking the right voice talent is a powerful way to make certain your brand is properly represented.

When to Use the Trademark (™) Symbol

There are legal implications to the proper use of various brand elements, especially those that have been registered as trademarks. Here are the most important things to keep in mind.

Protect Your Legal Rights

Trademarks are based on use. Failing to use a mark may result in losing your legal right to it.

Give Notice

You have to tell the person viewing the registered information that it is, in fact, a registered trademark. The easiest way to do this is to use the symbol ® (referred to as a *mark*). There are other ways—consult your inhouse legal counsel for the preferred approach, as it may differ from the above. Do *not* use the ® symbol if the mark has not been registered with the USPTO. Surprisingly, the government claims that to do so is a crime. Instead, use the ™ symbol for unregistered trademarks.

Use Marks Only as Adjectives

A mark should never be used as a noun or verb, never be pluralized, and never be used in the possessive form.

Include Registered Trademarks in the Distribution and/or Prominently Display Them on Usage

Traditionally, marks were affixed to goods and services. In the world of software, they must somehow be displayed to the user, so include them in the distribution, installation, and execution of your software.

Domain Names Can Be Trademarked, Subject to Certain Restrictions

If you've created an interesting URL for your product, service, or company, you may want to register it as a trademark. Additional information can be found at *http://www.uspto.gov/*.

Managing In-License Brands

In-licensed technology may have any number of branding requirements. The marketect and tarchitect should work together to ensure that brand elements of in-licensed components or technologies are properly handled.

Click OK to Continue

In one project I worked on we wanted to operate a key in-licensed technology as a service under Windows' NT. This would allow us to automatically restart the service if it failed. Unfortunately, the licensor required us to display a splash screen for at least 10 seconds, with an OK button, to ensure that a human operator would see the licensor's brand. The service wouldn't start until the button was clicked. The licensor was unwilling to negotiate this requirement, and we needed to make certain that the component could be started and managed as a service. We solved the problem by writing a manager program that would start the service and sleep for 11 seconds. If the splash screen was still displayed it would simulate clicking on OK.

Brand Element Customizations

Depending on the type of software you create, your target customer might have legitimate requirements to override or customize key brand elements. Some reasons for customization include software sold as a component in another system, software deployed in a service model (where the service provider wants its own brand recognition), or standalone software, integrated into a larger solution by a value-added reseller (VAR), where the VAR wants its own brand recognition. More generally, whoever supports the software or whoever is most visible to the user often wants brand recognition.

Marketects should be able to identify requirements for brand element customizations fairly early in the development cycle. Knowing which elements need to change is essential because you'll still have to install the software, name key components, and present messages to the user. In addition, make certain you know which brand elements *may* be customized and which *must* be customized. The former will require sensible defaults; the latter will require a way to handle the customization process.

Include precise details about every brand element that may or must be customized. These details include bitmap size, supported graphic file formats, default brand elements, and so forth. Keep in mind contract requirements in this process, as the specific requirements of brand element customization may be contractual.

Changing Brand Elements

Changing brand elements is usually harder than changing other parts of the system that are seen by the user, such as in an internationalized user interface that can be readily localized to different languages. There are two primary reasons for this.

First, brand elements change quite slowly and are therefore not generally required to support change. This is unlike internationalized software, which has been designed to support change. I am not advocating that you create requirements to support changing brand elements, unless this is specifically required as part of your overall strategy. Specific requirements to support changing brand elements are usually rare.

Second, brand influences a product and its architecture in very subtle ways. The product development team (marketing, engineering, QA, technical publications—everyone associated with creating a winning solution) often doesn't realize the full requirements when one or more brand elements are changed. I vividly remember the challenges one of my teams faced when we decided to change a product name. We debated, and eventually changed, a large number of items that didn't initially appear to be related to the change. These ranged from the labels used in our source code management system to the categories in our bug-tracking system (more on this later).

Of course, there are many legitimate reasons to change brands and brand elements. Products and components do change names. Companies change names, either voluntarily or because a company is acquired or a product line is sold from one company to another.

Product Areas to Change

When you're faced with changing a brand or brand elements, consider these product areas.

Subsystem Names

A tarchitect must name a subsystem or a component *something*. Ideally, the name is functional, but quite often it is related to the product or the brand. As described earlier, it also happens that functional or technical names become part of the product and brand. Changing the name of a product or any of its brand elements may motivate internal subsystem or other component name changes.

Source Code Repositories

It is easier for everyone if the product and brand element names either are not reflected in the source code repository (i.e., use code names) or match, as closely as possible, the product names. If you name repository structures after products, keep them synchronized. It is very confusing to track down a set of changes when the source code repository refers to a product that no longer exists!

QA and Technical Support Tracking Systems

Good QA and technical support systems provide bug categorizations. These categorizations inevitably reflect product and brand elements and should be maintained in close alignment with the actual products. This is especially important if you utilize any kind of customer self-service solutions, such as a Web site where customers can review problem case histories (which also reinforces that your brand is really your *total customer experience*, including technical support!).

Physical Location of Components

As described earlier in this chapter, it is often easiest to place physical components where they reflect the company, the product, and the module. Your upgrade process may have to account for this. If you change any components, be patient. I've worked on products where it took two full releases before all changes associated with the new product name were implemented, including upgraded versions of the product.

Naming and Structure Of APIs

APIs often reflect, either by name or by function, a variety of brand elements. Company or product names, for example, may appear as prefixes on functions and functions may be organized or grouped according to product-specific branding requirements. Because of this, changing the name of the product or any of its associated brand elements may even require changes to your APIs.

Error, Information, and Diagnostic Messages

Because any of these may contain references to corporate or product brand elements, each needs to be examined for potential changes.

QA and Test Automation Infrastructure

If you're changing any subsystems, error messages, or user interfaces, or your auto-mated build system or any externally visible APIs, chances are good that you'll also have to make some modifications to your QA and test automation infrastructure.

Sales Collateral

Sales collateral refers to all materials created to support sales. This includes Web sites, whitepapers, case studies, glossies, and so forth. These also require changes if the brand or brand elements change.

QA and Change

The QA effort to change a brand or key brand elements is often substantial. With so many parts of the system changing, and with the potential for tarchitectural change, you have to perform a full QA cycle. One of my teams had to track down a particu-larly nasty bug when the installer, under certain circumstances, put the new software in the old location! Fortunately, this was captured in the beta testing process (which is essential when brand elements change because it gives your customers time to adjust).

❏ ❏ ❏ ❏ ❏ ❏ ❏ ❏

Chapter Summary

- Brand elements have a subtle but pervasive impact on your tarchitecture, rang-ing from the icons that represent the product to the location where they are stored.
- Product names are the domain of the marketect. Good subcomponent and fea-ture names may come from developers (but are still controlled by the marketect).
- Internationalization poses special challenges to brand elements. It pays to hire a specialist if you're going to go international (and chances are good that you are).
- Understand how to use various legal designations associated with product names.
- Technology in-licenses may impose brand element requirements.
- Review all aspects of the total customer experience when considering changes to a product name.

Check This

- ❏ All required brand elements have been identified and approved.
- ❏ All brand elements have been internationalized as required.

❑ Error, diagnostic, and log files have been checked for approved brand elements.

❑ All marks, including ® and ™, are used properly.

❑ Any brand elements that may be replaced or changed by a partner or technology licensee have been identified and fully specified.

Try This

1. How are brand elements used in your application? Consider products and their names, graphics, URLS, and so forth.

2. Are there any plans for changing brand elements in the current or a near-future release? How do you intend to manage this process?

3. Do you work on software that requires you to give your customers brand or brand element control? How do you do this?

4. How do you coordinate brand elements with other product lines?

Chapter 10
Usability

Winning solutions are usable. They may not be perfect. They may not win design awards from fancy committees where people dress in black, sip champagne, and pontificate on issues like "convergence." But they are usable: With them users can accomplish necessary tasks easily, efficiently, and with a minimum of errors. Winning solutions enable people to achieve their goals with little, if any, frustration.

I've already touched on two important but overlooked aspects of usability: deployment and integration/extension architectures. Subsequent chapters will focus on usability in the context of operations and maintenance—notably, installations and upgrades. This chapter briefly explores some other important aspects of usability, concentrating on performance and scalability. Simply put, just about everything the tarchitect does affects usability in one way or another. Gaining an appreciation of usability, of how architectural decisions affect it, and of how it affects architecture, is critical to creating winning solutions.

As you read this chapter, keep in mind that usability is a very large topic, and several terrific books have been written about it. Even if you've read other books, however, you'll find this chapter useful because it discusses usability in the context of a winning solution. My primary focus is how tarchitecture impacts usability, with an emphasis on performance factors. This differs from books that address process or technology.

Usability Is about Money

Historically, usability was associated with the user interface, and human–computer interaction (HCI) professionals concentrated their work here. This makes perfect sense, because most of our understanding of a given system and its usability is shaped by the user interface.

But usability is much deeper than the user interface. In my view, it relates to the complex choices that users of the system make to accomplish one or more tasks easily, efficiently, enjoyably, and with a minimum of errors. Many, although not all, of these choices are directly influenced by your tarchitecture. In other words, if your system is perceived as "usable," it will be usable because it was fundamentally architected that way.

This view of usability makes certain demands on marketects and tarchitects. For different reasons, both must understand users and the context in which they work. The marketect needs these data to ensure that the system is providing a competitive edge, that it is meeting users' most important needs, and that it is providing the necessary foundation for a long-term relationship. The tarchitect needs these data to create the deeper capabilities—from performance to internationalization—that result in usable systems.

As a trivial example, consider users in different domains. An application designed to help a biochemist manage the vast amount of data created by automated experiment equipment is vastly different from the airport self-service kiosk where I obtain a boarding pass before taking a flight. A clear understanding of what makes these systems usable can only be acquired by understanding representative users and the context in which they work. The marketect needs to understand the use cases associated with user goals and motivations, how creating these systems will serve user needs, and so forth. The tarchitect must also understand the uses cases associated with these systems, even though the technology that underlies each solution is radically different.

More subtly, understanding users and the context in which they work is important for the quantitative and qualitative dimensions of usability. Quantitative aspects of usability address such things as performance and data entry error rates. Qualitative aspects address such things as satisfaction and ease of learning. Because no application can maximize every possible quantitative or qualitative value, tradeoffs must be made. Good tradeoffs produce usable applications and winning solutions.

There are a variety of techniques you can use to gain an understanding of users, including observation, interviews, questionnaires, and direct experience. The last is one of my favorites, a technique I refer to as *experiential requirements*. Simply put, perform the tasks of your users as best you can to understand how to create a system they find usable. This approach isn't appropriate for all situations (e.g., surgery or auto racing), but it is one of the best for many.

The fundamental, almost overpowering, reason to create usable systems is money. A large amount of compelling data indicates that usability pays for itself quickly over the life of the product. Whereas a detailed summary of the economic impact of usability is beyond the scope of this book, I will mention one system I worked on that was used by one of the world's largest online retailers. A single phone call to customer support could have destroyed the profits of a dozen or more successful transactions, so usability was paramount. Other applications may not be quite as sensitive to usability,

> ### Market Demands and Usability
>
> When you go to the store to purchase software, you can refuse to buy any application that does not appear to meet your needs—including your subjective preferences. This effect of market forces drives the designers of shrink-wrapped software to create systems that are increasingly easy to use.
>
> Unfortunately, software designers in large corporations are usually not driven by market forces. Instead, they typically attend to the needs of senior management. As a result, the usability of many applications in these corporations is abysmal: Poorly designed, manipulative, and even hostile applications denigrate the users' dignity and humanity.
>
> If you are a tarchitect working on an internal application in a large corporation, I urge you to pay special attention to the suggestions listed in the rest of this chapter. You may not be driven by the same market forces as are tarchitects creating shrink-wrapped applications, but the benefits of usability are as applicable within the corporation as they are in the marketplace.

but my experience demonstrates that marketects and tarchitects routinely underestimate usability's importance. Benefits of usable systems include any or all of the following, each of which can be quantified.

- Reduced training costs
- Reduced support and service costs
- Reduced error costs
- Increased user productivity
- Increased customer satisfaction
- Increased maintainability

It is generally not possible to achieve every possible benefit of usability simultaneously. For example, a system that is easy to learn for novices is likely to be cumbersome for experts who don't need simplified approaches. Because of this, it is vital that marketects and tarchitects work together to ensure that the correct aspects of usability are being emphasized in the project.

Mental Models, Metaphors, and Usability

Once you've gained a concrete understanding of how users approach their tasks, you can begin to understand the mental models associated with these tasks. A *mental model* is the set of thoughts and structures we use to explain, simulate, predict, or control objects in the world. It is shaped by the task and the tools used to accomplish it, which means that it can change over time. As far as I know, there is no language or notation that formally documents mental models. At best, mental models are informal observations that the development team can use to create more usable systems. Consider a designer creating a new project planning tool. Through several interviews she has discovered that managers think of dependencies within the project as a web or maze instead of a GANTT or PERT chart.

In creating the new planning tool, the development team will create one or more conceptual models to share their understanding with others. A *conceptual model* is some representation of a mental model, in words or pictures, using informal or formal techniques—for example, a UML class diagram of the primary concepts in the system.

An understanding of mental models, and the clarifying role of conceptual models, forms the creative foundation of metaphors that can be used in the creation or modification of a system. *Metaphors* are models that help us understand one thing in terms of another. Tarchitects often use metaphors to structure their application architectures. In one system I worked on, we had to support message passing between distributed systems in such a way that any system in the chain could add data to or remove it from the core message without altering the core message contents. To help explain this concept to potential customers, I created the metaphor of a Velcro-covered ball, where the ball represented the core message and the data that customers could add to the message were "attached" or "removed" much like we could attach or remove pieces of Velcro to the ball.

A well-chosen metaphor shapes both the tarchitecture and the user interface. In the project planning example described above, the system's underlying tarchitecture could easily have one or more functions to manipulate project plans in terms of a web or a maze. This choice, in turn, could provide creative ways of organizing tasks, displaying information, or providing notification of critical path dependencies.

Metaphors are often most apparent when considering the marketecture, primarily because those chosen by a tarchitect must be communicated in a targeted manner to a well-defined market. Metaphors can influence a variety of brand elements, including names and iconic representations of products or processes. They often affect the pricing model, by highlighting areas of the system that are of greatest value to the defined market segment. Entirely new products rely on metaphor to both explain how they work and provide marketects with the vehicle for shaping future customers' mental models about them, how they work, and the benefits they provide. All of these are reasons for close collaboration between marketects and tarchitects in the development of the system metaphor. In the example of a project planning tool, the marketect may prefer the metaphor of a maze over that of a web because a maze better fits the product's positioning.

The final benefit associated with well-chosen metaphors, and arguably the most important reason to pursue them, is their effect on usability. They substantially improve system usability by tapping into users' existing mental models of their work and how that work should be performed. Training costs are substantially reduced, satisfaction improves, and overall comfort with the system increases. An excellent catalog of prospective metaphors can be found in *Designing Object-Oriented User Interfaces* [Collins 1995].

Tarchitectural Influences on User Interface Design

You can find quite a lot of tarchitectural advice, including my description of layered architectures in Chapter 8, that recommends separating the user interface logic and design from the rest of the underlying system. This is good advice because elements of design such as business logic should be maintained in a manner that allows multiple representations. It is also true that the user interface should have maximum flexibility in presenting data meaningfully for the intended user. Consider an application that monitors processes on a factory floor. One of the monitoring devices may be a thermostat integrated with a specific piece of equipment. The user interface designer should be free to represent the thermostat in whatever way makes most sense: as a gauge, a dial, a simple numerical display, or perhaps something even more creative that hasn't been done before.

That said, my experience shows that in most applications there is no practical way to purely separate the user interface from the rest of the tarchitecture. In fact, as application complexity increases you often have to rely on the idiosyncratic benefits provided by a given kind of user interface, whether it be command line, graphical, haptic, auditory, or any combination thereof.

Areas of Influence

The next sections describe some specific areas where tarchitecture influences user interface design and usability.

Cardinality

Cardinality refers to the number of entities that participate in a given relationship. It is an important element of overall tarchitectural and user interface design because the techniques associated with storing, processing, and representing small numbers of entities vary quite a bit from those associated with storing, processing, and representing large numbers. As cardinality increases, the demand for visual representations of the data and their interactions also increases. Fortunately, the number of tools available for visualizing large data sets continues to increase. make certain you understand how cardinality may affect your user interface.

Feedback

One of the most important heuristics associated with creating usable systems is providing various kinds of feedback to the user. Feedback assumes a variety of forms, including informational messages, responses to user actions (such as a menu being displayed when selected by the user), progress meters, and so forth. The tarchitecture must be created with an awareness of feedback demands.

Consider the effects of a progress meter, which indicates that the system is processing a request or transaction that is going to take a fairly long time. The portion of the system servicing the request must be designed to allow periodic feedback on its processing status. This can be relatively simple, such as when you issue a request to perform some operation over a finite number of elements and processing each element takes a well-known amount of time. It can also be quite complex, as there are many operations for which you cannot predict in advance the time to complete. Note that this fact also influences the kind of progress meter chosen, another example of how underlying tarchitectural issues influence the design of the user interface.

A special form of feedback concerns early validation, in which the system performs partial validation or near realtime evaluation on every piece of entered data. A trivial example is a data input field for a numeric part number that only accepts numeric characters. A more complex example is an input screen that can partially validate data or an input screen that enables/disables various controls based on previously entered data. Early validation can't be performed on many Web-based systems because the underlying capabilities of HTML and a browser can't support it. More generally, the devices used to access the system do not affect usability in a uniform manner—the capabilities of every device must be separately understood to ensure you're getting the best usability.

Explicit User Models

One way to take advantage of your understanding of mental models is to create an explicit model of users' understanding in your system and adjust system behavior to it over time. This technique is used in everything from my word processor, which automatically corrects spelling mistakes, to my favorite online bookstore, which recommends books according to my previous purchases.

Workflow Support

System architectures and markets often mature together. This is one reason that so many initial system releases have poor workflow support and many mature releases have one or more elements that in some way provide explicit workflow support. As the market and use of the system mature, product development teams can capture *best practices* and codify them through any number of simple (e.g., wizards, animated help systems) or complex (e.g., scriptable workflow engines) workflow support structures. Workflow support usually builds on top of the understanding we develop of the users' mental models and is in itself a kind of explicit user model.

Transaction Support

Many of the operations performed in a system can be thought of as transactions—for example, simply typing a character into a program that supports undo. Inevitably, transactions, and transaction semantics, affect the user interface and vice versa. Consider a Web site that provides flight information, constructed according to the layered architecture presented in Chapter 8. In extending this system to support a voice-based user interface, you're likely to find that the underlying domain objects and many of the services are perfectly reusable but certain transaction-oriented services are not. This is because transactions are often designed to support a particular kind of user interface capability. For the interface just described, you can create a very large trans-action object that captures many fields from the user in a single screen. This is simply not possible in a voice-based interface, where user input must be obtained via small "chunks" because of the complexity of asking the user to correct errors.

Another example is the presentation of information to the user. In a graphical interface, it is easy to provide the user with cues as to how the information is sorted. Thus, your Web-based e-mail program might present all of the messages in your inbox, with simple visual cues as to how they are sorted. A voice-based interface probably won't be able to reuse this logic when presenting information to the user; the underlying logic to obtain the data will also need to change.

Error Response

How you gather, validate, and respond to user input errors is determined by a complex interaction between your underlying system architecture, your user interface, and the user's tasks. My favorite C++ compiler presents a hyperlinked list of errors in a win-dow; selecting an error takes me to the place in the source code where the compiler thinks the error occurred. This doesn't work for an e-commerce Web site, which must respond to errors with some kind of notification screen (perhaps the fields are in red or preceded by an asterisk). The choices made regarding error presentation will likely affect the underlying tarchitecture.

Internationalization and Localization

In internationalization the underlying tarchitecture supports multiple languages and localized data formats. In localization a given language and style of interaction and/or presentation is specified. The ramifications are substantial and range from formatting monetary values, dates, and numbers to hiring special firms to translate all user infor-mation into the supported languages. Operating systems and their platforms provide the infrastructure for determining the user's language. It is up to you to take advantage of this.

It is important to consider everything presented to the user when localizing an application: Error messages, informational messages, dialogs, input/output formats, log files, and even the names of external APIs are all internationalization candidates.

There are several areas in which the development team can make design choices that make internationalization efforts difficult. Some of the more common mistakes include using fixed-size dialogs and dialog components, embedding information dis-played to users within source code, and failing to use the services provided by modern operating systems to select the property localization information at run time.

Internationalization efforts include converting fixed-size dialog and dialog com-ponents to handle variable width text, allowing for text that flows right-to-left as well as left-to-right, and multi-byte or double-byte character sets. Information displayed to the user should never be embedded within the source code, but should instead be ref-erenced by an identifier that is passed to a component that converts the identifier to the appropriate output at runtime, based on appropriate localization settings. This component

Details, Details, Details

Some of my greatest challenges have been in creating software for use around the world. In a project in which our technology was embedded in other systems, one Japanese customer continually refused our deliverables because of spelling or grammatical mistakes. Their attention to detail was extraordinary, and I was generally glad to make their requested changes because I believed that it improved overall product quality. But when they submitted a change that reverted the user interface to a previous version, I realized that they were conducting their own beta tests to see which version their customers liked best—and forcing us to pay for it. Normally, I wouldn't have minded, but their beta testing was starting to negatively affect our other Japanese customers.

In another project we needed to localize the client to support 16 languages on both Macintosh and Windows platforms. We spent about a week chasing down bugs in the Macintosh translation. As it turned out, our internationalization vendor used a Windows character set when creating the files. The resultant bug was extraordinarily hard to find, but once found, it was easy to fix.

In general, localized software requires a strong beta program conducted with customers and/or partners who are experts in the highest-priority target languages. Most development organizations simply don't have the necessary diversity to properly test the results of the translations provided by your localization vendor.

can be used for everything from the information displayed in error dialogs to that written to log files (localizing log files can have dramatic effects in customer satisfaction). The foundation of all of these techniques is proper use of operating system facilities to select localization information and settings at runtime. This is an ongoing area of improvement, and tarchitects should routinely monitor operating system upgrades for internationalization/localization improvements.

Because of the far reaching impacts of internationalization and localization, marketects should specify their target languages very early in the development process as well as those languages likely to be used down the road. If in doubt, assume the possibility of Far Eastern and Right-to-Left languages, and design the architecture accordingly.

Canceling Requests

Usability in many kinds of systems can be substantially improved when requests that may take a long time to process or consume many resources can be cancelled. Users feel more in control, and overall system performance can improve as the system is not engaged in unnecessary work. The option to cancel an operation can also provide excellent hooks to system administrators to tune system performance, especially in multi-user systems.

If you're building a single-user, desktop application, creating a tarchitecture that can cancel requests can be pretty easy. If you're building any system that shares state with other systems or users, is based on a client/server architecture, or relies on cascading the request through multiple components, this can be hard or impossible. Creating cancelable requests in these systems requires careful tarchitectural design. When a client initiates a cancelable request, it must be given some kind of identifier to reference that request in the future. The server must be extended to associate request identifiers with requests, ensure that requests can be terminated, and properly recover system resources. This can be very challenging, especially when requests are distributed among third-party, in-licensed components.

To illustrate, one system I worked on allowed users to initiate requests that invoked the services of two in-licensed components: a database from one vendor and a search engine from another. Coordinating the cancellation process between these technology components took a fair amount of programming, but the results were worth it.

I am not differentiating between traditional kinds of enterprise class systems or those based on Web services and service oriented architectures. In fact, I'm concerned that many of the published approaches to creating Web services and service oriented architectures do not address request cancellation. Suppose, for example, that a Web service takes a long time to compute a result or consumes a large amount of resources doing so. It should be possible to cancel these requests once they have been initiated, for all of the reasons described above. Web services don't change this aspect of usability, and it is important to understand that request-cancellation semantics must be an early consideration in tarchitectural design.

Each request should be assessed to determine if cancellation makes sense. Small requests that can be quickly computed do not warrant the overhead associated with cancellation.

Undoing Requests

In addition to canceling requests, usability is generally improved when a user can undo the result of a request. Like cancellation, this can be pretty easy to implement in the domain of single-user, desktop-oriented software. In the domain of enterprise-class software, when system state is shared among technology components and users, the concept of undoing a request may not make sense or may be impossible.

Suppose, for example, you've created a system that allows users to collaboratively work on documents stored into folders on a shared server. At time t_0, Pradeep adds a document. At time t_1, Sally deletes it. While Pradeep may think that he can undo the operation, in reality he cannot. This example can be extended to a large number of scenarios and can occur whenever two or more entities share state.

Sophisticated tarchitectural design, especially in the domain of transaction management as well as the use of publish–subscribe protocols, can enable you to provide substantial undo capabilities, even in the presence of a shared state. For example, in the previous example the system could keep track of the number of entities that have access to the shared folder. If a single entity is using the folder then single-user semantics, including such things as undo, could apply. Transactions can be extended to attempt an undo operation on behalf of a user; chances are probably good that it will succeed. Finally, rich user interfaces that maintain close correlation with the persistent state of the application can provide users with the information they need to determine if undo makes sense.

Compensating Transactions

Certain classes of business transactions cannot be cancelled or undone. For example, suppose your employer incorrectly calculates your payroll and automatically deposits the amount in your account. Chances are good that the money will be in your bank account before you receive the payroll stub and notify your manager of the error. The operation can't be undone or canceled. In this scenario the system must be extended through the use of compensating transactions. I've included compensating transactions in the section of usability because most business systems that fail to include them are very hard to use. You can't escape the effects of a compensating transaction, and adding them early in the design substantially improves usability.

Timeouts

Systems that require a session with another system or the user often have a variety of timeouts. Choosing the wrong value can lower usability, consume unnecessary system resources, and ultimately require the user to work more to accomplish her desired tasks. This is one area where sensibly chosen defaults can really help your application be perceived as truly usable. Default values are not enough, and session-related parameters must be under the control of the system administrators.

Network Availability/Speed

Many architectures use networks, but they don't have the luxury of an always-on connection, speed guarantees, or notification of a change in these states. Consider the context of the user as you address network issues. Chances are good that their context will differ from yours—plan accordingly.

Shared Resources

All systems have one or more resources that are shared. For example, I've worked with searching systems that take over all available processors in a multiprocessor system, leaving none for other work. A better design would enable the system administrator to tune the number of processors the search service consumes. Make certain that your system's concept of usability extends to other system's.

Failure Recovery

Systems can fail in a variety of ways. Tarchitectural choices make certain kinds of failures more or less likely. Once a failure occurs, how your system handles it directly affects usability. Ideally, your system handles and recovers from the failure in a reasonable manner, such as when your printer driver attempts to retry your print job. Failure conditions also are fodder for enhancing system design, especially when you can convert previously unhandled failure conditions into automatically handled failure conditions that do not disrupt the user.

Even if you handle as many failure conditions as possible, you will likely have to alert the user to some of those associated with your system. You can inform users of any of the following: potential negative effects of the failure and their magnitude, potential and/or recommended recovery procedures, and future preventative actions.

The Need for Speed

An important aspect of usability is performance, both actual and perceived. Unfortunately, this is quite misunderstood. It is beyond the scope of this book to provide detailed advice on how to create high-performance systems. Instead, my focus will be on precisely defining performance-related terms so that the marketect and tarchitect can communicate clearly, and on showing what performance information the development team needs to provide the marketect.

Let's Be Clear on What We're Talking About

The terminology I use to describe performance is presented in Table 10-1. All of these terms are related to each other. To illustrate, let's say that you want to calculate results for some of these terms for one of your systems. Your first step is to specify, or "fix," one or more of your system configurations. This could mean specifying underlying hardware, amount of disk space, memory size, operating system, database, Web server, and any other applications required. As for configurations, consider the following:

TABLE 10-1 Performance Terminology

Term	Definition
Throughput	Number of bits/transactions per unit of time
Performance	Time per unit (inverse of throughput)
Latency	Wait time for response
Capacity	Number of users (entities) system can support in a given configuration at a fixed level of performance
Scalability	Ability to increase capacity by adding hardware
Reliability	The length of time a system can run without failing
Response time	Total perceived time it takes to process requests (an emotional, subjective qualitative rating, the "human" dimension of performance)

- Below: below the minimum specified configuration—just for testing.
- Minimum: the minimum specified configuration. This should be well below the average configuration in your target market (market configuration).
- Average: slightly below the market configuration.
- Ideal: the market configuration of early adopters and influential end users (demo).
- Max: The best system you can (practically) assemble.

The next step is to identify the transaction or operation you want to test, complete with reference data. If you're going to test the performance of a spreadsheet recalculation, the same data must be available for every test run!

In this example, I'll assume that your system is server based and constructed in a manner similar to that described in Chapter 8. Once the server is up and running, you can program a test or driver program to simulate a request. Let's say that when you send a single request for a specific, common operation your system responds in .1 second. This is a base level of performance. If you configure your test driver to stimulate your system with up to 10 requests per second, and it runs without failing for 24 hours while maintaining the same performance, you also have some baseline data for reliability.

As you begin to increase transactions you'll probably notice more interesting things. You might expect the system to fail when the number of transactions exceeds 600 per minute (since $600 \times 0.1 = 60$ seconds). In reality, the system may not fail until the number of transaction exceeds, say, 700 per minute. This shows the difference between latency and throughput on the *total* system, because parts of various transactions are held in different components as they pass through the various layers.

Let's further assume that you can separate the transaction logic from the persistent store. This means that you should be able to increase capacity by adding more machines. You add more machines, but because you have a single, shared database all of these transaction servers are pointed at it. You might find that you can now handle 2,500 transactions per minute before some kind of failure, such as a completely dropped request. This is a measure of the scalability of your system—that is, its ability to add more hardware to improve various performance factors. If you find that you can't improve beyond this, you know you've reached the database server's maximum. Improving this may require you to optimize the server in some special way, such as installing special disk-processing hardware, changing database vendors, or tuning or optimizing it by adding indices or profiling SQL queries.

Note that in this example the mechanism used to improve performance shifts as various limits are reached. This is common in complex systems. More memory might buy you better performance—to a point. Then you have to get a faster processor or perhaps faster disk hardware.

You might also find that your system does not exhibit linear performance. In fact, complex systems seldom exhibit linear performance curves. Most often, you will have linear responses for small areas of the various curves that are plotted from these data. Don't be surprised if your system "falls over" or "cliffs" when certain tolerances are exceeded. This is the reason for a scalable system (one that you can "throw hardware at" to increase capacity at an acceptable level of performance).

My example thus far has assumed that the driver program sends requests uniformly. This does not match reality, in which most non-batch-processing, server-based systems have *bursts* of activity. Since servers queue requests, it's possible to handle bursts that are significantly higher than the steady-state throughput limit without failure. For example, your original configuration may be able to handle 1,400 requests during the first minute as long as no requests come in during the second minute. Since different servers vary in the number of requests they can successfully queue, it's also a good idea to know the queue limit. That will give you the maximum burst that can be handled by the server, which is another factor in reliability.

The system's perceived response time may not actually match the performance just described. Performance is typically measured at a layer below the user interface, because the user interface layers can add any number of additional processing steps or transformations that are considered a realistic part of performance. Moreover, response time may be more unpredictable. Still, response time is important, and having a good response time matters because it is associated with our perception of the system and our ability to use it for useful work. Subsecond response times are often required to create the perception that the system is responding to our needs instantaneously. Response times of less than 5 to 10 seconds are needed to enable the average user to maintain an uninterrupted flow of thought. Users may lose focus if the response time is greater than 10 seconds.

Reliability also deals with the graceful handling of failure. If a server crashes when its peak load is exceeded, it's less reliable than a server that sends back an error code in response to the messages it can't handle or that simply refuses to allow a user to log in.

Note that it is rare for a system to process only one kind of transaction or operation. Since most systems support a variety of operations, each taking different amounts of time and resources, the ideal way to measure performance is to define a user model that helps you understand the effects of an *average* user on your system. Some authors recommend a stochastic model of system usage, but this is only appropriate when requests are truly random. Most systems do not have random distribution of requests, so a random model can give misleading data. A better source for good user-model data is the log files associated with the operation of your system in a production environment.

In addition to the complexities of testing the system, you should also learn to be conservative in your performance estimates. Real-world conditions can vary quite a bit from lab conditions, causing potentially misleading results.

What a Marketect Really Wants with Respect to Performance

It is tempting to think that what a marketect really wants is the fastest possible system. This is most obviously true: *Of course,* everyone wants that. A good engineer hates waste, and poor performance is wasteful. Also, poor performance is harmful to customers, as it forces them to purchase unnecessary and unwanted equipment and/or to limit growth. Still, the fastest possible system is not what a marketect *really* wants.

What a marketect really wants is a way to confidently, reliably, and above all accurately answer performance-related questions. *That* is more important than simply building the fastest possible system because this is what is needed to create a winning solution.

To illustrate what I mean, here are sample questions that I've received from customers regarding various performance attributes. Each of these questions was asked relative to a specific, customer-defined system configuration (hardware, storage, network, and so forth).

- How many simultaneous users/connections/sessions will the system support? What is the load on various components?
- How many transactions can be processed with my current hardware [where the hardware is precisely detailed]?

The biggest reason that marketects need good answers to such questions is that most of the time customers don't have raw performance queries. Instead, they come with some basic understanding of their needs and their environment and ask for help in creating the required infrastructure support. The marketect needs some way to respond. To get a sense for what I mean, consider the following questions, abstracted from real customer requests.

- We anticipate 200 active and up to 500 casual users. What hardware configuration do you recommend to support these users?
- We estimate that our system will need to support 800 downloads per hour during the new product release. How should we structure our Web infrastructure to support these downloads?
- We estimate that our system will initially handle 2,500,000 requests annually, with a projected 25 percent growth rate. Make certain your hardware estimates account for a three-year period and that your design provides for at least 98.5 percent (or 99% or 99.9%) overall system availability.
- If the database size were to grow faster than anticipated, what impact would there be on the system? Where would possible bottlenecks occur, and how would you scale the proposed system to handle them?

Questions such as these form the foundation for a long and complex sales process. Answering them well usually requires additional information from the customer, but ultimately, the marketect must have the necessary data to provide accurate answers.

One of the most effective ways to communicate this information is through case studies or whitepapers, with an appendix outlining additional performance scenarios. Another method, suitable for complex performance scenarios, is a program that estimates performance under various conditions.

Any performance data published by the marketect must be recalculated for each new release or when advances in hardware motivate changes in recommended system configurations. This last point is especially important. As consumers, we have been collectively conditioned by the hardware industry to expect that performance will continually improve. It doesn't matter if we're an end user installing old software on a new computer, or a Fortune 2000 enterprise installing the latest release of their CRM system on a new multiprocessor server. Whenever we invest in new hardware we expect that performance will improve.

Of course, we also expect that new releases of existing software will exhibit better performance on existing hardware, even if new features are added. This can be challenging, but reducing performance can seriously lower customer satisfaction. Performance always matters.

Responding to the User

One of the timeless pieces of advice from the usability literature is that, unless the system can respond truly instantaneously, you're going to need some feedback mechanism. In general, there is a strong correlation between good user feedback and problem/application/system complexity. What has worked well for me is to first broadly characterize the feedback you can provide. Table 10-2 lists the two most important categories.

Percent-done progress are your best choice when you need to provide continuous feedback to the user. They reassure the user that the system is processing their request and ideally, they allow him to cancel a task if it takes too long. The very best progress indicators also provide a reasonably accurate estimate of the total amount of time needed to complete the task. Be careful of your estimates—tarchitects are notoriously bad at estimating how long something will take, and if you estimate wrong you're going to choose the wrong kind of feedback.

TABLE 10-2   Feedback Mechanisms

Feedback	Examples
Immediate: task is expected to take less than 1–2 seconds	Visual changes to common objects, such as briefly changing the cursor to a "mail has arrived" icon when your mail client has downloaded a new e-mail message in the background
	Auditory responses, such as a beep (use sparingly and put under user control) Information messages or other changes displayed in status bars
Continuous: task is expected to take more than 2 seconds	General animation in an animation "loop;" appropriate when you don't know how long a task will take, such as the spinning globe that appears in Microsoft Internet Explorer when it is loading a Web page
	Percent-done progress indicators that estimate time or effort to complete a task. These can be shown in a status bar (if the task cannot be canceled) or in a separate dialog (if the task can be canceled)

> ## Feedback Eliminates Unnecessary Work
>
> One client/server system I worked on didn't provide users with enough feedback about their requests. As a result, users would submit the same request over and over, at times overloading the server. The problem went away once we implemented appropriate feedback mechanisms, illustrating the main point of this discussion: Response time and feedback are *qualitative, emotional* perceptions of system performance. You are far better off creating the right emotional perception of acceptable response before making a large investment to provide cold facts and figures about system throughput.

Performance and Tarchitectural Impact

The authors of *Software Architecture in Practice* [Bass 98] note that the performance factors just described are affected by both architectural and nonarchitectural choices. Architectural choices include the allocation of functions among various components, the manner in which these components interoperate and are operationally deployed, the management of state, and the management of persistent data. Different architectural choices affect different factors, and the needs of the overall system must be considered as choices are made. For example, converting a *stateful* architecture to a *stateless* one may increase latency but dramatically improve scalability.

Nonarchitectural choices include the algorithms for key operations within a single component and any number of technology idioms related to the specific implementation. Examples are implementing a more efficient sort algorithm or slightly restructuring a database to improve query performance

Managing performance factors is a complex topic that is beyond the scope of this book. That said, there are some basic tools and tricks that every tarchitect should have when considering them.

Throw Hardware at the Problem

In many of the systems I worked on, the easiest way to solve a performance issue was to throw some hardware at it—sometimes a bit more memory, sometimes an extra CPU rather than a faster one. The specific ways that you can use hardware are nearly endless, so architect your system to take advantage of the ones that matter most to your customers.

Of course, there is a fine balance. Too many engineers believe that throwing hardware at the problem justifies sloppy development practices. I vividly remember a conversation with an engineer whom I ultimately fired because of his poor coding. He worked on a system made up of CGIs written in C++. His coding style produced massive memory leaks, which he claimed were acceptable because all we had to do was purchase additional memory to "cover up" his mistakes. There is *no* justification for such sloppy development, no matter how much hardware you have at your disposal!

Finally, hardware will only work if you understand the scalability of your tarchitecture.

Use Large-Grained Transactions

Performance is typically enhanced in distributed systems when the transactions between components are fairly large.

Understand the Effects of Threading on Performance

Multi-CPU systems are pretty much the standard for servers. UNIX-based operating systems, such as Solaris, have proven that they can scale to dozens of processors. You should understand how multiple CPUs affect the performance of your architecture. It may not be what you think. In one application we relied on a rather old search engine, thinking that adding processors would help performance. It didn't, because the search engine wasn't multithreaded.

Use a Profiler

Performance can only be reliably increased if you know what is too slow. One technique is to use a profiler. Be forewarned, however, that a profiler can only identify and improve situations involving nonarchitectural bottlenecks. When it reveals an architectural problem, it often means that you either live with it—or rewrite.

Another technique is to run your program on a small number of data elements and then extrapolate the results to a larger number. This can tell you fairly quickly if you're headed in the wrong direction.

Handle Normal Operations and Failure Conditions Separately

This is a variant of advice I first read in Butler Lampson's excellent paper *Hints for Computer System Design* [Lampson 1984]. In general, normal operations should be fast. Failure conditions, which presumably happen much less frequently, should be handled appropriately. There is usually very little motivation for quick recovery.

Cache Results

In its simplest form, a cache saves some previously computed result so that it can be reused. Caches can have an enormous impact on performance in an extraordinary number of circumstances, from operating systems to companies that improve performance factors on the Internet, such as latency, by caching Web pages. If you use a cache, make sure you understand when and how a cached result should be recomputed. Failure to do so inevitably means that your results will be incorrect. The ramifications of this vary considerably by application, but in any case you should know what can go wrong if you are using poor results. Lampson refers to wrong cached results as a hint. Hints, like caches, are surprisingly useful in improving performance.

Make sure your architecture has a programmatic ability to turn caching on and off on-the fly so that you can test its impact. Cache problems are among the most insidious to find and fix.

Perform Work in the Background

In one system I worked on, one of the most frequent customers requests was to issue print commands as a background task. They were right. We should have designed this in right from the start. There are many processes that can be handled as background tasks. Find them, for doing so will improve usability.

Design Self-Service Operations

One of most striking examples of improving efficiency in noncomputer systems is self-service. From ATMs to pay at the pump gas, we consumers have many opportunities to serve our own needs. Although not necessarily their intent, self-service operations can improve any number of performance parameters. I've found that this concept also helps in tarchitectural design. For example, by letting client components choose how they process results, I've found ways to dramatically simplify client/server systems. Consider an application that enables the user to download prepackaged data into a spreadsheet and then utilize any number of built-in graphing tools to manipulate the results. Of course, you may have legitimate concerns regarding the distribution of data, but the performance benefits of self-service designs cannot be ignored.

Learn the Idioms of Your Implementation Platform

Your implementation platform—language, operating system, database, and so forth—all have a wide variety of idioms for using them efficiently. Generally techniques such as passing by reference in C++ or preventing the creation of unnecessary objects in Java, can have a surprisingly large impact on performance. I am *not* advocating that you simply design for performance. Instead, I'm merely saying that one of the ways to improve overall performance is to make certain you're using your implementation technologies sensibly. The only way to do this is to thoroughly understand your platform.

Reduce Work

Perhaps this advice is a bit trite, but it is surprising how often an application or system performs unnecessary work. In languages such as Java, C++, and Smalltalk, unnecessary work often takes the form of creating too many objects. In persistent storage, it often means having the application perform one or more operations sequentially when restructuring the data or the operations would enable the database to do the work or would enable the application to produce the same result through batching. A related technique is to use stored procedures or database triggers. The non-database world provides such examples as precomputed values or lazy initialization.

❑ ❑ ❑ ❑ ❑ ❑ ❑ ❑ ❑

Chapter Summary

■ Usability is about systems that allow users to accomplish necessary tasks easily, efficiently, and with a minimum of errors. Usability means that users can achieve their goals with little, if any, frustration.

■ Usability is a core feature of your product brand. Like your brand, it touches every aspect of the product.

■ Winning solutions are usable; usability contributes to long-term profit.

■ A *mental model* is the set of thoughts and structures that we use to explain, simulate, predict, or control objects in the world.

■ A *conceptual model* is some representation of a mental model, in words or pictures, using informal or formal techniques.

■ *Metaphors* are models that help us understand one thing in terms of another.

■ Maintainability is enhanced by separating the user interface from the rest of the tarchitecture, even though there is no absolutely certain way to separate the influence of the user interface from the rest of the tarchitecture.

■ Performance matters. This isn't a justification for pursuing design decisions purely in the context of performance, but rather an acknowledgment that performance is always important.

■ Marketects want a way to confidently, reliably, and, above all, accurately answer performance questions. This is especially important in enterprise software.

■ There are a variety of techniques you can use to improve performance, including caching, working in the background, offloading work to other processors, or avoiding work entirely.

Check This

❑ We have tested the usability of key tasks within our system.

❑ We have captured a conceptual model (perhaps using UML), which we have used, along with our understanding of the user's mental model, to create a system metaphor.

❑ The system metaphor is readily apparent in the design and implementation of the system.

❑ We have agreed on the terms that define performance. We have provided a way for marketing and sales to estimate configurations.

❑ We know when and how to "throw hardware at the problem" and what will happen when we do!

Try This

1. Do you have a user model? Are both your team and the marketing and development teams familiar with it? Is it based on real users, or what people think are real users?

2. Pick a reference configuration for your current system. What are the various values for the performance factors described above?

3. What was the last article or book you read about usability?

4. Where could improved usability help you improve your product or service the most? What is the potential economic impact of this improvement?

5. What kinds of feedback does your system provide? How do you know that this feedback is helpful?

6. Ask your marketect for a copy of a recent RFP and her response to it.

Chapter 11
Installation

Most software must be installed in order to run. Unfortunately, many development organizations defer installation and installation issues as long as they can. When they do get around to it, the results are often perplexing and error prone. The economic implications of poorly designed installation is very real, ranging from tens of dollars for each support call to thousands of dollars for professional services fees that could be avoided if the installation process was easier. Indeed, one of my reviewers pointed out that you can *lose* a sale based on an onerous evaluation installation.

In this chapter I will consider some of the unique challenges associated with designing and implementing a good installation process and the business motivations for doing so. In the next, I will cover upgrades.

The Out of Box Experience

Usability experts have coined the term "out of box experience" (OOBE) to describe the experience a person has using a computer or other device for the very first time. Some companies excel in creating superior OOBEs, mostly because they *care* about being excellent in this area. Apple computer has a well-deserved reputation for creating superior OOBEs, starting with the original Macintosh: Simply take it out, plug it in, turn it on, and you're ready to go. This tradition continues with the popular iMac series.

In software, the OOBE begins when the person who is going to install the software first acquires it. This could be through purchase of a CD-ROM or DVD at a local store. Alternatively, and increasingly, it could be when the user downloads the software directly onto her machine, either through a technical process, such as secure ftp, or through a more user-friendly distribution process, such as any number of software programs that manage downloading of large files for a user.

The Cost of Poor Installation

Our enterprise-class software worked great when the server was *finally* installed. I emphasize finally, because our initial server installation process was so complex and error prone that it required sending at least one, and usually two, members of our professional services team to the customer's site to install the system and verify its initial operation.

We didn't think this was a problem because we charged our customers for installation support. Once we created this standard charge, we thought no more about it. Fortunately, our director of customer support challenged our assumptions and analyzed both their real and their opportunity costs.

The real-cost calculation showed that we didn't make any money by charging for onsite professional services. Most of time we just broke even; the rest of the time we lost money. Even if we didn't lose any money, however, we certainly lost an opportunity to improve customer satisfaction. The opportunity cost, which measures the alternative uses of a given resource, presented a more sobering analysis. Simply put, was it better to have a member of our extremely limited and valuable professional services team doing "routine" installations or some other activity, such as a custom integration? In this case, common sense was supported by reasonable analysis.

The opportunity costs of our poor installation process were substantial, so we took it upon ourselves to improve it to the point where a customer could install the system with no more than one phone call to our technical support team. This turned out to be a bit harder than we expected. At first, we thought we knew all of the problems and how to fix them. We didn't. We eventually used Excel to build a dependency matrix that identified each step of the install and their inter-dependencies. It enabled us to redesign the installation process, removing unnecessary work and identifying good candidates for further automation. The team also did some real out-of-the-box thinking on automation, and used Perl to execute the install. One trick was that the Perl executables were included in our distribution so that Perl could be run from the CD without installing Perl on the target system. This worked surprisingly well (for our server; our client was installed using InstallShield). We eventually achieved our goal, improving customer satisfaction and our profitability at the same time. Perhaps, if I'm lucky, someone from Oracle will read this chapter!

The OOBE continues as the customer attempts to install the software. Common packaged software, such as video games or basic productivity tools, is often installed automatically when the user inserts a CD-ROM and an autorun facility starts up. For high-end professional software, installation can be substantially more complex, possibly requiring one or more programs to be executed to verify that the software can be installed properly (more on this later).

It is helpful if the marketect establishes some clear goals for the tarchitect regarding installation. One useful goal might be for an "average user" to be able to perform installation without having to make any phone calls to technical support. Of course, the definition of an "average user" varies substantially based on the kind of software you're building. It could be a schoolteacher with basic computer skills or an MCSE-certified system administrator with extensive knowledge of operating systems. For companies that employ use cases, I recommend at least one that captures software installation.

Ouch! That Might Hurt

We humans are so pain averse that we often attribute pain sensations to only potentially painful events. This, in turn, causes us to fear the event itself. Even if the event doesn't happen, we may still claim to have experienced some mental anguish. Pain, indeed! Understanding this is helpful in understanding how customers may approach the installation experience.

Customer Fears

Here are some fears that customers have expressed to me about software installations.

Too Hard

Many users perceive the installation process as too hard. They are justified in this when the installation program advises them to do things that sound dangerous ("Shut down all applications before continuing or you will irreparably damage your computer") or ask them to do things they don't understand ("Do you want to update the system registry?"). In older days, installation was often physically hard, especially on personal computers. I remember shuffling as many as 30 high-density floppy diskettes to install a large program! Fortunately, the difficulties have largely disappeared as the software industry has moved to CD-ROMs, DVDs, and the Internet to distribute software.

Too Complex

The simplest installation is just copying the right file to the right location on your computer. However, in today's modern operating systems, something as simple as this just doesn't work anymore. Proper installation usually requires a sequence of complex steps, and the entire process can fail if any individual step is not completed perfectly. Mitigate this by providing both typical or standard options and more advanced or custom options.

Too Easy to Break Something

A major installation concern is for the state of the system if something goes wrong during installation. Too many software applications leave the system in an unknown or unstable state if the install process fails to complete (for whatever reason). This is an unnecessary result of a sloppy or careless installation program. Because it is unnecessary, it is unacceptable.

Unknown Amount of Time

Users often express frustration because they don't know how long a "typical" installation will take. As a result, they can't plan various activities around it. For example, if I know that installing some software will take more than 20 minutes, I will probably wait until lunch before I begin unless I need the software right away.

Too Much Data, Too Many Forms

There are few things as frustrating as an installation process that requires you to enter the same data multiple times, or one that requires you to fill out endless forms, and then tells you that you forgot to enter some important code, such as a product serial number. Get all the answers you need up front. Your users and technical support organization will thank you.

Installation and Architecture

The various definitions of "software architecture" provided in Chapter 1 don't correlate strongly with the concept of installation or installation process. I don't have a problem with this, because the primary reasons "architecture" is of concern deal with such things as efficiently organizing the development team or choosing the best tarchitectural style for a given problem or problem domain.

Forces and Choices

That said, there are a variety of ways that marketectural or tarchitectural forces and choices influence the installation process, as the next sections describe.

Managing Subcomponents

In a component-based system, all required components must be present, in the right version and configured the right way, in order for your software to work. Quite often this means making tough choices about whether or not you should install a component or require that the user install it. I've done both.

In-Licensing Requirements

Some technology license agreements (see Chapter 5) have terms governing the installation of the technology, such as contractually requiring you to use their installer. Of course, the license agreement could state exactly the opposite and require you to write your own installer subject to its terms.

License Agreements

Your legal department will want to associate some or all of the license agreement with your installation program. This is commonly referred to as an End User License

> ## We Pick up after You're Done
>
> The specific technologies chosen by the tarchitect can affect the installation process in a number of ways. For example, it is common in well-designed tarchitectures to partition persistent storage in a separate subsystem, both logically and physically. If a relational database is used for the actual storage, quite often the only configuration data needed is the database connection string, a user ID, and a password—provided the database has been properly installed on the target system, the appropriate permissions have been set, and the database is available for your application's use. If the database hasn't been installed, you're going to have to do it.
>
> In one application in which we supported both SQLServer and Oracle, we created a two-step installation process. The first step required customers to install and configure a variety of software, including the database, before they could install our software. To help them, we provided detailed instructions.
>
> The second step was installing and configuring our software. To make this easier we had several steps, including creating a preinstallation program that ensured that each required technology was properly installed and configured.

Agreement (EULA). Make certain you're including a EULA as part of the installation process in the manner your legal department requires. For example, you may be required to have a "scroll to the bottom and click" screen that presents the license agreement to the user and halts installation until the user indicates acceptance (usually by clicking on a button).

Business Model

Some licensing models, such as per-user volume licensing (see Chapter 4) track installation events to count the number of licenses consumed. Others track access or use of a component that may affect the installation process. For example, many large applications offer small features that are installed only when the user attempts to use them (on-demand installation). More generally, your business model can affect how you create your installer, and your installation process can make supporting your business model easier.

Partitioning Installation Responsibilities

A general tarchitectural concern is the partitioning of responsibilities among various system components. As component capabilities change, the responsibilities we assign to a component may also change, which ultimately can affect the partitioning of components in the delivered system.

The increasing sophistication of installation programs, such as InstallShield's Developer, provides a great case study. In the early days of Windows, writing a really great installation program required the tarchitect to create a variety of components to check for the right versions of key files, necessary disk space, and so forth. Such tasks, and many more, are now performed by installation programs. Learning to let these programs do as much work as possible is a practical strategy for handling many complex installation tasks.

Installation Environment

The environment you're installing into, as well as the environment you're going to support, can have a substantial impact on your installation architecture. Consider an e-mail management tool for the growing market of knowledge workers who work from home. If the tool is really useful, it is inevitable that corporate users will want to adopt it.

While both home and office users may require the same core features, the context associated with each is very different. This difference will be expressed in a variety of ways, including the installation process.

The home user may be content to install the software via a CD-ROM or a DVD, or through an Internet download. The corporate user, on the other hand, is working in a very different environment. His machine is likely to be under the control of the corporate IT department, and the system administrator will probably want to be in charge of installation—among other things, by installing the software from a centrally controlled server on the internal network; by controlling one or more installation parameters such as where files are stored; and by controlling the specific features installed. When designing your installation process, make certain that you account for the environment of the target market.

Installation Roles

Many enterprise customers are comprised of people having different roles. System administrators have different responsibilities than database administrators, and both are distinguished from security and network engineers. To make things easier for you and your customers, organize complex installations according to these different roles. For example, database setup and data load scripts (environmental, schema DDL or DML, or data) should be separately organized, allowing database administrators full visibility and necessary control over your installation. This actually saves you time, because chances are each administrator will want this control before installation proceeds anyway.

Sensitize Developers

Have each developer run through the install process at least once so that they're sensitized to how their work products affect installation. Do this when they're first hired, so that they enter the team with an appreciation of installation issues.

How to Install

A general algorithm for installing software goes something like this:

1. Installation data collection and precondition verification
2. Installation
3. Postinstallation confirmation

Let's review each step in detail.

Installation Data Collection and Precondition Verification

In this step you collect all data needed in the installation. I really mean *all*. There's nothing worse than starting a one-hour installation process, walking away for lunch, and then returning to some subcomponent holding up the entire install by asking a minor question, with 50 minutes still to go.

To help make certain you're getting all the data, ask your technical publications department to create a simple form that captures all of the necessary information in writing. An even better approach is to capture all of this information in a file for future reference by your customer and your technical support group. Augmenting these forms with case studies of installations on common configurations is also helpful. Ask for all vital configuration information and important customization data, including where the product should be installed, database connection strings, proxy servers, and so forth. Storing these data in a file enables you to easily support corporate installation environments, because you can use this file as input to mass installations.

Once you've collected the required data, verify as much of it as possible before you begin the actual installation. Don't start the install until you know that everything works. Your verification activities should include any or all of the following.

Free Space

Although storage systems continue to make astonishing leaps in capacity, ensuring adequate free space is still very important. It doesn't matter if you're installing into a PDA, a cell phone, a laptop computer, or a server farm. Make certain you have enough free space for the target application, its associated data and working storage, and enough "scratch" space for installation.

Connections

If your software requires any connections to other entities, check them *before* you begin the actual installation. I've gone so far as to create installation precondition verification programs that simulate database or external internet server access to ensure that the provided connection information is accurate. I've put the installation process on hold until a valid connection was established.

Configurations of Required Entities

If you're relying on a specific database to be installed, you're probably also relying on it to be precisely configured for your application. One of my teams spent quite a bit of time debugging a nasty error in which our software wouldn't run on SQLServer. The root cause of the error was an improper SQLServer installation—the default collating sequence was the exact opposite of what our software required! Had we checked this setting before installation, we would have saved a lengthy debugging session.

Access Rights

Operating systems with sophisticated rights administration capabilities often restrict the modifications associated with installing software to users with appropriate administrative privileges. This is entirely appropriate when software is being installed in an enterprise. Whether it is a server or a desktop, enterprises have a legitimate right to know that the person with the proper training and authorizations is making changes. Unfortunately, what works well for organizations doesn't work nearly as well for end users, who can become confused when installation programs ask for certain kinds of permissions or fail entirely because of inappropriate access rights. While there is no easy or universal solution for the challenges associated with managing access rights, an awareness of the issue can help you choose approaches that minimize the requirements for privileged access.

Installation

Now you can begin the actual installation, which might be as simple as copying a few files to the proper locations or as complex as reconfiguring several system parts. Here are some things to consider during the installation process.

Provide Indication of Progress

The user needs to know that the installation is proceeding. In common end-user applications, this is usually achieved through a progress meter. In complex enterprise applications, this is often achieved via a command-line user interface. In either case, provide some form of feedback.

Provide a Visual Map

Very complex applications organize the installation into steps to give users a form or a map on which they can check off the completion of major activities.

Track Progress in a Log File

Log files (see Chapter 14) are useful for recording the operations performed and the actions taken during installation. They make recovery from installation failures as well as subsequent removal of the installed software substantially easier. At the very least, your customer/technical support personnel will know what happened. Don't forget to capture user responses to questions raised by the installation.

Make Installation Interruptible

With many enterprise application installation processes it is assumed that the installer, usually an IT system administrator, is going to be devoting her full and undivided attention to the installation process. This is, at best, wishful thinking, as IT system administrators are extraordinarily busy people. Instead, I recommend that you create your installation process with the expectation that it will be interrupted *at least* once.

This perspective is invaluable in motivating the team to choose interruptible installation options. The best way to do this is to make the installation *hands free*. That is, after you've gathered and verified the information you need to install the software, everything runs without intervention once it has been initiated. The next best approach is to make the installation process *self-aware*, so that it can monitor its own progress and restart itself at the appropriate place as needed. You can also provide an installation checklist that tracks each step or explicitly breaks up the installation process into a series of smaller, easily performed and verified, steps.

Follow Platform Guidelines

Most platforms have specific guidelines on designing your installation process/program. Learn them and follow them.

Avoid Forced Reboots

If you must force the user to reboot, give them a choice as to when.

Avoid Unnecessary Questions!

If you can resolve a question or a parameter setting at runtime in a reasonable way, do so! Often the person responsible for the installation is doing it for the first time and so they are probably not familiar with your program. Asking unnecessary or even esoteric questions ("Would you like your database indexed bilaterally?") is therefore, useless at best, and harmful at worst, to your system operation. It is far better to pick

There Are No Cross-Platform Guidelines

One exception to the admonition to follow platform-specific guidelines is software that must run under various platforms. In this case, it may be substantially easier for the development team to write a cross-platform installer. I've done this on server-side software using Perl. For client-side software, I still recommend following platform guidelines even if it takes more time and energy. The effort is worth it.

sensible defaults that can be changed later, after the user has gained appropriate system experience.

If you must ask the user a question, make certain they have sufficient reference material to understand it, the effect a particular answer might have, and whether or not the answer is inconsistent with answers to other questions. Since many people simply choose the default answer, make certain your defaults really are the most reasonable values.

Postinstallation Confirmation

Installation isn't complete until you've confirmed that it was done correctly. This may be as simple as verifying that the right files were copied to the right locations or as sophisticated as executing the installed software and invoking any number of manual and/or automated tests. Unlike installation precondition verification, which focuses on the context in which the software is installed, postinstallation verification should focus on actual system execution. Is it giving the right results? If not, why not? Make certain you log the results from your postinstallation confirmation, so you can use them to resolve any problems.

Once the installation has been verified, *clean up!* Many installation programs create or use temporary storage. Some do a poor job of cleaning up after themselves. Set a good example and clean up any files or modifications.

Now that things are working and you've cleaned up, you can do other things to enhance your product's usability. Consider the following.

- *Read-me or notes files:* Most people probably won't read them, but write them anyway. You'll gain critical insights into your product by doing so.
- *User registration*: Many user registration processes are initiated after the software has been installed. You may, for example, check for an active Internet connection and automatically launch a Web page that allows the user to register your product. From a marketing perspective, you should provide some reasonable incentive for registering other than spam!

Finishing Touches

Here are some techniques I have found useful in improving software installations.

They Don't Read the Manual

That's right: The people who install your software often *don't* read the manual. This is not an argument against installation manuals. They are vitally important, for no other reason than that they provide development and QA teams with a concrete, verifiable description of system behavior. Of course, I've found that great technical writers can substantially improve manuals and thus the odds that they'll be read.

More generally, users don't always do the things we recommend. While this may be unfortunate, it is also part of the reality you must deal with. There are other things you can do to make installation easy. One is to provide some kind visual roadmap of the installation process that can be combined with the checklist described earlier. This gives the installer the context for what is happening and provides them with an overall sense of what is happening at each step of the process. A well-done roadmap can also provide an estimate of how much time each step will take, which can help the installer manage his tasks.

Test the Install and Uninstall

Both installation and the uninstall must be thoroughly tested. Yes, I know this is common sense, but I've found that many QA teams don't adequately test one or both. This is a very poor choice given the adverse economic effects. Keep in mind the following when testing these options.

Test the Installer in the First Iteration

Agile development processes (XP, crystal, and SCRUM), and iterative-incremental development processes, share the idea that a system is developed in "chunks." A best practice is to start the installation very early in the product development cycle, usually by the third or fourth iteration.

The benefits are substantial. Done properly, it can be included as a step in your automated build process. With each build, the "actual" installation program can be run and configured to install the product correctly. This allows you to begin testing the installation, using it more easily in sales demos, customer evaluations, or even alpha/beta programs. Developing the installation process early can shake out dependencies among system components, ensure that the build is working correctly, and reduce the installer's overall complexity (instead of trying to do it all at once, you're doing it like the rest of the system—a little at a time).

Try Various Options

Your users will; your testers should. Hopefully, if the development team understands the complexities of testing the various options, they won't provide so many.

Automate

Complex installations alter the target machine in a variety of ways, from copying files to setting various parameters (such as registry parameters in Windows). The only way you can reliably check the effects of the installation is through automation. Write programs that can accurately assess the system before and after installation or uninstallation.

Follow Platform Guidelines

As stated earlier, modern operating systems offer guidelines for installing software. They also have guidelines for uninstalling it. Make certain you follow platform guidelines *and* properly remove what you add or change.

Make Installation Scriptable

If your product will be installed more than once by a single organization or person, provide automation scripts for your setup. Most installation generators allow you to feed a script to the setup apps they generate so that they run automatically.

Even better, provide a way for the installer to take the log from a successful install and generate the installation script from it for future ones. Anyone who has to do 200 identical installs will thank you.

Chapter Summary

■ Installation is about money. A poor installation usually costs you more than you're willing to admit or quantify. A good one saves you more than you're *able* to admit or quantify.

■ Many users find installation scary. They don't understand the questions and often can't make sense of what's going on.

■ Your installation deals with the structure of your architecture. All components and component dependencies must be handled properly.

■ Make certain your proposed installation process is supported by all of your license agreements.

■ A general algorithm for installing software is
  – Installation data collection and precondition verification
  – Installation
  – Postinstallation confirmation

■ Automate your installation process for internal testing, and make it automatable for enterprise environments.

■ Test, test, test.

Check This

❑ We have defined how each subcomponent will be handled by the installation process.

❑ Our installation process meets all technology in-license requirements.

❑ We have defined the level of skill required of the software installer. This level is reasonable for our product.

❑ We have a way of verifying the correctness of the installation.

❑ Our installation process adheres to target platform guidelines wherever possible.

❏ An average user can perform the installation without referring to the documentation.

❏ We have tested both installation and uninstallation.

Try This

1. Starting with a fresh computer, grab copies of your documentation and your software. Install your software. Perform a standard operation or use case. How do you feel?

2. Who installs your product? What is the definition of an "average installer"?

3. Where is your software installed?

4. How is it installed?

5. What is the expected/required skill level of the installer?

6. How long does it take to install your software? Can lengthy portions be easily interrupted?

7. Can you undo/remove what was installed?

8. How can you diagnose install problems?

Chapter 12

Upgrade

Chapter 11 covered installation; this chapter focuses on upgrades. Upgrades are often more problematic than installations because they can cause customers substantially more pain: Data can be lost, stable integrations with other systems can break, and old features may work differently (or even not at all). Handling upgrades well is key not just to creating winning solutions but to sustaining them through multiple releases. Given that more money is made on upgrades than on initial sales, and that one of the primary functions of marketing is finding and *keeping* customers, it is surprising that upgrades receive so little attention from marketects and tarchitects.

Like Installation, Only Worse

Chapter 11, I discussed some of the fears users may experience when installing your software. Upgrading a software system takes these fears and adds new ones to them.

Upgrade Fears

Here are some of the upgrade fears I've had to deal with during my career.

Pain of Rework
Many times an upgrade requires the user, the system administrator, or IT personnel to rework one or more aspects of the system and its underlying implementation. This can take many forms, but usually centers on how your system is integrated with other systems. For example, I have created systems that relied on data produced by various government agencies. In an astonishing case of poor customer management, these agencies occasionally change the format of the data being distributed to customers such as

myself, breaking the programs we had written to reprocess it. When this happened we had to scramble, rapidly rewriting a variety of software to maintain business continuity. Clearly the agency knew of these changes before they were instituted. The pain and cost to my company, and to other companies that relied on these data, could have been minimized or avoided had the agency simply considered our needs beforehand. At the very least, they could have warned us of the changes!

Ripple Upgrades

A *ripple upgrade* is one that forces you to change otherwise stable system components. The impact can range from changing hardware (e.g., more memory, more or faster processors, more disk space or different peripherals) to changing software (e.g., new operating system, different version of a key DLL). They are caused when you upgrade your software and new features mandate these changes or when a key vendor forces you to upgrade a key in-licensed technology (an inverse ripple).

Ripple upgrades are a painful part of technology reality. If you're going to in-license technology—and you will—then you're basing part of your future offerings on one or more in-license components. In many circumstances there is simply no alternative to a ripple upgrade.

What you *can* do is make the ripple upgrade as painless as possible. Clearly identify all dependencies associated with an upgrade. Use ripple upgrades to simplify your matrix of pain by discontinuing support for one or more configurations.

Data Migration

Data created in version n of the system often requires some kind of transformation to be fully usable in version n_{+1}. New features typically require new schemas. The upgrade process must be constructed in such a way that the user can move data relatively easily from the old schema to the new one. Remember that data migration may go in the other direction. Users of version n_{+1} may have to create data that can be used by users of version n. The tools for doing this vary considerably based on the application and your choice for a persistent storage. In shrink-wrapped software for personal computers, data is primarily stored in files. In this case you will have to provide facilities for converting files between formats. You should also clearly define the features lost when moving from version n_{+1} of the system to version n.

In enterprise class software, the bulk of the data is stored in relational databases, which usually means you will have to provide special tools for migrating data between versions. In an upgrade, this data is usually converted in one operation. In a conversion, this data may be converted in one operation or on demand as various features in the system are exercised.

My friend Ron Lunde points out that careful schema design can dramatically reduce the effort of migrating data between releases. The goal is to separate those aspects of the schema that rarely change, or that shouldn't change at all once created, from those that may change frequently. For example, in many transaction-based applications it is rare to upgrade the transaction data, so carefully separating transaction data from nontransaction data in the schema design can substantially reduce data migration efforts.

Data Retention

Old data is rarely deleted. It is retained according to some corporate policy. Reasons for such policies include the fulfillment of specific legal requirements, such as tax laws. Your customers may require you to produce valid archive copies of the data, and you may need to verify that you can access these copies for anywhere from three to seven years after the upgrade.

Certification

Upgrades, especially of enterprise-class software systems, must pass through stringent internally defined customer certifications before they can be put into production. This process usually takes at least one to two months and often considerably longer, which is why it is so rare to see enterprise-class software upgraded more than once or twice a year.

New APIs

New APIs are a special form of rework that must be carefully managed to customer needs. Changing them introduces a variety of pain, usually resulting in the upgrade being delayed. For everyone concerned, it is best to avoid this pain if at all possible. Refer to Chapter 8 for a discussion of API management.

Once Integrated, Never Upgraded

It was a tough decision, but we knew that the changes we made to our underlying server were going to invalidate earlier APIs. In the long run, these changes, and the new APIs, would provide our customers with much more flexibility and functionality. And, since the APIs were rarely used, most customers were not going to be affected. Unfortunately, our analysis indicated that the proposed changes would negatively affect a small number of our largest and most important customers, who had done a lot of custom integration work with the old APIs. The development team found a way to create a partial compatibility layer between the previous API version and the new one, easing, but not erasing, the burden of migrating their systems. Ultimately, for customers upgrading to this new version using these APIs substantial changes would be unavoidable.

Most of our customers realized the benefit of the new server and the new APIs, and decided to upgrade. Some, however, held out for a surprisingly long time. One in particular had spent almost $40K in consulting fees to integrate our system with another one, and they didn't want to spend this money again. I knew that they were serious when they spent $20K to fix a bug in the older, unsupported version. Eventually, they did adopt the new system, not by upgrading but by converting to managed services.

New Features

While customers may be excited to learn that your latest release has several new features, they may not be so excited to learn how to use them. Learning takes time and effort. It requires changing behaviors. Depending on the size of your customer and the magnitude of the upgrade, the cost of learning new features can motivate customers to delay or even cancel the upgrade.

Inaccessible System

Unless an application is truly mission critical, the upgrade process is likely to make it unavailable to users. This can range from a minor inconvenience, as when I'm upgrading a desktop application, to a major inconvenience, such as when I'm upgrading my operating system, to a completely unacceptable risk, such as when my business is upgrading its customer relationship management (CRM) or employee benefits system.

Reversion

Change management protocols for important or mission-critical applications must always define how to revert to the previous version of the system should *anything* go wrong in an upgrade. Your architecture can help make reverting relatively easy . . . or very dangerous.

Often, many complicated steps must be followed exactly or the overall process will fail. The order in which these steps are performed, and their management, represents a special kind of customer pain. Understanding the upgrade process by mapping out each step gives you a chance to simplify it.

My Pain Is Different

The problem with the list of upgrade fears presented is that it is relatively abstract, covering situations that more than likely don't correlate with your specific circumstances. I don't like this because alleviating upgrade pain depends on managing the specific kinds of pain associated with upgrading your system.

Therefore, if this chapter is to have any real value, you must create your own list of upgrade pain. Each of the companies I've worked for, and each of my consulting clients, has one. (Not surprisingly, each of them also had a unique architecture!) Until you've created this list, you can't critically examine what you're doing and how you can improve it to make certain you're meeting customer needs.

Making Upgrades Less Painful

As with installation, there are a variety of ways to make upgrading less painful. For starters, review the algorithm for installing software presented in Chapter 11. Upgrading software typically follows the same steps, and this algorithm will help ensure you're not missing anything important and that you're asking your customer to do things in an orderly manner.

Choices for Painless Upgrades

Upgrading raises some additional issues best handled by the entire development team working together. Consider the following.

Number and Timing

Customers can't absorb releases that occur too quickly, and they get frustrated and concerned if releases happen too slowly. You have to understand the events and rhythms of your market (see Appendix B) to know how frequently you can create and distribute upgrades.

Upgrade Readiness

All of the steps I recommended in Chapter 11, such as checking for the necessary disk space and verifying configuration parameters, still apply. In addition, and depending on the upgrade, you may want to examine how the customer is using the current version to determine the best upgrade approach. For example, suppose that your system is composed of several optional features that can be installed as part of a custom configuration. Before simply upgrading various components, you should check what has been installed to make certain you only change what must be changed. A good rule of thumb is that it is best to make the least amount of changes possible when performing either an installation or an upgrade.

Data Migration

It sounds simple: Take data from version n_{-1} and migrate it to version n. It might actually be simple, depending on the changes being made in the system. Unfortunately, in the real world of working systems and customer environments things are surprisingly complex.

Recall that data is typically stored in two basic formats: Semi-structured data in files, and structured data in a database management system. Data migration for these formats differs in a number of ways, including when the data has to be upgraded and how much work the customer must do during the migration process.

It's Easier to Say Yes than No

I've earned a reputation of fairly ruthlessly assessing application features. Simply put, if a feature isn't needed, *take it out.* Of course, like so much advice this is easy to say but hard to do. Removing a feature is usually traumatic because it raises all sorts of questions: Which customers are using this feature? How are they using it? How will they react if we take it away? Attempting to answer all of these questions can be costly and time consuming. Even asking the question can alert customers to a potential change, and there are times when it is best to deal with customers affected by such a decision in a very controlled, and subtle, manner.

Virtually the only way to remove a feature is during the upgrade process. Features often correlate in some way with the application's persistent data. By carefully assessing the persistent data of an existing installation, you can often determine if a feature is actually used. If the data indicate that it isn't being used, then you can often relatively quietly drop support for it.

In one application we allowed our customers to associate keywords with certain data. We thought this implementation was good enough, but it really wasn't. It was too hard to use and the results weren't all that useful. A more thorough analysis showed that making this feature better would be much more work than originally expected. So, since it wasn't as important as other features, I decided to remove it. The team modified the upgrade procedure and analyzed the database. No keywords meant no use of the feature and safe removal.

More generally, it is a good idea to write a program that assesses the current installation to determine the best way to upgrade it. A good assessment will let you know how the system is being used (based on persistent data) and may tell you about any modifications, integrations, or extensions, and it will help you identify any ripple upgrade requirements. Log files, configuration and customization files, and even corporate settings (such as LDAP servers) are sources of potentially useful information that can help you plan a sensible upgrade, including the removal of features.

Finally, if you use this technique to help you remove features, remember that removing a feature is more complex than examining persistent data and removing some software. Feature removal requires coordination among the entire development team: Printed and on-line technical documentation needs to be updated, services must be informed, and training programs may need to be added. In other words, removing a feature is at least as hard as adding one, often more so (which makes you wonder why features are added so easily in the first place!).

For data stored in a database, you have to work out the data migration process because chances are that all of the data must be migrated at once. This can be pretty simple if you're absolutely certain that the customer hasn't modified the schema in any way. If they have, you're going to have to find a way to handle the modifications. You can require your customer to do all of the work (e.g., export all customizations and associated data and then import them after the upgrade), but then, if your customer doesn't want to do this work, you may have to create the tools to do it automatically. I've had the best results with a middle-ground approach, in which developers write special tools that the professional services organization then uses in the field. It is imperative that the services organization understand these tools because there is a good chance they will have to modify them in the field to deal with unique problems that occur only in customer environments.

Data stored in a flat file can often be upgraded on demand, such as when an application opens a data file from a previous version but stores it in a new version. It is good practice to warn the user that you are doing this.

Upgrade Configuration and Customization Information

Like many users of Microsoft Office products, I customize these products according to my personal preferences. Unfortunately these settings are not preserved when I upgrade from one version of Office to another, which is very frustrating. Don't make this mistake with your users. Make certain that you upgrade configuration and customization information.

Previous Versions

A big problem with migrating data from a previous version to the current version is that probably not all of your customers are going to be running the same version of the old software. If you're releasing version 3.7, you may have to deal with customers who are upgrading from any prior release. Only a careful examination of your customer base will let you know how many previous versions you need to handle.

There are two basic strategies for dealing with older versions, and a sensible approach often combines them. The first is a single-step migration, in which you provide a direct path from any previous version to the current version. The second is a multistep migration, in which you pick a subset of the previous versions that can be upgraded to the current version. Customers whose version isn't within this subset must first migrate to one of the versions in the supported set. To make certain you're managing all of the prior versions, draw a directed graph that includes all versions—even versions that are not supported but may still be in use.

Coexist or Replace?

A special issue in upgrading existing software is whether or not the new version should completely replace one or more existing components or co-exist with them. Resolving this requires a detailed technical understanding of the dependencies between

> ## Which Version Do I Use?
>
> As mentioned in Chapter 6, allowing multiple versions of the same application or product on the same system increases testing complexity (the matrix of pain) and often increases support costs. For example, I was confused when I installed an AOL upgrade on my laptop and found that my desktop had two nearly identical shortcuts—one referenced the old version; one the new version. They looked identical, and even more frustrating, not all of the data I had entered into my old version was transferred so I had to do it by hand. I don't mean to single out AOL. All of the applications I use on a regular basis have a variety of upgrade-related problems, ranging from data migration to unknown or unstated ripple upgrade requirements. Given that more money is made in upgrades over the life of a successful application than in its initial sales, you would think that marketects and tarchitects would take the upgrade process more seriously.

system components as well as marketing's input on the user experience. While successful systems have used both approaches, I recommend replacing components if at all possible. If you don't, you'll confuse your users, who won't know when they should remove the old version (if it wasn't safe to remove it during the upgrade, when *will* it be safe to do so? And who will remind the user when they should do this?).

Market Maturity and Upgrades

In earlier chapters I observed that innovators and early adopters are more tolerant of the many problems in an immature product. They can deal with difficult installations; they can handle APIs that don't work very well; and they often accept poor performance in the expectation that it will improve in a future release. Given that innovators and early adopters are willing to tolerate so many shortcomings, you may be tempted to think that they will also tolerate a poor or faulty upgrade process.

My experience tells me that this is not the case. One area in which innovators are just as demanding as the late majority is in software upgrades, *especially as it relates to data migration.* Simply put, you cannot screw up their data. Innovators may put up with a lot, but trashing their data is beyond even their considerable level of patience.

Of course, this is not a justification for a difficult-to-use or otherwise faulty upgrade process. Innovators and early adopters may be reluctant to upgrade precisely because they have invested considerable time and energy into making the application work within their environment. A faulty upgrade process also creates nasty problems in the future, regardless of market segment. If you've ever struggled through an upgrade, you know from personal experience that you're unwilling to upgrade to a new version of anything unless absolutely needed. I once used the same laptop for more than four years simply because I managed to create an extremely stable and reliable environment. Don't provide your customers with a reason to avoid upgrading their software by using their last upgrade against you.

□ □ □ □ □ □ □ □ □

Chapter Summary

- Upgrades can cause considerable customer pain in a variety of ways. Make certain yours doesn't.
- Ongoing technology evolution motivates ripple upgrades. Detail these requirements carefully.
- Don't ever screw up your customers' data during an upgrade.
- Understand just how frequently your customers can absorb an upgrade. They may want an upgrade, but they may not be able to absorb one as quickly as you can create one.
- It helps to have tools to assess upgrade readiness, upgrade impact, and whether or not you can easily remove any unnecessary or unused features.
- All market adopter segments require a good upgrade.

Check This

- ❑ We have identified all potential areas where an upgrade can cause pain and have tried to minimize them.
- ❑ We have tested all data migration paths.
- ❑ We have defined the manner in which *any* customer with a previous version of the system can upgrade to the current version.
- ❑ We have defined how long the system will be down because of an upgrade.
- ❑ We have provided detailed instructions on how to completely uninstall an upgrade and convert all data to the previous version.
- ❑ We have provided tests to confirm successful upgrades and to identify any areas in which the upgrade may have failed.

Try This

1. Find a computer that has the second-most-recent version of your software. Use it. Build at least a sample dataset. Now take the most recent version of your software and upgrade to the current system. How do you feel?

2. What kind of data transformations are required by your upgrade process? Is each transformation essential? Can the schema be redesigned to minimize or eliminate these transformations?

3. What was the last feature you removed from your solution? Why did you remove it?

Chapter 13
Configuration

Complex systems need to be configured to be useful. Unfortunately, *configurability* is not one of the more commonly discussed ilities, so systems end up much more difficult to configure than they need to be. For that reason, ease of configuration is a worthwhile goal for both the marketect and the tarchitect. In this chapter I will discuss configuration parameters and some of the things you can do to make your system as easy to configure as possible.

Configurability—An Element of Usability

The primary reason to care about configurability, which is a dimension of overall usability, is cost. Difficult-to-configure systems

- Are harder to use, increasing operating costs.
- Are harder to tune, resulting in lower actual and perceived performance, which can increase costs by forcing customers to do such things as purchase unnecessary hardware.
- Result in more calls to technical support, increasing technical support costs.
- Require more complex professional services, increasing direct costs to customers because professional services take longer than they should, and decreasing employee satisfaction because very few professional services people get excited about configuring a complex system.
- Increase overall customer frustration, putting you at a competitive disadvantage.

A related reason to make configuration easy is based on the architectural nature of the systems you're creating, which are increasingly built using modular approaches.

Modular systems increase configuration requirements—a fact that becomes increasingly true in architectures based on Web services. Without a strong commitment to easy configuration, you're going to see configuration costs increase over the life of your application. This is *not* a pleasant prospect.

You must architect ease of configuration. Doing so is in everyone's best interest. In terms of usability, configurability is having the right number of configuration parameters—not too many and not too few—and choosing parameters that affect the system in ways that are material to the user.

The System Context

Before worrying about the technical details of structuring configuration parameters, let's take a step back and consider what should be configurable. The basic information that needs to be captured in these parameters is the *system context*—that is, all aspects of the contextual information you need for a properly functioning system. By capturing these data and making them configurable, you provide your customers with the ability to set key parameters at deployment instead of during development. This process of late binding makes your system more flexible and far easier to deploy.

Contextual Information

Identifying contextual information is the job of the tarchitect, as informed by key members of the development team. Here are some specific areas to consider.

Location of Key Files and/or Directories

Many complex systems rely on predefined or well-known files and/or directories whose locations are set during system installation and captured in configuration files for the runtime environment.

Bootstrapping Data

Most technical systems require various kinds of bootstrapping information. Your computer requires a BIOS. Your application requires an entry point for the operating system to begin executing the program. Enterprise-class systems usually require bootstrapping data stored in files in precisely named files and carefully located directories. The most common choice is a subdirectory under the subdirectory containing the application, with one or more well named configuration files. Note that even these bootstrapping data can be lost, and a good defensive design technique is to ensure that the system can perform a reasonable minimum set of functions without it.

Portability Switches

A special context is one that deals with system portability. For example, a team that worked for me designed a system that could be configured for use with Oracle or

SQLServer. The choice was important because the system used slightly different SQL statements that had been tuned for the performance characteristics of each database.

Compatibility Controls

Development teams face challenges in determining how to support older versions. Instead of making this decision arbitrarily, turn it over to your customer and let them decide via any number of configuration parameters.

Performance Parameters

Performance parameters range from timeout values to in-memory storage requirements to the number of database connections the system should automatically maintain. Truly sophisticated applications can adjust these parameters based on self-monitoring system performance, but most of us can get away with allowing the user to configure with simpler parameters specified at system startup.

Too Much of a Good Thing

It started with a well-intentioned development team trying to peacefully resolve differences of opinion on everything from how much default memory should be allocated to the default layout of the user interface. By the time they were finished, I feared that I would need an expert system just to help a customer install and configure our software.

We had too many optional configuration parameters. In isolation, each parameter made good sense. In total, they presented to the system administrator a bewildering array of choices. We managed to arrive at a workable solution by creating sensible parameter groupings, with rock-solid in-line help and plenty of examples on how changes to the parameters would affect system performance. Still, I learned my lesson and am more cautious about putting something into a configuration parameter.

A good rule of thumb is that something should be a configuration parameter only if the system can't function without it being set, such as a proxy server. If something can vary in a sensible way, or if you simply want to give your users greater flexibility, make it a customization parameter and provide a reasonable default. The difference is subtle but important. Configuration parameters have to be set correctly for the system to operate, which usually means that they must be set by a person who knows what he's doing (e.g., a system administrator). Customization information, which should be an attribute of some object, may never be set at all.

By the way, in case you think I'm being overly dramatic about needing an expert system to manage configuration parameters, keep in mind that one of the most famous expert systems ever—XCON—was created specifically to configure DEC VAX computers!

Initialization versus Execution

There are basically two times when a system needs to be configured: before execution and during operation. As discussed in the previous section, much if not all of the configuration parameter information is processed during initialization. In addition to reading these data to obtain the required context information, the system must also handle gross errors and/or configuration inconsistencies. A proven approach is to ignore an inconsistency, choose a sensible default, and log the error. If you can't ignore the error, stop processing and inform the user.

One drawback of requiring that configuration data be processed during system initialization is that the user may have to shut down and restart for seemingly trivial changes. This may be acceptable for simple systems, but is likely to become intolerable for complex systems. For example, it is often best if log data (discussed in greater detail in Chapter 14), can be turned on and off while the system is running. Or consider configuration data in high-availability systems. Such systems need to be designed so that there is a way to notify the system of important changes to configuration data, or so the system can discover important changes during normal operation on its own. A key consideration is any data that may be useful for problem diagnosis—it's always best to gather the data needed while the system is running, when the error occurs.

A special case of complexity in configuration parameters deals with pass-through parameters, that is, parameters set in the context of your application but are actually passed through to in-licensed components. Suppose, for example, that your system relies on a third-party text searching engine. The structure of its configuration parameters will constrain the structure of yours, including whether or not you can set its parameters during system operation. Because of this, the tarchitect must consider which configuration data are best handled during initialization and which are best handled while the system is operating.

Setting the Value

Once you've determined what values need to be configured and when, you need to consider who can set them. Three entities are common: a human, such as a system administrator; another system, as when two systems negotiate a value or receive commands for inter-operation; or the system itself, when it is architected to auto-configure one or more values. A system can rely on any combination of the three to get the job done.

It is assumed that the entity setting the value has been authorized to make changes to configuration parameters, but this doesn't mean that every entity should have this authority. Make certain that each parameter, or each class of parameter, is reviewed so that the full ramifications of changing it are understood.

You may not want any individual user to be able to change any given parameter. If not, require configuration data to be stored on a system with administrative access protection, although this isn't a guarantee that the right system administrator will be changing the right value. If needed, you may want to consider creating an audit trail of these data by putting them into a database—a database will give you all the facilities you need to manage the audit. Later in the chapter I will recommend storing configuration data in easily accessible, human-readable files. Unfortunately, these are conflicting recommendations, and the development team will have to choose what is best for your situation (no one said being a tarchitect was easy).

Interesting challenges can emerge when one or more entities are granted authority to change the same parameters and you have to choose the circumstances under which one entity can override the other. This can be a sticky problem, and it is best to involve the marketect in its resolution as her input will consider your market. I created applications in which the number of active database connections is set either by the system administrator or by the system itself based on an assessment of its own performance. We allowed the system to adjust the value automatically in case the administrator set it to an absurdly low or high value.

Setting the Right Value

In discussions regarding configuration parameters, the tarchitect and marketect must together meet both the needs of the user affected by the parameter and the needs of the user (or system) setting it.

In general, most users are not aware of the full range of configuration parameters that exist for their application. They don't need to be. In writing this chapter I did a quick search on my computer for all files with the extension .ini (I'm writing this book on my trusty laptop running Windows 2000). I had expected to find two to three dozen, so imagine my surprise when I found more than two hundred! A cursory review revealed that most of them weren't really storing configuration parameters of the kind I'm talking about in this chapter but instead were using the Windows facilities as simple persistent storage.

However, some, were clearly configuration files as defined in this chapter, with various settings based on user needs. In considering those needs here, remember that increasing the number of configuration parameters increases the likelihood that they may be set to improper or useless values and generally detracts from usability because of increased complexity.

The previous sections provided the information you need to give to the entities setting the values. Simply put, they need to know what values to set, how to set them (including formatting and valid values), why to set them, and their effect on system operation. Give this information in the file, not in some external document or hidden on a Web site. Let the entity using the file understand what is happening.

The caps.ini file, distributed as part of the Microsoft Platform SDK provides almost all of the answers that a user needs to modify these values. Here is an extract under the section [CAPS FLAGS]. The file could be substantially improved by adding some information about the effect of setting each of these parameters on or off.

```
[CAP FLAGS]
# CAP accepts the following parameters:
#    *  profile        = (on/off)
#    *  dumpbinary     = (on/off)
#    *  capthread      = (on/off)
#    *  loadlibrary    = (on/off)
#    *  setjump        = (on/off)
#    *  undecoratename = (on/off)
#    *  excelaware     = (on/off)
#    *  regulardump    = (on/off)
#    *  chronocollect  = (on/off)
#    *  chronodump     = (on/off)
#    *  slowsymbols    = (on/off)
#
# Anything value other than on or off is encountered
# and the default values will kick in:
#                  profile        = on
#                  dumpbinary     = off
#                  capthread      = on
#                  setjump        = off
#                  loadlibrary    = off
#                  undecoratename = off
#                  excelaware     = off
#                  regulardump    = on
#                  chronocollect  = off
#                  chronodump     = off
#                  slowsymbols    = on
#
# Please notice there are no spaces between the keyword
# and the value (either 'off' or 'on')
#
```

While the instructions provided in this document are clear (at least to me), they do contain some minor grammatical mistakes. Because such mistakes will happen, involve your technical publications department in preparing configuration file documentation (including its internal documentation). They shouldn't write the initial description of these parameters—that's the job of individual developers as reviewed by the tarchitect. However, they should be involved in the final review process because they know how to structure and communicate important information.

Configuration Parameter Heuristics

The following heuristics are useful when designing configuration parameters.

- Make them easy to change, even when the rest of the system is down. This means storing them externally, in a simple, easily managed, nonbinary format.
- Store all of the data in one location. If you think you *must* have them in multiple locations, find a person you trust and convince them that storing the data in multiple locations is a good idea. If both of you continue to think this is a good

idea, go ahead and do it. If you are lucky, your trustworthy friend will convince you that this is a poor design choice and will help you choose a better one.

- Store the file in an obvious location with an obvious name. I recommend names like "System Configuration Data" and places like the root directory of the installed application.

- Platform-specific file formats, such as .ini, are okay, but why not use XML? It's simple, as verbose as you need, and easily managed.

- Be careful of things like registry entries. They aren't portable and can be difficult to change for nontechnical users. I don't see a lot of value from use of the registry.

- Make configuration data easy to capture and forward to technical support. It's amazing the number of problems a sharp technical support person can solve once they understand how the system has been configured.

- Make it hard to get the values wrong. If they are wrong, notify the user as soon as possible and either stop execution or continue with sensible defaults.

The most resilient designs are based on the idea that configuration parameters are persistent attributes of some entity or object. This enables other objects or subsystems to deal with the information within this object and not worry about how to manage INI or XML files. Because these attributes can often be affixed to different objects, the tarchitect should consider that any of the following may be useful.

- A system context object, for storing information about overall system context

- Per-computer, per-service-instance, per-user, or even per-selectable-user profile objects

- Objects that capture the semantics of the configuration data

Keep in mind that, while you don't have to get all of the configuration data you need right at the beginning of the system, retrofitting can be cumbersome, and may require architectural changes.

Chapter Summary

- Configuration is an essential aspect of usability. If your system is difficult to configure, your customer won't be able to use it to its fullest capacity.

- Configuration parameters should be designed to capture the system context, which is all of the contextual information needed for the system to function properly. Examples include the location of key files and directories, portability switches, and compatibility controls.

- There are two times when a system needs to be configured: before it begins execution and during its operation. A system that can process value changes while running is good for debugging.
- Customers need support in setting the proper value. Give it to them.

Check This

❑ We have defined all system configuration parameters. For each parameter, we have defined its security and auditability requirements and whether it is used only during initialization or can be changed while the system is running.

❑ We have documented how to set each value and have provided guidance for setting it correctly.

Try This

1. How do you choose when to add new configuration parameters? Who in the team is allowed to do this?

2. Where is the documentation for your configuration parameters stored? Can your users obtain everything they need from the configuration file?

3. How tolerant is your system when the wrong values are set? What happens? Have you tested this?

Chapter 14

Logs

You just hit your favorite Web site, but it's taking a bit longer than normal to download the start page. You're wondering if the system is *hung* or if it's just responding more slowly than usual because of increased load. Chances are the site's system administrator is wondering the same thing, and unless the system can log or otherwise display its operational status and related performance data, she may never know.

Better Late than Never

Sometimes the pressures of getting the release done on time can consume all of your energy. Instead of carefully thinking things through, your overwhelming motivation is just to finish the $@#%&@ software. Since you may not be able to pull yourself out of this line of thinking, it helps to have senior developers who can.

We were just completing our first release of a brand-new enterprise-class system. I wasn't thinking about log files at all. Fortunately for me, and our customers, Dave Smith, one of my senior developers, was, and he took it upon himself to add some of the foundation needed for them. Myron Ahn, another senior developer, extended the log file format and structure and made sure that many parts of the system were logging useful information. I can't claim that this first release was a model of logging tarchitecture beauty, but I do know that it served our initial needs very well and was a very useful foundation for logging data in future releases.

The importance of this lesson has served me well over time. I've added logging, or have substantially enhanced it, in any number of systems since then. Each time the results were worth the effort.

Well-designed logs can help you with a variety of tasks crucial to the marketectural goals of your application. This chapter explores logs, covering such topics as the purpose and audience of log data, the specific content of log files, and log format and management.

I Want to Know What's Happening

The fundamental motivation for logging data is that someone wants to know something about the system. Table 14-1 captures what people want to know according to category, purpose, and audience.

Developers often misuse log files by storing one category of data in a log designed for another—debugging information in the operational status log file, say, or behavioral data in the system configuration log file. These mistakes, whether intentional or

TABLE 14-1   Log File Motivations and Audiences

Category	Purpose	Audience
Debugging/Error Logs	Provide information on system operation as an aide in debugging.	During construction, developers are the primary audience. After release, technical support and professional services personnel can use this information to resolve problems in the field.
Error Recovery	Capture information that can be used to restore the working state of a system in case something crashes.	Almost exclusively the domain of the application. An example is a database management system transaction log.
Performance Tuning	Provide information on one or more aspects of performance, usually with the goal of improving it.	Professional services organizations, customer IT organization sites, and end users.
Capacity Planning	Provide information on actual resources consumed during system operation.	Customer IT organizations and end users.
Behavior Tracking and Auditing	Provide information on how various actors (end users, system components, other systems) interact with the component in question.	Marketing organizations (for user/feature profiling) and security organizations (for audit trails). In these cases the content of the log may be similar but how the log is used is different.
System Configuration Management	Provide information on the system context. These logs are often symmetric with configuration files.	As a subset of debugging information, it has the same audience.
Operational Status	Provide information on the current operational status of the system (e.g., how many transaction requests are in the queue, how many users are connected to it).	IT and professional services organizations.

No Categories Are Better than Two

Log data categories are not hard boundaries. Sometimes you're just not certain where the data should be stored because it could be used for more than one purpose or you're not certain who will be using the data or how. One option for handling this situation is to store log data in a single log file that has appropriate identifiers for each type of log event. Postprocessing tools can then read only one file to obtain the data they need.

In one application I worked on, the system administrator specified the locations of various files required at initialization and used during operation in a configuration file. As the system processed these files, it logged the results. These log data were used in several different ways.

- Developers used them while creating and debugging the system.
- Technical support used them to help customers recover from a system crash.
- Professional services used them for performance tuning and capacity planning.

We didn't spend a lot of time debating where to store these data. Instead, we just put them in a single file.

not, dilute the value of the data, invalidate or seriously complicate postprocessing analysis, and contribute to overall system complexity.

A more serious misuse of log files is when a developer uses them for storing non-logging data. The most flagrant abuse I ever experienced was when one developer used a log file to store persistent data! A good rule of thumb is that log files only be write only from the perspective of the system generating the log file. There are exceptions to this rule, such as when a system can process its own log data (I've worked on systems that can self-tune key performance parameters based on log file analysis), but they are fairly rare. Application processing of log files should be completely optional: If someone deletes a log file and your application crashes, you've got a design problem that needs to be fixed.

Not Just the Facts

A wide variety of information can be included in a log. Table 14-2 details some of it according to the categories described in the previous section. As you look at this table, keep in mind that Murphy's Law really applies here. Specifically, you may not know what you need in a log until you need it, so try to create log data with enough context to make sense of what is happening. In other words, if you are logging information about a complex transaction, don't just log when the transaction started and stopped: log each processing step so that you can understand transaction states. As an alternative, use an approach common in rule-based systems, in which the system should be able to "explain" its behavior.

Log data may be provided in real time, or nearly real time, to other applications. This will help you create such things as dynamically updated dashboards that show the status of the system in a rich graphical format.

TABLE 14-2 Techniques to Improve Log Utility

Category	Suggested Contents
Debugging/ Error Logs	• Contextual information. Consider the following entry (from an MS Windows Dr. Watson error logging program—(DrWtsn32)).

```
*----> System Information <----*
        Computer Name: LUKELAP
        User Name: Luke Hohmann
        Number of Processors: 1
        Processor Type: x86 Family 6 Model 6 Stepping 10
        Windows 2000 Version: 5.0
        Current Build: 2195
        Service Pack: None
        Current Type: Uniprocessor Free
        Registered Organization:
        Registered Owner: Luke Hohmann
```

	• Inputs and outputs to each function call or equivalent. Consider multiple debugging levels and whether or not you should record parameter values. Recording parameter values takes some planning because you can't simply dump complex data structures into a log file and expect it to be useful. Serializing these data into XML is a good choice, but you have to be careful about how much data you're adding to the log and how much of a performance hit you'll take in the process. This issue is so complex that you probably won't be able to establish a uniform policy but will instead have to approach each log entry on a case by case basis.
	• All main components—for example, in a heavy client client/server system, both the client and the server.
Performance Tuning	• Each command and how long it took to execute. If possible, track both elapsed and actual processing times.
Capacity Planning	• Complex systems use a variety of resources. Monitoring usage levels in log files allows you to tune performance. In one application I worked on, the system administrator could specify the initial number of database connections in a configuration file. During operation, the system would create additional connections as needed. By recording the number of connections used and any connections that were created in a log file, we provided system administrators with the data necessary to tune their performance. If they specified 50 initial connections but never used more than 30, they could lower the number and improve performance by freeing up valuable resources. If they specified 50 initial connections and consistently required 80, they could increeas the initial number of connections, again improving overall performance (because creating the connections at startup is faster than creating connections on the fly).

Category	Suggested Contents
Behavior Tracking and Auditing	• Reports of operations/features used, including optional features *not* used. For example, it is easy to add information to a log file when an optional feature structured as a DLL is invoked. Scanning the log to identify if these features are invoked at all is trivial. • Highly used features may be sources of new revenue by creative licensing programs, including feature-based licensing. Unused or little used features may be removed in a future release or may become the target of marketing and/or educational campaigns designed to increase use. Logs used for auditing purposes must be trustworthy.
System Configuration Input and Processing	• Data in configuration parameters. If any are processed by your system in an interesting and useful way, add the input and the resultant output or effect to a log file. Many inappropriate configuration parameter values can be overridden by the system. Any resets should be logged for further review and analysis.
Operational Status	• Operational status logs, being most closely associated with enterprise server applications. These applications have specific status requirements. Transaction-based systems may log transaction states (beginning, processing, ending), cumulative requests, outstanding requests, and so forth. Enterprise applications based on concurrent user business models may log logins and logouts, graceful or abrupt session termination, failed login attempts, or total number of users, etc. Operational status logs often correlate to the business model.

Logs Are Not Glorified Trace Statements!

Once the decision has been made to create any log files, developers usually start stuffing a variety of them with data that is generally useless to anyone but them. To maintain coherence and integrity, especially of logs used by customers and/or technical support organizations, and to meet the team's legitimate debugging needs, I recommend a separate log for developer-centric data. Once this is done the tarchitect can periodically review the contents of a sample log and work with developers to see that the right data ends up in the right log.

Log Format and Management

Log data can be structured in a variety of ways, including flat files, databases, and direct input from the system to a formal monitoring system, such as HP OpenView or the Windows event log.

Log Format

Here are some general observations on log format.

• *Internationalization:* Creating log data in the user's target language can substantially improve usability. It can also score points with customers who prefer to use their native language for all system operations.

- *Start with a time stamp:* The first entry in a log file should be a time stamp.
- *Always add a unique identifier, traceable to the actual source location:* Log data are most useful when you know you can return to the source code to interpret what is happening.
- *Provide a way to identify transactions:* Many log entries are associated with various kinds of transactions. Once an ID is assigned to a transaction, put it in the log. This is the best way to tie together a single transaction's logging data.

Flat Files

The flat format is probably the most popular for log files. It's faster and more malleable than a database and usually trivially ported. Indeed, when I did a casual search on my laptop for .INI files, (mentioned in Chapter 13) I also did one for .LOG files. Once again I was surprised by the results. I had expected to find, at most, a dozen or so files. Instead I found 132, created by programs ranging from MS Outlook to Adobe Acrobat and my REX6000 PDA.

Here are some principles of good flat file design.

- *Easy parsing:* The contents of the flat file should be easily parsed. A little thought here can save a lot of work later. A good rule of thumb is that it should be trivial to import log data into a relational database or analysis tools like MS Excel.
- *Easy reading:* Log files that are easily parsed are often—but not always—easy to read. Again, with a little bit of planning you can create log files that are parsed easily by both computers *and* humans.
- *Sensible location:* Don't put log files where a user won't expect them, such as the root directory. Put them in a sensible location, preferably one associated with your application or that can be configured by the user/system administrator.
- *Sensibly named:* I prefer that log file names be easily understood, but sometimes this just isn't possible—for example, when a separate log file is created for each invocation of an application. In these cases, you may want to generate a random name for the file, put it in a sensible location, part of which should be the date the log was created. The format YYYY-MM-DD-HH-MM-<log file name> has the advantage of automatically sorting log files by date (using a 24-hour clock).
- *No garbage or special characters:* Avoid putting anything into the log file that isn't a "normal" character. Use Unicode characters if you're concerned about multibyte languages.
- *Documentation:* Like configuration files, log files need precise documentation to ensure their proper use. Explain what logs are created and when and how they're created, what different settings will produce, and so forth.
- *Reconciliation or audit ID:* If you're using different log files, create some kind of identifier than can tie related entries together. If at all possible, use this identifier with third-party applications.

Log Management

Log management refers to such things as how and when logs are created, updated, and/or deleted and responses to error conditions. Consider the following.

Dynamic Logging

Complex systems benefit from the ability to configure logging parameters (such as level of detail or kind of operations to log) during operation. This allows customer support to work with customers in real time to resolve key issues. An even more sophisticated approach is to construct your system so that *it* can decide if you need to log data. If your fraud detector notices that something is amiss, have it log additional information for awhile.

Per-Thread Logging

Complex servers that distribute operations over multiple architectural layers often service each request in a separate thread. The net result is that log entries from several different components, each running multiple threads, may have to be correlated to produce useful results. If you're using multi-threading, make certain you support per-thread logging.

Logging Levels

In addition to starting/stopping logging, consider making the level of detail configurable. This is often expressed as *logging levels*, where you set a number to indicate the amount and kind of information that should be logged. For example, you might set developer logging to the highest number and default logging to something else. This helps prevent your logs from filling up with data that is only needed in specific or special circumstances.

A complementary approach to logging levels is to label the various logging data. These labels can be used with levels to create a very flexible system. Here are some examples of labels.

- Debug: usually reserved for extended data; turned on when conducting error diagnosis
- Info: provides noteworthy information
- Warning: logs an entry when a potential error condition has been detected, such as when the system has detected a lower-than-desired amount of a critical resource
- Error: logs an entry when an error has occurred

Logging levels and labels should work with the categories defined earlier. Thus, a *warning* entry for performance purposes might be generated when the system takes longer than expected to process an event; whereas, a warning entry based on operational status may be generated when the system becomes low on memory or disk space. Not all combinations make sense—there is no good definition of a warning or an error for behavioral tracking and usage (unless you're concerned about a feature being over-used).

APIs

Controlling the behavior of the system with logging levels and labels should be through an appropriately designed set of APIs.

Configurable Syntax

There are times when a different format is easier to process. For example, Web server logging facilities, like those found in Apache, are completely configurable in syntax and contents.

Log Exceptions

Exceptions and logging are closely related. Log every exception.

Removable

Many logs outlive their usefulness, unnecessarily cluttering machines and potentially confusing log consumers. If the date the log was created is part of the file name, removing unnecessary logs becomes that much easier.

Security

Log data can be sensitive, so you may have to encode it or store it in a privileged location. Depending on the contents of the log, customers may not be willing to share it with your company.

Automatic Forwarding

Conversations between technical support and customers can become pretty tense when something goes wrong. Asking your customers to collect and forward log files to your support organization may result in additional frustration: Nontechnical customers may not know where log files are, and they may not know which ones are needed or how to send them. To make things easier for your customer, consider providing facilities to automatically capture and send log data to technical support. You'll not only get better results, you'll get happier customers.

Logging Standards and Libraries

Logging standards are either platform independent (such as the W3C Extended Log Format or the Common Log Format for Web servers) or platform dependent (such as Windows Event Logs). Basing your log files on these standards enables you and your customers to use a wide range of freely available analysis tools. An alternative is the several logging libraries available, such as log4j for Java. You should roll your own logging facilities, formats, or external viewers only after you've proven that the readily available, and often no-cost tools won't work for you.

> ### Be Careful about Repurposing Log Data
>
> Users often discover a variety of uses for log files. Unfortunately, these new uses can subtly conflict with a file's original functions, causing any number of problems. In one system I worked on, we recorded various user operations for performance monitoring. It was suggested that we could also use them for billing. While it appeared that all of the data were available, this would have been a dangerous choice. Because the logs were simple flat files, they could be easily changed by the user, completely changing their bill. We had to come up with a different tracking mechanism for billing.

Postprocessing Log Data

Simply creating log data is often insufficient to meet users' needs as described at the start of this chapter. Many times additional post-processing tools are needed to make sense of log data. Consider any of the following.

- *Compaction services:* Log data can quickly consume a *lot* of disk space. Web servers on high-traffic Web sites can easily generate hundreds of megabytes of data per hour. Sophisticated tools, such as compaction services, can substantially reduce the amount of disk space you need. Simpler approaches, such as a rolling log, in which data is maintained only for a specified reason and then replaced, can also keep logs under control. An example of a rolling log might be one in which only the last 60 minutes of data are stored.

- *Synchronization tools:* Logs created by several different applications may require synchronization to produce a useful result. A synchronization tool can help ensure that logs will be synchronized properly.

- *Log viewers:* It often makes sense to create tools that view the contents of logs for users. Of course, if you're using system management tools, such as the Windows Event Manager, these tools are handled for you.

Logging Services

I've found it helpful to think of logging as a service provided to the development team that abstracts the complexity of implementing good logs. The actual implementation of a logging service varies from architecture to architecture, but in most cases it can be some form of Singleton. Implementing the log file as a centralized service has the following advantages.

- *Internationalization:* Within the source code you can invoke the logging service with an identifier associated with a given log entry, passing in any additional data as necessary. The logging service can use this identifier to look up any internationalization of the log entry and write these data to the log file.

- *Unified time ordering:* Logging requests in multi-threaded applications can appear to occur out of order because of slight differences in thread execution. A logging service can help make certain that log requests are written to the log file in a sensible manner. In addition, because only one component has generated timestamps, chances are further reduced that log entries will appear out of order.

- *Flexible destinations:* The logging service can choose the destination(s) of log entries at run-time via configuration files. This allows developers to concentrate on what should be logged and allows operations personnel to choose where it should be logged.

- *Consolidation across multiple instances or servers:* If you're operating in an environment in which multiple instances of your application are running on one or more servers, consider augmenting log file names or contents with additional information that allows you to disambiguate various data. Examples of such data include the process or thread ID and the IP address of the host machine.

Chapter Summary

- Logs help provide information or aid activities in the following areas:
  - Debugging
  - Error recovery
  - Performance tuning
  - Capacity planning
  - Behavior tracking and auditing
  - System configuration management
  - Operational status

- Logs must be constructed from the perspective of their *consumers*. This often means you should add additional, contextual information to the log file to aid in its use. It also means you should construct a log file so that it can be easily analyzed.

- Assess the operational impact and/or environment of your log files. Make certain you can handle any error situations such as insufficient disk space.

Check This

❑ We have defined the purpose of each log file.

❑ We have confirmed the utility of each log file with its intended audience (i.e., it contains the right data in the right format).

❑ We have taken care to remove all developer-specific debugging information from our log files.

❑ Our log files follow the same guidelines for internationalization developed for other parts of the user interface.

❑ Our log files follow the same guidelines for portability developed for other parts of the system.

❑ Our log files are easily parsed.

Try This

1. Perform a log file assessment of your current system. What logs does it produce? Why? Who uses these logs? For what purpose? Are these logs secured? If not, do they need to be Are they plain text? If not, why not?

2. How big are your logs? How much data are you generating?

3. Is any data redundantly logged (e.g., a Web server is already logging some data)?

4. Are logs unique to each day? Are they rolling?

5. Open a sample log. Are there any "silly" or out of context entries relative to the target audience? An example would be the name of a function and all of its parameters in a log file designed for behavior tracking and analysis. Such an entry isn't useful to the marketect unless a postprocessing tool can convert it into an appropriate entry.

Chapter 15

Release Management

Release management ensures that the correct artifacts are shipped to the customers wanting or needing them. It does so by identifying, organizing, and controlling these artifacts; assigning them descriptive labels, and integrating these labels into the appropriate back-office systems through SKUs and/or part numbers.

Release management is strongly related to configuration management, which is the process of identifying, organizing, and controlling the various components and related artifacts during system creation. Release management is more effective when it is based on well-known configuration management practices. This chapter discusses important topics in release management, including identification, SKUs, serial numbers, and tarchitectural implications.

Yes, You Really Need This

Properly organized and executed source code and related artifact configuration management are vital to the success of any development, regardless of idiosyncratic system architecture, development methodology, or implementation language. Practically, this means managing change: tracking changes to system artifacts in a coordinated way, communicating these changes to the people who need to know about them, and sometimes even preventing or delaying changes. Fortunately, there are many best practices in configuration management as it relates to workgroup productivity (I list several good books and Web sites in the bibliography).

Configuration management extends beyond promoting teamwork. In a component-based system, components usually don't work with all possible versions of other components. (Just ask your QA team—they'll tell you about the ones they've tested, not every possible combination.) It's a lot easier for a customer or technical support to prevent or diagnose problems when components know their prerequisites. In message-passing systems, messages should have version identifiers so that changes in content or processing rules can be managed.

You need release management because your customers need it. They need to know which version of a system should be ordered and which is compatible with previous versions, the patches and/or upgrades that are available and which apply to their situation and in what order, and so forth. The issues are complex, both from the standpoint of the underlying technology and because some of the choices have nothing to do with the underlying technology, as I will describe later in this chapter.

Establishing a Baseline

Practioners of software configuration management have defined a few basic terms that are useful in managing external deliverables. These are presented in Table 15-1. Managing dependencies or prerequisites is *central* to effective configuration management, as even very simple software often has components that depend on specific versions of other components.

TABLE 15-1 Configuration Management Terms

Term	Definition
Program Family	The total of all versions of all product components. This chapter focuses on the subset available for external distribution.
Component/ Artifact	The smallest discrete entity identified in the system. Each component or artifact distributed to a customer must be uniquely identified and versioned. The tools the development team uses can track components at a much finer level of granularity, even down to each function or method. A well-managed project places more than just the source code under configuration management: Interfaces, test plans, test cases, technical and end-user documentation, MRDs, and even project plans on large, important projects are all candidates. A good rule of thumb is that any independently replaceable component should be uniquely identified.
Version	A fixed or "frozen" component or other artifact. In software, it is important to maintain versions of source artifacts (e.g., source code) and things that can be derived from them (e.g., object code, API documentation), because we typically don't distribute the source artifact but the derivations. A derived version can be uniquely recreated from the source. You may need to establish both internal version and external version identifiers.
Revision	A new version of a component or artifact that is intended to supersede the old. Revisions are usually linearly ordered and are often sequentially numbered to reflect this ordering (e.g., as in a sequentially increasing project build number).
Variation	An alternative implementation of a component or other artifact. An example is a software component designed to perform the same task on different operating platforms that require slightly different implementations. Variations are *not* sequentially ordered—they are alternatives.

Term	Definition
Distribution	A version created for distribution to a set of customers, usually made up of one or more certified components and/or artifacts. By definition, a product contains a list or configuration of its components.
Release	A named and versioned collection of components and artifacts that are generally for external distribution to one or more customers and that have been certified. (It is what tarchitects commonly think of as the product, although marketects use a slightly different definition of "product.") A release can be simple or complex and is often recursively structured. Unlike revisions, releases may not be strictly linear, especially in the case of patches to a major system.

Of course, the easiest way to manage dependencies is to make certain that the release has the correct version of all of required components. In practice, however, this is often impossible because of licensing agreements and because not every release contains all components. I'll discuss this issue in greater detail later.

Release Management

Managing releases involves three factors: what you're releasing, who you're targeting, and why they want it.

What You're Releasing

You may be releasing something as small as a single patch to one component or something as large as the complete product. A *full* or *complete release* is of the entire product, usually to be installed on a fresh system or used to upgrade an existing system. A *partial, module, update,* or *fractional release* is some subset of product functionality usually designed to extend the capabilities of a base system, such as an optional module. A *patch or update release* is some subset of the product, that usually precisely replaces one or more existing components in a working installation that have known errors. In general, patch releases should not be used to add new functionality to an existing system.

The determination of a full, partial, or patch release can be quite fluid. You might be in the midst of planning a full release with two major milestones when a competitor makes a major announcement about one of their releases. Your plan then changes to preempt your competitor by converting the first milestone into a full release and the second milestone into a partial release. These factors and a host of others strongly influence a marketect's decision on what to release.

Full, partial, and patch releases are all subject to the same release processes—however you've defined them. For example, most release processes require the team to do a virus scan before shipping any bits to a customer.

Who You're Targeting

You may be targeting internal users in an alpha release; external users, in a beta, limited, or general release. A *limited*, *managed*, or *controlled release* has been targeted to a specific set of customers. An example would be a patch release to customers who have a bug on a single hardware platform. A *general release* is intended for all of your customers.

Marketects and development teams often confuse *who* they're targeting with *what* they're releasing. "Who you're targeting" is about scope, whereas "what you're releasing" is about size. When a new virus is discovered, anti-virus vendors want to update their virus definition files quickly. What is being released is relatively small in size but large in scope. It might be referred to as a generally available update on the Web site of the anti-virus vendor.

I've found that many companies have trouble targeting their releases, mostly because they don't know enough about their customers. Let's say that you support Solaris and Windows XP and find a relatively easily fixed bug in the XP release. Unless you've kept track of which customers have Windows XP, you'll have to send out the announcement to all of them. It would be far more efficient, and far more compelling, if the announcement only went to the people who should get the patch.

Why They Want It

Customer motivation can range from actively working against accepting and installing the release ("we can't install that patch in our production system ten days before the holiday shopping season—it's too risky") to overwhelming your Web site because the demand is so great ("We must have it *now*"). Most releases fall into a middle ground, and usually the marketect has to use carrots (new features, improved performance, reduced bugs, greater reliability) and sticks (lack of support for discontinued platforms or releases, license agreement compliance) as a way of motivating the customer to accept and implement the release.

Choosing the right combination of carrots and sticks is one of the marketect's most complex tasks. For example, a new release is often made backward-compatible with a previous release. But should it be made backward-compatible with software that was released three years ago? Probably not, as the aggregate costs of such compatibility, including regression testing, operation verification, and associated support, can be enormous. Of course, losing important, major customers who may not be interested in upgrading their software to a new release can be just as risky, which makes keeping the installed base as current as possible a major job of the marketect. No matter how you keep track of these things, you're going to have "version skippers" and you're going to have to define the upgrade path from whatever version they've got to your current version, regardless of how painful the individual steps in the upgrade are.

Release Identification

Unlike component identification, which may or may not be publicly exposed, release identification concerns the manner in which a release is identified to a customer. The full identification consists of the product name (see Chapter 9) and versioning information that captures the appropriate product revisions and variations. The goal is to get all of the necessary information in as few names and identifiers as possible, which helps improve overall efficiency.

Over the years, I've learned that there is no single, universal algorithm for creating release identifiers. Moreover, you need slightly different algorithms for what you're releasing and who you're targeting. With these caveats in mind, here are algorithms that have worked well for me and proven to be considerably more useful than the seemingly arbitrary identification schemes used by many vendors.

Full or Complete Releases

Regardless of who you're targeting, full releases are best identified using

- The name of the product
- The four-digit tuple of *x.y.z.build* to capture revision information
- An arbitrary number of variation identifiers pursuant to the needs of the product

The parts of the four-digit tuple *x.y.z.build*, are defined in Table 15-2. Note that this scheme takes advantage of the natural linear ordering of revisions.

It's usually best for marketing to promote only the major and minor identifiers to customers. In other words, when customers are told they'll be receiving version 3.4 of the product, they might really be receiving version 3.4.2.129 or 3.4.7.13. The primary motivation for this is the expense of trying to manage the full tuple in promotional materials, license agreements, sales collateral, and so forth. You don't want to incur the expense of reprinting all these materials because of a maintenance release.

By definition, a full release distributed to an existing customer is a complete upgrade. You'll find that customer satisfaction is improved when you only modify components that absolutely must be modified, especially in the case of a dot release.

Some people recommend including the target of the distribution in this scheme by inserting an appropriate identifier. For example, you might have *A* for an alpha/internal release, *RC* for a release candidate sent to QA, *MR* for a managed release, and *GA* for a general release, all inserted to the right of the *y* or *z* designator ("SuperDraw 4.5A"). I prefer not to do this because it makes the overall naming convention unnecessarily complex and because it mixes what is being released with who is being targeted. I've also had situations in which a release originally intended only as an alpha was later distributed to a trusted external customer. This change in scope invalidated the release identifier and thereby limited its usefulness.

TABLE 15-2   Release Tuple Definitions

Tuple	Definition

x	A *major* release. One motivation to increment the major release number is when there is some extensive, customer-visible architectural or feature change. These changes, in turn, must be defined and agreed upon by the marketect. Consider a system that manages very large databases. In such a system you might define a major release as any release that
	
	• Changed the structure of these databases because of the rather severe impact upgrading the system had on your customers;
	• Modified the published API in a way that makes it incompatible with previous versions;
	• Removed functionality (yes, a good marketect will remove unwanted functionality); or,
	• Added substantial new functionality, such as support for a new operating system.
	
	In systems that rely on multiple components, incrementing x on one might mean incrementing x on the other. An example is a client–server system, in which clients at release x.*.* are guaranteed to work with servers x.*.* and x_{-1}.*.*, but not servers x_{+1}.*.*.
	    x can also be incremented for purely business reasons. For example, a customer's support contract might state that that their software will be supported for 18 months after the next major release. By incrementing x, you put the customer on a forced path to upgrade (one of the sticks I mentioned earlier). In one company I worked at, we designated our first release of a major enterprise-class system as 5.0, to both build on a legacy of previous releases of a related product and to help us avoid the concerns that many IT administrators have regarding a 1.0 release of the software.
	    Most marketects should establish strong goals to distribute major releases to all customers as quickly as possible. If it is a major release, treat it as such.

y	A *minor* release, usually associated with desirable features or other improvements. The minor release number is incremented when marketing deems it justified by the set of features in the release. The decision to increment x or y can seem arbitrary. The marketect should define the events that trigger any increments. (It is easier to define the trigger associated with x than with y.).
z	A maintenance or "*dot*" release. Maintenance releases are made available to all customers affected by the contents of the release. Any given dot release should be compatible with other dot releases that share the same major and minor release numbers.
build	The specific *build* number associated with the product. For compiled languages, it is easy to compute the build number. For interpreted languages, the build number can be created by a simple program that labels a fully checked-in code base. The build number is rarely presented to the customer unless needed for precise identification purposes, usually in relation to technical support. The build number may be optional if the main component is an aggregate of subcomponents. Suppose a product comprises two subproducts: one, release 1.3.2.29, the other release 3.6.2.19. It might be acceptable to identify your release as 3.4.0.0 or anything else that indicates the composition.

Partial Releases

Determining the identification scheme for a partial release mostly depends on marketing factors. If the component or artifact can be purchased separately or as an option in the main distribution, it is usually best to have it evolve under its own *x.y.z.build* identification scheme according to the guidelines given in the previous section. Naming consistency makes it easy for customers to build a mental model of the various optional components. It also makes it easier to construct an overall list of available products.

Partial releases that are not sold separately, such as updated anti-virus files, and not expected to be revised in the future, don't have the same complexities associated with a naming convention that revisions do. In this case, partial releases simply need a unique identifier. For most products a specially defined name and a date are usually sufficient.

A key issue in creating partial releases is managing the dependencies between their components or functionality and those of the main product. These dependencies may be captured through rules that govern release identifiers or through the design of the architecture, as described later in this chapter. As an example of the rules approach, you might require that every release of a component at version $x.y$ be compatible with every version of the main system designated $x.y_n$, where y_n is greater than or equal to y. Thus, "SuperDraw Enhanced Rendering Tool 4.5" would be compatible with "SuperDraw 4.5," "SuperDraw 4.6," and so forth. Rules won't do you or your customers any good if you fail to follow them: If SuperDraw were to go through a major upgrade and be released as "SuperDraw 5.0," you would have to modify the release identifier of the enhanced rendering tool to match, even if the code didn't change. While this may seem like busy work, it will save you and your customers a lot of pain (and license agreements may require this).

Patch Releases

Recall that a patch release is some subset of the product that usually precisely replaces one or more existing components in a working installation that has known errors. Identifying patch releases represents special challenges. Everyone involved usually has a strong opinion on how to identify a patch release, everyone thinks that their way is the best way, and everyone feels like arguing over each point for an endless amount of time! Many poor choices can be made when identifying patch releases. This section provides guidance on easily creating a sensible patch release identification scheme. Patch releases are always associated with something in use, which means that they deal with a customer in a potentially stressful situation. Moreover, the team that creates the patch may not be the team that created the system and so may not be familiar with previous release identification schemes.

Because patches are highly dependent on an existing product, it is usually convenient to refer to that product in the patch identifier. At the same time, you don't want to adopt the $x.y.z.build$ numbering convention because patches are rarely revised unless a serious mistake was made in the QA or release process. More important, the linear ordering associated with revisions implies that everything included in the previous release is included in the next highest release unless specifically stated otherwise. Thus, we expect that version 4.5 of our favorite compiler includes and extends the functionality in versions 4.2, 4.3, and 4.4. This is *not* necessarily true with patch releases. A given patch may or may not include the modifications of a previous patch. Patches are not cumulative unless designed as such.

Patches are often associated with emotionally charged events or bugs that take on a life of their own. Since some aspect of these events or bugs usually becomes associated with the patch, I recommend leveraging this by referring to patches by name and possibly by date. The net result is patch names of the form *product—x.y{.z{.build}}—patch name*. Note that the maintenance release and build number are optional in this naming convention, which in practice allows customers to easily identify the patch they need. The external, customer-facing name might be something like "SuperDraw 4.5 Repaginate Long Documents patch," which means that this patch can be applied to any SuperDraw 4.5.* system. If the patch is focused on a specific dot release, you refer to it in this scheme as "SuperDraw 4.5.2 Repaginate Long Documents patch."

Especially complex products may call out those areas affected by the patch, primarily because it makes it easier for customers to identify which patches they want to download from a self-service technical support Web site. Let's say that you have a client/server system with an optional workflow module. You might augment the naming convention to be *product—x.y{.z{.build}}—product area—patch name*, as in "SuperDraw 4.5 Repaginate Long Documents Server patch" or "SuperDraw 4.5 E-mail Client Notification Workflow patch."

Patches that are dependent on other patches can call out those dependencies via documentation. If a large number of patches are associated with a product, I recommend collecting them all in a maintenance release. If this isn't possible, another approach is a service pack that does the same thing. Make certain your documentation is clear on whether or not service packs are cumulative.

Note that not everyone agrees with naming patches. Imagine that your patch has an error (yes, it happens). This means that it needs to be versioned, and versions are best handled through numbering. You might version the patch but not include the version identifier unless it's absolutely needed. Thus, your patch would be in the form *product—x.y{.z{.build}}—patch name.patch version*. If you have a problem with the first version of "SuperDraw 4.5 Repaginate Long Documents Server patch," you can release a second version called "SuperDraw 4.5 Repaginate Long Documents Server patch, version 2." However you choose to resolve this, do not impose an arbitrary limit on the naming, because you'll eventually run into a situation where the limit is exceeded.

Very sophisticated architectures are smart enough to package patches together, tracking what is installed and not installed. Some companies do this in their software and allow automatic updates (think of anti-virus software as a simple example). Other companies (such as ManageSoft) do this on behalf of corporate administrators, taking snapshots of the software on various desktops.

Let's assume that you want to extend your architecture to include patch management. If so, it will need to be smart enough to understand what is and is not installed. It will need some mechanism for communicating with a remote server, preferably over the Internet, to obtain updates. It should be able to detect if prerequisites are

---

Bug Fixes Don't Have to Be Free

When bug fixes are not included as part of the license, the marketect must decide when to fix them. Sometimes the right choice is to fix them as a way to build good will with a customer. Sometimes the right choice is to charge for the fix, which can also build good will with a customer.

I once had a customer with an extremely urgent request to fix a bug on an unsupported product. Specifically, they had a perpetual license to use the product, but the version they had installed was no longer supported. In a very real sense, they brought this problem on themselves because they had failed to upgrade their system over the course of several releases. When they contacted us to fix the bug, I originally said "No, if they want the bug fix they can upgrade."

As the saying goes, "Money talks . . .," and my original No turned to Yes once I was able to negotiate a substantial fee for the fix. My team hustled and fixed the bug in record time (even I was a bit surprised at how quick they were!). The customer was so impressed with this service that they subsequently executed the major upgrades they had delayed far too long.

---

available, and if not, install them. It needs to be able to determine that an automatic update was installed correctly—it didn't break the system or any settings—and roll back the change if something is wrong. These are very complex requirements, which is why I don't generally recommend this approach.

Variations

Variations, like patches, don't have monotonically increasing revision numbers. Naming them and inserting or appending the name into the overall identification string in a way that makes sense is the best way to handle them. For example, suppose that our SuperDraw client/server system supports Linux and Solaris. The binaries for these operating systems are functionally equivalent but physically different. Thus, you might call a full release of version 4.5 "SuperDraw 4.5 for Linux" and "SuperDraw 4.5 for Solaris." If you require a patch to this release for Linux, you call it the "SuperDraw 4.5 e-mail Notification Workflow Patch for Linux."

Things become more complex when the system or component supports multiple variations, usually associated with portability, internationalization, or performance characteristics. Suppose that SuperDraw supports six languages and has two performance options: single- (default) and multiple-CPU. Here are some of the ways this might be handled.

- "SuperDraw 4.5, German Language for Linux" for a full release of the single-CPU version

- "SuperDraw 4.5, German Language for Linux, multi-CPU," for a full release of the multi-CPU version
- "SuperDraw 4.5 email Notification Workflow Patch, German language, for Linux"

As a general rule, the more options, the more complex the name. I consider this a good thing because customers don't deal with these names every day and they often have trouble clearly remembering what they want or need. Verbosity ensures that they are getting the right artifact.

SKUs and Serial Numbers

Except in the very smallest of companies, products shipped to customers must be identified for a variety of purposes, including inventory tracking and sales reporting. Most companies rely on SKUs (stock keeping units) to manage these functions in the various corporate systems that help them perform. Software sold in high volumes may also be serialized for unique identification, tracking, and some limited copy protection.

SKU Management

The changing nature of releases and variations, and their potentially long and descriptive names, puts a great deal of pressure on other corporate systems that must account for sales, shipments, upgrades, or other customer activities. The easiest way to manage this is to establish SKUs. These are unique release identifiers that enable one release to be distinguished from all others within corporate tracking systems. As an identifier, a SKU is independent of the various textual descriptions of releases that I've described in previous sections.

SKUs are used in a variety of circumstances. One example is orders for specific releases. Another is prices, which are not part of the release identifier or product name and must be obtained from a pricing database or system; the primary key to find the price is the SKU. Inventory levels for physical goods are also usually managed through SKUs. Inventory for electronic software distribution doesn't make sense, but since chances are good that you'll do some physical and electronic distribution, SKUs have a place in your inventory management system.

Teams often struggle with when to assign a SKU to a release. SKUs introduce many additional tasks into the overall release process, so it is understandable that marketects avoid them unless absolutely necessary. The following guidelines have worked well for me.

- Always assign a SKU to any release that can be sold, regardless of its scope (patch, partial, or full) and target (controlled or general).
- Try to assign a SKU to any general release (a release targeted to all customers), regardless of scope (patch, partial, or full). This makes for convenient tracking of what is globally available.

- Always assign a SKU to any release if your primary customer-tracking and distribution systems are keyed to SKUs *and* you can track who gets the release. This allows you to know who has what release.

- Avoid SKUs for releases simply posted on self-service Web sites, such as technical support or free-download sites. You're not selling these, so there is no need to create SKUs in your financial systems, and you're not keeping track of who gets them (although perhaps you should).

Of course, these recommendations should be followed only if they fit with corporate policy. If your company mandates that all releases, no matter what, have SKUs, then by all means, create them.

You can't mandate the format of a SKU, because it is usually under the control of corporate IT, fulfillment, accounting, and the like. You can, however, tell these groups how many SKUs you need and work with them on a format that will enable you to accomplish your objectives.

Returning to our example, SuperDraw is one of four product lines at SuperSoft. Other parts of the company, such as accounting and order fulfillment, don't care about the product names or version identifiers. Accounting just wants to track sales results by product line and division, while order fulfillment just wants to make certain that the right deliverable is shipped to the customer. What they care about is the SKU, which is their way of tracking these products. For various reporting reasons, accounting has defined a SKU format—*NNNN-MMMM-#*, where *NNNN* is a four-character division identifier, *MMMM* is a four-character product identifier, and *#* is a unique product number of arbitrary length—and has defined the division identifiers. Together product management and accounting have defined the product identifiers; product management alone is responsible for assigning unique product numbers. Product management might define the SKUs as shown in Table 15-3.

Table 15-3 contains three key logical components: the SKU, the external name, and the fully qualified release identifier. The last component should be extended as needed by product management to ensure that all aspects of the product are properly managed. For example, you may want to include the location of the build in your internal network (e.g., \\buildmaster\SuperDraw\4\5\1\{build} if you're building every day).

TABLE 15-3 Example: Assigning SKUs to Products

SKU	External Name	Internal Identification
DRAW-SERV-0001	SuperDraw 4.5, German Language for Linux	SuperDraw 4.5.1.21, German Language for Linux
DRAW-SERV-0002	SuperDraw 4.5, Russian Language for Linux	SuperDraw 4.5.1.20, Russian Language for Linux
DRAW-SERV-0003	SuperDraw 4.5, English Language for Linux	SuperDraw 4.5.1.20, English Language for Linux

Backend systems often need an estimate of how many SKUs you might need. The number of SKUs associated with a product can be estimated by adding the following:

- The number of full releases multiplied by the number of full release variations (remember to count each kind of variation, such as language, operating system, or platform, separately). For example, if SuperDraw 4.5 runs on 3 operating systems and supports five languages, this produces 1*3*5 = 15 SKUs *for each release*. You may have to adjust these numbers as releases often add or subtract variations or variation classes.

- The number of partial releases intended to receive a SKU multipled by the number of partial release variations.

- The number of optional components multiplied by the number of optional component variations.

- Any other SKUs that are generated for other reasons.

As you can see, SKUs can quickly grow to hundreds or thousands of identifiers—plan accordingly.

Serial Numbers, Registration, and Activation

A SKU is an identification code that allows a class of products to be tracked for inventory purposes. It can't identify an individual product sold to an individual customer. For that you need a *serial number*, a unique identifier that does distinguish individual products. *Registration* is how a customer, who has purchased the unique product, makes themselves known to the vendor who sold it, with the serial number acting as a key that binds the customer to the company. *Software activation* is a kind of forced registration in which various product features, and possibly even the entire product, are inaccessible until the customer completes an approved registration process. Software activation is closely related to license enforcement (see Chapter 4) as one of the goals of software activation is to ensure that only properly licensed software is allowed to function.

In the physical world, serial numbers range from the lot numbers and associated codes printed on vitamin bottles to the identification tag affixed to my PDA. As a digital good, software cannot easily be identified with a unique serial number. Unlike physical goods, digital goods are often trivially copied, and embedding a serial number within the object code at production often represents an expensive change to internal processes. Moreover, unless you've adopted one of the license enforcement schemes described in Chapter 4 to prevent copying or modification of your software, serial numbers can be easily changed.

Although serial numbers can be a bother, there are real benefits to using them. By associating a serial number with a product and asking the user to register it with your company, you can collect vital demographic statistics and tailor your marketing campaigns. Consider that once your customers have registered their serial number you can use it to notify them of product upgrades, bug fixes, and product and service offers.

Registered customers may be willing to provide you with additional valuable information, including their preferences for new features or their willingness to participate in beta programs.

Properly registered serial numbers can help reduce piracy. In the past, when serial numbers were printed on CD sleeves, the sheer size of programs and the difficulty in duplicating CDs were deterrents to piracy, but technological advancements have made such deterrents ineffective, and software developers are continually looking for new ones.

Software activation is effective at deterring piracy while increasing the number of users that register their software. Activation processes vary according to need or by software activation vendor. Generally they work something like this.

1. The software publisher prepares the software for distribution. A serial number may be assigned at this time, although serial numbers can be generated dynamically instead. The software is protected in some way to prevent execution until it has been given the proper activation code.

2. The customer purchasing the software, a consumer or an enterprise, installs the software, binding it to the machine. The binding process takes a unique "fingerprint" of the machine, such as the processor ID, motherboard serial number, or MAC address of the primary Ethernet card. This information is usually stored in a secure location to help prevent illegal copying of the software.

3. To use the software, the purchaser contacts the publisher with the serial number or the machine fingerprint, or some combination of the two, and requests an activation code. This process may also force the entity to register with the publisher. The publisher should provide several channels for acquiring the activation code, such as the Internet, e-mail, phone, and fax. During this process, data from the target machine are stored in various corporate databases and the software associated with that serial number is marked as activated. Registering the serial number ensures that it is uniquely identifying a product, while storing the machine fingerprint and binding the software to the machine helps prevent piracy.

4. The activation code is given to the software and stored in a secure location. Depending on the technology that was chosen, it or the license allows the software to be used but only on the designated machine.

Adopting a software activation process is a strategic decision. Most companies don't have the resources to create effective activation systems, but several vendors provide them. Offerings must be evaluated relative to existing and planned backend systems and workflows. Managing the backend systems is likely to be a much bigger job than choosing a software activation vendor.

Release Management Influences on Tarchitecture

Knowing what the release management requirements are can improve your tarchitecture by encouraging choices that make release management easier. Consider the following.

- *Recreate everything.* The most important rule of release management is that everything shipped to the customer must be either derived (such as building an executable from source code) or created (such as printing a manual from a Framemaker file). This can create some funny behavior among dedicated workers, especially if they don't trust that IS is backing up their machines. I once had a director who copied every aspect of the source tree, along with all of the tools necessary to build the product, to multiple machines as well as burning multiple CDs, simply because she didn't trust our IT department to properly backup our source code machines. I'm glad she did this, because our IT department failed us more than once—and her backups saved the day.

- *Use existing solutions and infrastructure wherever possible.* Chances are good that some aspects of your deployment architecture can handle any number of issues associated with technical configuration management. Microsoft, for example, has an extensive (some would say nightmarish) infrastructure for managing components packed as DLLs and their associated dependencies. Learn these infrastructures and leverage them when you can.

- *Put version information in your tarchitecture as early as possible.* Once you've identified the need for version information, put it in without delay. Retrofitting version information is expensive and painful.

- *Components should know their dependencies.* In component-based systems, your components should know which versions of other components they can work with. This is easiest with a data-driven approach, perhaps through a special dependency-checking component that processes dependency information stored in a configuration file—for example, when a client is directed at a server that can't support it, instead of failing outright, the client can inform the user of the problem and ideally provide him with some information on how to rectify the situation.

- *Messages and protocols should be versioned.* Messages sent between components should be versioned so that changes in content or processing rules can be managed.

- *Databases and tables within them should have versions.* One way to do this is to create a system table that contains the version identifier of each table in the schema. It can be extended to provide release information for specific columns within tables as needed by your application. Versions facilitate upgrading schemas in the field, detecting changes made to released schemas, and ensuring that components that read from and/or write to the database do this properly.

- *Any component that can be updated should be versioned.* Versioning makes certain that your technical support organization can quickly assess whether a component should be updated in response to a customer problem. It also simplifies the installation of partial and patch releases.

- *Internal components should understand the versions of the external components they require.* If your system requires Solaris 2.8, check for it. If you know your system has problems running on Windows XP, check for that.

- *There must be a way of obtaining versions of all versioned artifacts.* This enables technical support to help the customer and is the foundation for customer self-service and automatic software updating.

- *Beware the testing and support implications of patches.* Creating more components, and providing support and/or backward compatibility for previous releases, can increase testing and verification complexity at an exponential rate. Just because you can provide backward compatibility support, don't think that you must.

□ □ □ □ □ □ □ □ □

Chapter Summary

■ *Release management* ensures that the correct artifacts are shipped to the customers who want or need them. It is based on the following concepts:
  - Program families
  - Components and artifacts
  - Versions—a fixed or frozen component or other artifact
  - Revision—a new version intended to supersede the old
  - Variation—an alternative implementation
  - Distribution—a set version created for distribution to a set of customers
  - Release—a named distribution

■ Release management involves three factors: what you're releasing, who you're targeting, and customer motivation.

■ Releases must be identified. The four-digit tuple *x.y.z.build* is a proven way to create release identifiers.

■ SKUs are used to manage releases within back-office systems such as accounting and order fulfillment.

Check This

❑ For each release, we have defined what we're releasing and who we're targeting. We have also estimated the customer's motivation for obtaining the release.

❑ We have a defined system for identifying releases.

❑ Each release that needs a SKU has one.

❑ Each release that needs a serial number has one.

Try This

1. What corporate systems track releases and SKUs? How do these systems inter-operate?

2. Does your system require serial numbers? Should it?

3. Should you require your customers to register their software? Why or why not? Should you require your customers to activate their software? Why or why not?

Chapter 16
Security

with Ron Lunde
System Architect
Aladdin Knowledge Systems, Inc.

Most of what you're trying to accomplish with your tarchitecture is making things easy. You want your products and systems to be easy for your users—to install, to configure, to use, and to learn. You want them to be easy for your developers—to understand, to change, to extend, and to repurpose. If problems occur, you want them to be easy to detect, diagnose, and fix. And, you want them to be easy for the ecosystem that inevitably develops around a winning solution—easy for solution providers to extend, easy for system integrators to integrate, and easy for operations to install, maintain, and extend as necessary.

The main difference with software security is that it's not about making things easy. It's about making things hard. You want your software to be hard to steal, hard to misuse, and hard to fool. You want to make certain that no one is cheating your business model or using your software against the terms of the license agreement.

Security is an essential part of a winning solution, yet it is often overlooked until the system is nearing completion. Just like an effective error- or exception-handling scheme, security must be taken into consideration during the design of tarchitecture. It isn't icing on a cake; it's eggs in the batter, and if it isn't in there at the start, you can't go back and add it when you take it out of the oven and serve it to your customers.

In this chapter we'll explore the ways in which software and the data that it manages can be misused and some of the techniques and technologies that can be used to prevent misuse.

Keep in mind that security is a huge topic. Many excellent books have been written about security, and on specific aspects of security, such as cryptography. You should find this chapter useful even if you've read those books, since our focus is on how to create a winning solution using the technologies available to you rather than on the details of the technologies themselves.

Viruses, Hackers, and Pirates

There are four main types of security you need to consider.

- *Digital identity management.* Most enterprise systems provide services to either humans or other systems in fulfillment of a larger transaction. If you're building an enterprise application, some of the things you're going to be doing include defining different capabilities for different users and the roles that they assume, formally tracking their actions, and verifying that a given user is who he or she claims to be.

- *Transaction security.* Communication between the various parts of your system must be secure so that those parts cannot be replaced by unauthorized components, and so that messages cannot be intercepted, altered, or hijacked. Hackers can exploit holes in transaction security or simply prevent your transactions using denial-of-service attacks. You'll also need to protect against these.

- *Software security.* You have to protect your software from viruses or hackers. Nobody should be able to alter your software except those you specifically authorize, and nobody should be able to exploit holes in your security to gain unauthorized access to one of your customers' systems. Software security protects your work from viruses, software pirates, and some hacking. One aspect of software security, software piracy (the illegal copying of software), was covered in Chapter 4.

- *Information security.* The databases and information repositories used by your system need to be secured against unauthorized access or use. In many circumstances, the real target isn't the software that manages the Web site but the detailed transaction history, including such things as credit card numbers, that the software has stored in a database. Unless you take explicit steps to prevent unauthorized access, these data may be at risk.

Each type of security requires its own tools and techniques, which we'll cover in greater detail later in this chapter. Some techniques, such as maintaining confidentiality through encryption, can achieve higher security in more than one area. For example, to maintain confidentiality of messages or database records you can encrypt them.

Sometimes you may pay very little attention to one type of security and focus all of your attention elsewhere. At other times, you're going to have to explicitly account for all types of security. While information security may not be a strong requirement for a family financial management application running on a personal computer, it is likely to be of paramount importance to an enterprise application that maintains payroll records. While digital identity management isn't needed for a game that you play by yourself, it is critical when playing a multiplayer game for a monthly fee over the Internet! Getting clear on elements of security that are important for your application is key to creating a winning solution.

Managing Risk

The first thing most security experts will tell you is that there is no such thing as a secure system. You can increase the level of security, but you can never be 100 percent sure that your system is safe from all types of attack. For example, firewalls and intrusion detection tools are commonly used to prevent unauthorized access, but hackers are not the only concern. Disgruntled employees and others with physical access to your computers can create serious problems while completely bypassing the firewalls that are meant to keep hackers out. In fact, the risk management consulting firm Kroll estimates that 80% of all attacks happen from inside the firewall (you did perform a full background check of the temporary secretary before you let him borrow your corporate ID, didn't you?). Just as it is physically impossible to cool matter to absolute zero, it is also exponentially harder to make your system more secure. And you'll never be able to say that you're absolutely secure: You can't prevent every element of crazy human behavior.

You can't eliminate risk, but you can manage it. Usually, it isn't difficult to make hacking your system prohibitively expensive so that no real hacker will have the time or money to succeed. Consider software piracy. When large programs were first distributed on CD-ROM, piracy wasn't that bad. You couldn't copy a CD-ROM, and no one wanted to download 100Mb on a 56Kb modem. Those times are long gone, and copying software onto a variety of media or downloading it on high-speed Internet connections has led to a piracy explosion.

Just like anything else, it's possible to go too far with security. Storing all of your data in an encrypted format might make your system more secure, but will certainly prevent reasonable integrations with other systems. Security is an area where the marketect and the tarchitect must work together. The marketect must lead the assessments of risk by determining what harm will befall the customer, the company, or other entities if one or more elements of security are compromised. The tarchitect must inform the marketect of ways to handle these problems, as well as make her own assessment of risk (not too many marketects are going to worry about transaction security). Once the perceived risks and mechanisms to handle them are known, the marketect and the tarchitect can make the tough calls on how to deal with potential problems.

See No Evil, Speak No Evil

How big a problem is security? After all, it's fairly rare to hear of a large corporation having a major security problem. Maybe security is not a wise investment, and everyone would be better off putting their time and efforts in improving other aspects of the system.

According to the seventh annual joint FBI/Computer Security Institute (CSI) Computer Crime and Security Survey, 75% of the companies surveyed do not report security problems to law enforcement agencies because of negative publicity or fear of giving their competitors an advantage as a result. The same report showed that of the 500 corporations surveyed 40% reported denial-of-service attacks, 20% reported theft of proprietary information, 12% reported financial fraud, and 8% reported sabotage. In fact, security lapses result in hundreds of millions of dollars lost annually. The time to start considering security is right at the start, when you're designing the tarchitecture.

If you're working in an environment that doesn't worry about security, start shouting.

Digital Identity Management

This section explores the most important building blocks of digital identity management, including authorization and authentication.

Authorization—Defining Who Can Do What

Like many elements of security, there are static and dynamic aspects to authorization. The static aspect deals with defining which entities get rights to perform an operation, access part of the system, or access part of the database. The most common approach is to have a trusted user, such as the system administrator, define user rights by individual or by class. For example, if you're designing a medical records system, you might permit a patient to access all of his own history but not any data about anyone else.

The dynamic aspect of authorization concerns checks made to ensure that a given user or entity has the necessary rights to perform the operation or to access a certain part of the system or database. In sophisticated systems these checks need to happen at runtime because the authorization rules may be based on a variety of runtime parameters, including the role the user has assumed while accessing the system, her prior behavior, the state of the system, or even the behavior of others using the system at the same time.

There are a number of technologies and rights management systems that you can use, or tie in to, to provide authorization and access control. Lightweight Directory Access Protocol (LDAP) is a common one. Another is role based access control (RBAC), a generic name for technologies that provide authorization based upon user role. If you need to provide file system authorization, ACLs (access control lists) may be all you need. It's a good idea to isolate the systems you use for authorization by wrapping them with your own authorization layer. This way you can swap out one type for another as the requirements of the system change over time.

Authentication—Proof of Identity

Authentication is the process a system uses to ensure that an entity is who or what it claims to be. This can be important as the precursor to authorization, or it may be required to simply engage in a trusted transaction. The most appropriate authentication technology depends on whether you have a closed or an open system and whether or not you require third-party certification of identity.

Closed Systems

In closed systems, there is little or no need for an independent third party to certify an identity. The system itself, by its structure and/or operation, provides for acceptable levels of authentication. Many enterprise applications that grant specific rights to authenticated users are closed. Once the system administrator has registered a user ID with the system (either directly or through a directory) and provided it with the necessary system access (e.g., a password and a token), that user is now recognized as an *authenticated*, certified user whenever she successfully logs in to the system.

Authentication in closed systems is usually based on one or more of the following:

- *Something you know*—for example, a password
- *Something you have*—for example, a smart card or a computer that has been uniquely identified, either through a machine fingerprint or an actual unique identifier stored in the processor or the motherboard
- *Something you are (biometric)*—for example, a thumb print or a voice print

A combination of any two is normally considered strong authentication. Extremely secure environments may require all three, or multiple applications of each.

Of course, the most common, and certainly most insecure, authentication mechanism by far is a simple password, which is usually easily guessed. When system administrators mandate secure passwords, users often make the system even less secure by writing theirs down on a scrap of paper or allowing their favorite Web browser to save them for easy reference. Don't be lulled into a false sense of security because your system requires a password!

From a tarchitecture perspective, we recommend abstracting the approach you use for authentication. Many systems start with a simple password system and evolve through use or customer demand to require something stronger.

Open Systems

Unlike closed systems, open systems require an independent third party to authenticate a user. Examples of open systems include a secure e-mail between two parties, and secure communication links between applications on the Web. In this case we need some kind of certification by a third party that the communicating entities are who they claim to be.

We've faced the problems of open systems before, and we've solved them in similar ways. In the 18th century, a gentleman scientist who wanted to visit a member of the Royal Society he hadn't met, to study in his library, for example, brought a letter of introduction from a colleague known to both to show that he could be trusted. If the host wanted to be extra sure that his visitor was who he claimed to be, he would compare the signature of the letter with the signature on correspondence from the mutual colleague, to make sure that the letter hadn't been forged. We do the same thing today, except that we now use certificate authorities and digital certificates instead of venerable gentlemen and parchment and ink. These certificates and the trusted third party provide the necessary levels of authentication for open transactions.

The idea is that you prove who you are to a trusted third party, who gives you a digital certificate signed with their private key. Anyone can use the trusted third party's public key to verify the certificate, and since they trust the signer and the signer is saying that you are who you claim to be, they can trust you. This hierarchy of trust can extend in a certificate chain—each certificate signed by an agency that vouches for it, until it reaches the top; the certificate authority.

Certificate authorities support certificate revocation, which means that if you lose your private key or someone up the certificate chain has their security compromised, the certificate corresponding to the lost key can be revoked. Then you get another certificate, and everything continues as usual—except that anyone presenting the revoked certificate will not be authenticated.

The problem with certificate revocation is that sometimes you have to be able to talk to the certificate authority in real time to make sure that a certificate you want to authenticate has not been revoked, and for isolated subnets or disconnected applications this isn't possible. Also, if you run your own certificate authority, you must ensure that your system will work 24 hours a day, 7 days a week.

For this reason, you should carefully consider whether your system needs revocable authentication. If you combine certificate-based authentication with other information, it may not be necessary. For example, in one system we know of, the server checked the IP address of the caller as well as the caller's certificate. Even if the client's certificate and private key were stolen, the server would log and disallow the transaction if the originating IP address was incorrect.

There are several challenges associated with certificate-based authentication. Let's start with the first step, proving who you are to the trusted third party. Some certificate authorities have a very poor record of verifying these claims, and several multi-million dollar lawsuits have been filed over inappropriate verification procedures. In addition, some certificate authorities have hurt themselves through deceptive marketing practices. Simply put, how can you trust a certificate authority who deceives customers? There is no undisputed world-wide leader in certificate management. There are several for-profit, not-for-profit, quasi-governmental, and governmental certificate authorities, all of which hinder the search for global solutions.

In addition to these technical and operational challenges is the challenge of complexity exposed to average users who may wish to use, or who are forced to use, digital certificates. The usability associated with acquiring, managing, and using certificates is abysmal. Until it improves, the use of certificates will continue to remain relatively low.

Hybrid Systems

Your application may have aspects of both an open and a closed system. Consider corporate e-mail. It is closed, in that a user can probably be acceptably authenticated with the same user ID and password that gave him access to the corporate network when he first logged in. When receiving an e-mail from another internal user, he can be fairly confident that the person who purportedly sent the mail did send it.

The system is open, in that this user may need to send and receive secure e-mails to and from external entities. Suppose this same user receives a distressing e-mail from his outside attorney. It would be good if there was a way to certify the identity of the sender. Hybrid systems will increase as we find ways to use Web services and open our business processes to trusted and semi-trusted partners.

Transaction Security

Transaction security is of utmost importance in a client/server application or a Web service. Its objective is to support auditability, integrity, confidentiality, and accountability. It is likely that you're going to employ authentication and authorization as discussed in the previous section in combination with these four security techniques.

Auditability—Proof of Activity

An auditable system requires authentication and behavior tracking. Together, these enable the system to generate credible reports of activity that can be used in a variety of ways. Consider financial applications that use proof of activity to spot suspicious behavior. For example, a velocity check will spot a sudden higher-than-expected transaction volume coming from the same source, which may be an indication of fraud. Often, audit data is copied to an offsite location managed by a trusted third party, so that it can't be tampered with to remove evidence of transactions.

Three motivations dominate the creation of auditable systems. Reactive motivations include the need to respond to government or industry regulations or guidelines. Proactive motivations include the ability to create one or more unique features based on auditable data. Discovery motivations include the desire to analyze data over time in the hope of discovering interesting trends. Each of these are related to the other. A marketect may require that certain parts of the system be auditable to meet a key government regulation, but do so in a way that provides a significant edge over his competitors and provides interesting data for long-term trend analysis.

Integrity—Preventing Tampering and Alteration of Data

A digest function (also known as a one-way hash) takes a block of data and returns a small byte sequence that represents it. Good digest functions are very random, so that any change to the original data results in a different digest value and so that it is very difficult to find a different block of data that has the same value. Algorithms such as SHA1 and MD5 are well-known digest functions, and they've been exposed to public scrutiny to make sure they meet the above requirements.

Digests are normally encrypted with a private key, to create a digital signature. Anyone with the public key can decrypt them running the digest algorithm on the block of data to produce a new digest. If the digests match, the source data has not been altered. The reason we don't simply encrypt the data itself with the private key is that private key encryption is expensive and would take far too long for large blocks of data. The digest algorithm is very fast and produces a small result that is easy to encrypt. The signature for a block of data need not be attached to the data or even stored with it.

Generally speaking, integrity is easy to provide—the code that implements the algorithms used is readily available, and much of it is open source—so there's little excuse not to use it if there's a chance it will be needed. Integrity is often correlated with auditability, as a way of proving that the record of system behavior has not changed.

Confidentiality—Keeping Data Away from Those Not Entitled to It

Encryption also comes to the rescue when you want to make sure that nobody can intercept your messages or the data stored in your system. Consider the difference between a log file that tracks system activity for billing, and a message sent between two systems, or a record that contains credit card information. In the case of a log file, you may only need to implement an integrity mechanism to prove that it was not altered. In the case of the credit card information, you not only need to prevent a devious person from altering a message or record that contains the number—you also need to prevent him from reading or accessing it in the first place!

The most common approach to encrypting data, and one used by systems such as Secure Sockets Layer (SSL), is a two-step process. The first step relies on symmetric key encryption, which is very fast. The sender of the message generates a symmetric key and uses it with an algorithm like RC4 to encrypt the data. In the second step the sender encrypts the symmetric key used in the first step with the public key of the receiver. Public key encryption is much slower than symmetric encryption, but the data being encrypted is so small that it happens very quickly. The sender then sends both the encrypted data and the encrypted key to the receiver. The receiver decrypts the key using his private key and then decrypts the data.

This process is a good balance of speed and cryptographic strength. Since SSL is very widespread, we recommend its use whenever possible. We also expect that SSL implementers will adopt even stronger cryptographic algorithms, such as Rijndael instead of RC4. Using the standard means that you get its benefits as it improves (you also get the drawbacks if it's cracked, but, although this is possible, we're comfortable in recommending this standard).

Accountability—Holding People Responsible for Their Actions

One of the objectives of transaction security is to provide a mechanism for non-repudiation. That means that if you send a message to me, I can later prove that only you could have sent it. Public/private key operations alone permit nonrepudiation, but any operation that relies on public/private key operations will supply that capability. Read that sentence again, slowly. Suppose, for example, that a user logs into a multiuser system using a two-factor authorization scheme (such as a smart card with a password). Even though you have authorized this user, you may not be able to hold her accountable for her actions—unless your system requires strong authentication.

Strong accountability requires strong authentication—if all you need to send a message is a smart card containing a digital certificate, someone could steal your card and use it. On the other hand, if you need to enter a password as well, the chance that someone else can send the message decreases.

Digital signatures are used along with strong authentication to provide strong accountability. Nobody without your private key can send a message signed by it since all they have is your public key. That means that by saving a digitally signed message a service can later prove that you sent it.

Software Security

Some of the issues associated with software security were raised in Chapter 4 in the discussion of how license managers enforce the terms and conditions of business and licensing models. In this section we'll cover the topic more thoroughly.

Software Security Techniques

The first thing most software developers think of when it comes to software security is preventing piracy. This is a good thing, because no matter which reports you read, piracy is a multi-billion dollar problem. Several techniques have emerged for making software more secure, each a bit more complicated and a bit more effective at deterring thieves.

Serial Numbers and Activations

Recall from Chapter 15 that a serial number is a unique identifier that distinguishes individual products, and that through activation you can bind a legal copy of the software to a specific machine. A more advanced technique uses a digitally signed license with software, so that an application or a service will not run unless a valid license with a valid signature is present.

Most people aren't hackers, and most people don't frequent hacker pages on the Internet. Most illegally copied software is passed on by friends and relatives, who may have few qualms about passing along a serial number or a license as well. Serial numbers, software activations, and digitally signed licenses all cut down on casual copying—after all, a serial number can be traced to its official owner if it's posted on the Internet or otherwise gets away.

Hackers attack these schemes in a number of ways. The most damaging attack is reverse-engineering the serial number generation algorithm and writing their own. That opens the door for actual software piracy—the selling of illegal copies.

Digitally signed licenses are much better—the private key needed to sign the licenses will not be available, so the hacker must either modify the program to bypass software security or replace the embedded public key with one for which the pirate has a private key. That way, the pirate can generate his own licenses.

Protecting the Validation Code

All of the schemes we've discussed thus far are based on embedding one or more checks in your code that confirm the presence of a valid license. A typical code fragment that does this might look like the this:

```
if (!LicenseIsValid(licenseFileName))
{
    ComplainAndExit();
}
```

Surprisingly, it's often trivial for a hacker or a software pirate to bypass this kind of security check, even if you have a highly secure, digitally signed license and even if your license validation routine is difficult to reverse-engineer. All the software hacker has to do is use a disassembler, find the code corresponding to the **if** statement, and insert a jump around the test or replace the test with no-ops. That means that you can't just use a Boolean return to check your license—you have to be a lot trickier to foil a hacker.

Instead of just asking a simplistic yes/no question, more secure approaches actually store something that your application needs to run as encrypted data within the signed license. This might be a critical function, such as an initialization routine or a function that registers subcomponents within the application. The application then verifies the license and decrypts this data, which in turn controls the behavior of the software. You then have to protect the software that performs the license validation and decryption, which is when you realize that the professional license managers described in Chapter 4 are actually pretty hard to write!

Hardware Binding

Hardware binding, as discussed in Chapter 15, is the process of associating or binding information about the software with some kind of hardware. There are two basic choices for hardware binding, each with its own advantages and disadvantages.

In *machine binding*, the software is bound to the machine it runs on. The binding process works by taking a hardware fingerprint of the machine. If too many parameters change, the software stops working. The chief advantage of machine binding is its low cost. The chief disadvantage is that it may prevent users from easily upgrading their machines or moving software to a new machine. It is also the easiest kind of binding for a cracker to crack.

In *hardware binding*, the software is bound to a physical device connected to a serial or USB port, commonly referred to as a dongle. The device must be connected for the software to work. The chief advantage of a dongle is portability and strength of security. The chief disadvantage is cost and management.

Software Security Costs/Benefits

An important thing to remember about piracy prevention is this: Many, if not most, of the people who run illegal copies would not have bought the software if they hadn't gotten it free. You don't want to make life difficult for your legitimate users, possibly driving them away, in a futile attempt to prevent people from using your software who would never actually buy it.

Software security can add significantly to the cost of developing, maintaining, and supporting your software. Obfuscation is often helpful in foiling attempts by hackers, but it can make your programs extremely difficult to debug. Even running a certificate server as a certificate authority can add tremendous cost, given its 24/7 operational requirements.

This doesn't mean that we endorse software piracy. Casually copying an application from your work computer to your home computer, purchasing one copy of an operating system and installing it on more than one computer without the necessary license rights, and posting an application on a Web site or making it available via a P2P network are all *illegal* activities. The best way to address software piracy is to weigh the risks of implementing strong anti-piracy tactics against the potential for lost revenue. If you're selling enterprise-class software or providing your software as a service via an xSP, piracy is not likely to be a problem, partly because of the intense integration and support requirements and partly because of the ease with which piracy can be determined through nontechnical means. If your software requires regular updates of code or data to be useful, piracy may not be that much of a problem.

However, if you're losing, or even suspect you're losing, thousands or millions of dollars because of software piracy, do something about it. Explore a new business model, such as a rental. Implement a lightweight protection mechanism and see who breaks it. If you find your software freely available on the hacker Web sites or Usenet lists, (use Google groups to view alt.2600.*), implement stronger forms of protection. You may even be justified in using a hardware-based software protection device.

Information Security

Many of the same techniques used for transaction security can be adapted for information security, although they are far less effective.

To understand information security, ask yourself the question, What if someone had open access to all my files and databases? If your data is encrypted, and you've stored the encryption keys in the database or in a file in the same system, the hacker has the keys to decrypt it. If your data is signed, the hacker can alter it since he has the keys needed to sign it again after it is altered. You can, and should, store these things outside the database or file system managed by the application, but this is an operations nightmare. In addition, other systems frequently want to manipulate these data, and encryption makes them useless for this purpose.

As a result, the primary approach to information security is not to protect the information once it's been accessed, but to prevent access to it in the first place. The main tools for doing this are network tools such as firewalls and intrusion detection software and user management tools such as password policy checkers.

Password security is an interesting area in itself. Many companies never store passwords in a database—instead, they run a digest algorithm over them and store only the digests. That means that no hacker can steal a whole database full of passwords, since the passwords themselves aren't there. Unfortunately, it also means that if a user loses a password the best you can do is generate a new one—you can't derive it from the result of the digest function any better than a hacker can. Many Web sites operate that way, especially the ones that ask you for a special question they can use to authenticate you should you lose your password and require a new one.

Another technique is to store passwords on an internal system not reachable from the Internet but reachable only from a server on a local file system. If a hacker is going to get passwords, he must first hack into the outer system and then use that as a way to get at the inner system. Intrusion detection systems can often foil such attempts.

One of the common things that we think of in information security is theft. In the digital world, information theft boils down to illegally copying bits from one computer to another. This may not be your most serious threat. Semantic attacks, in which hackers alter data stored in a database to gain an advantage, are on the increase. For some reason, these attacks seem less harmful, perhaps because Hollywood has created too many cute movies in which the nerdy hacker changes his grades. When that nerdy hacker is changing bank accounts, altering credit histories, or changing voting records, things aren't so funny.

Information security should guide your system architecture, but don't attempt to write your own tools—there are many excellent ones already available for that.

Secret Algorithms or Secret Keys?

The techniques for achieving security are usually based on a mathematically complex algorithm itself in the public domain or whose underlying logic is in the public domain. This may not matter to you—unless you're the one picking the algorithm! In fact, choosing an algorithm can be so daunting that you might not want to do it at all

You might think that a secret algorithm would be the ultimate in security. After all, one of the best kept secrets of World War II was the Enigma machine, which the Germans used to encrypt and decrypt information. It was only after an Enigma machine was captured intact that the Allies were finally able to start decoding messages. This is why you shouldn't use a secret algorithm. Generally, "security through obscurity" is one of the weakest forms of security available as your secret algorithm can be found, reverse-engineered, or leaked. Given the tremendous ongoing improvements in raw computing power, no algorithm is safe from a brute force cracking attempt. A better choice than a secret algorithm is any of the excellent publicly available algorithms. Public algorithms are under continuous scrutiny. In fact, many mathematicians are hoping to make a name for themselves by finding a cracking method that doesn't require brute force (i.e., try every key).

Smart security managers avoid any product or service that uses a secret security algorithm, because it provides no guarantees. On the other hand, secret keys are used all the time and nobody has any issue with them.

It can be tempting to come up with your own encryption algorithm, but it's pointless—even if your algorithm is significantly better than others, nobody is going to spend time and money to verify that. Use standard algorithms and secret keys—until quantum computers are readily available, you'll be perfectly safe.

Back Doors

Another temptation is to put back doors in your code so that a customer service representative (for example) can get at secure data, even if the customer has lost a password or a certificate. With just the little extra effort it takes to put in a carefully controlled back door, you look like a shining hero, saving the customer from her own foolishness.

That's possibly the case. On the other hand, back doors are often poorly implemented and can give way to easy hacks. The result is a lot of wasted time and effort on security.

To illustrate this, we'll use the 100th Window Problem. Let's say your company has a large building with 100 windows that are all open, and you rush around locking them all before you leave for the day. Unfortunately, you actually lock only 99 windows, having overlooked one. Even if you have excellent locks and burglar alarms on all the locked windows, a thief can slip in the 100th window and make off with all your corporate goods. The more windows you add, the harder it is to make sure that everything is secure.

Generally speaking, there's no point in securing less than 100 percent of the relevant portion of your system. If you're going to do it at all, you must be committed to securing everything. It's better to offer your customers secure offsite escrow of passwords and keys than it is to build in back doors. That way, if they don't take you up on your service and they lose their password or certificate, they can only blame themselves.

Also, you're not saying, "By the way, our software is really secure, but we can break the security if you need us to." You're saying "We'll try to help you avoid costly mistakes, but our software is so secure that even we can't break the security." This is a better technical message and a *much* better marketing message.

> ## Customer Support Shouldn't Sneak in through the Back Door
>
> One customer of our enterprise-class software system was having trouble managing their database. Customer support was having trouble diagnosing the problem because our customer was unable to run the necessary SQL commands to diagnose the problem. They just didn't have the necessary skill.
>
> One of my developers created a very clever solution. He wrote a program that could send an arbitrary SQL to another program installed at the customer's site. This program would apply the query to our customer's database and return the results to technical support. Once installed, it would periodically check for any commands, roughly every few minutes.
>
> We sent this program to our customer. They installed it, and a short time later the customer support team resolved the problem. In fact, the solution was so well admired by both customer support and the development team that they lobbied hard to put this into the next release. I said, "No." The risk of creating an inappropriate command and sending it to an unsuspecting customer was simply too great. Even when intentions are good, you have to guard against back doors.
>
> —Luke

Security and Marketecture

The marketing implications of choosing appropriate levels of security are far-reaching. Companies get hacked and, along with their customers, suffer real losses. In fact, in certain domains security can be a significant perceived competitive advantage (just ask Sun's marketing department to tell you about the security of Windows).

Areas of Interaction

Here are some of the areas in which security most directly interacts with marketecture.

Authentication, Business Models, and Operations

Two key areas in which strong two-factor authentication can have a significant impact are your business model and your operations model. Business models based on named users should consider strong authentication; when users share user IDs or passwords you lose money. xSP operations personnel, such as an xSP system or network administrator, often have tremendous access to sensitive data. To ensure that you're creating an environment your customers can trust, make certain they know that all activities on their systems are protected through strong, two- or three-factor authentication.

Regulatory Impact

Applications in many domains are either regulated by specific standards or required to adhere to them (such as the U.S. Federal Information Processing Standards, or FIPS, for many kinds of applications). Clearly, you have to know the standards. Of course, you can exceed a standard's minimum legal requirements, which means that you may be subject to technology export regulations.

Industry Growth

One of the major reasons for the success of the Internet is its open standards, such as TCP/IP, HTTP, and SMTP. Over the next several years, the security industry is going to see a proliferation of standards. By proactively adhering to key standards, some related to the Internet, some not, you're going to give your solution a better chance at being adopted by customers, primarily enterprises, who are beginning to demand standards-based security approaches. Note that many security related standards are already available, such as X.509.

Trust

While compliance with regulatory requirements may be required, it may not give your application a true competitive advantage, as your competitors are also subject to these requirements. Beyond compliance, which can be thought of as the minimum necessary to be seen as competent, lies *trust*: the confidence your customers have in your character and integrity and in the ongoing quality of the relationship you've established with them.

You've got a competitive advantage when your customers can entrust their data to you, secure in the knowledge that you won't allow inappropriate access or disclosure. You've got a competitive advantage when system administrators can establish and provision user rights in such a way that sensitive corporate information is made available only to those individuals who should have such access. You've got a competitive advantage when your application seamlessly and usably integrates with digital certificate infrastructures in such a way that users can rely on them without becoming mired in incomprehensible technical jargon.

All of these, and more, are elements of trust, which is an elusive but extraordinarily powerful element of your corporate brand. When you've got your customer's trust, you have a powerful competitive edge. Approaching security with care and building a strong, secure solution, only enhances that trust.

Dispute Resolution

Disputes are common in business, and software systems are often involved in or even cause them. Security techniques such as integrity and accountability help ensure that disputes are resolved in a timely manner. Examining your business model, licensing model, and technology in-license agreements can provide you with additional ideas on how security techniques can help in dispute resolution. For example, providing digest functions on log file entries can prevent fighting among technical support teams ("No, it's your bug, and we can prove it—here's our log file!"). Ask your legal team for help in identifying areas in which security technologies can avoid problems.

When You Have to Prove Your Point

I teach a variety of seminars and classes, and it is always interesting to hear how various parts of a winning solution affect a company. In one class, a student worked for a company that created automated drug dispensing units. She related a story about how the company was involved in a lawsuit that they eventually won.

The lawsuit was initiated by the family of a man who was killed because of a drug overdose. The family sued the doctor, who in turn sued the company that made the drug dispensing unit. The key issue in the case was who was at fault: The doctor, who claimed he input the right dosage level but that a faulty unit dispensed too much, or the company, who claimed that its unit performed flawlessly and that the doctor input a lethal dose.

The verdict was decided in favor of the company. The proof lay in a close examination of the secured, auditable log files generated by the unit. In constructing the unit the company had foreseen this circumstance, and had consulted with their legal team to make certain they were building a legally defensible log file.

—Luke

Chapter Summary

- An overall security plan for your application must take into account appropriate risk factors.
- There are four main types of security:
  - Digital identity management
  - Transaction security
  - Software security
  - Information security
- The primary tools and techniques associated with digital identity management include
  - Authorization—defining who can do what
  - Authentication—proof of identity. Authentication approaches vary tremendously based on whether you're dealing with an open or a closed system
- The primary tools and techniques associated with transaction security include
  - Auditability—proof of activity
  - Integrity—preventing data tampering and alteration

- Confidentiality—keeping data away from those not entitled to it
- Accountability—holding people responsible for their actions
- The primary tools and techniques associated with software security include
  - Preventing software piracy and enforcing license compliance (see also Chapters 4 and 15)
  - Binding the software to a machine or a hardware token
  - The primary tools and techniques associated with information security are the same used for transaction security, but are far less effective. The main technique is to make certain that the environment in which the data are placed is properly secured.
- Don't invent your own security algorithm. Chances are it will get cracked. Use a publicly available algorithm with a well-formed key.
- Never put in a back door.
- Use security to your advantage. The ultimate brand element is trust, and security can help you get it.

Check This

❏ The accompanying table provides you with a way to check the various kinds of security discussed in this chapter. How do you fare?

Type of Security	Assessment
Digital identity management	
How much security is needed?	
Why do you think you need it?	
How have you addressed this need?	
Transaction security	
How much security is needed?	
Why do you think you need it?	
How have you addressed this need?	
Software security	
How much security is needed?	
Why do you think you need it?	
How have you addressed this need?	

Type of Security	Assessment
Information security	
How much security is needed?	
Why do you think you need it?	
How have you addressed this need?	

Try This

1. Imagine who might attempt to defeat the security of your software. Is it a software pirate? An information thief? A temporary worker for whom no background check was performed? A competitor after company secrets? A vandal? Write a one- or two-sentence biography of each. One at a time imagine that you are them. How would you attack your software?

2. Look for mention of your software and your competitor's software in the hacker Usenet groups. Are there serial number generators, or cracks, available? Are people asking for them?

3. Ask yourself what is the worst that can happen. Imagine the worst-case scenarios. Try to put a dollar value on the damage that can be done, and try to estimate the likelihood that the worst case will come to pass. If there's a high likelihood of very expensive damage, it's time to increase your security efforts.

4. Using at least five typical installations of your software, create a picture of how your customers secure your system. How do they manage access to your system? Can you help your customers improve security? How are other elements of your system managed? Even if your application is secure, there may be other routes to your data through third-party tools, and hackers can exploit them.

5. How secure are the components you've licensed?

About Ron Lunde

Ron Lunde is an amateur orchid grower, a humorist, and an inventor of strange and typically useless things, who is currently employed as a system architect for Aladdin Knowledge Systems. He has 19 years of software development experience as a software architect, a software manager, or a senior engineer in electronic software distribution and license management, digital video editing, source-level debuggers for in-circuit emulation, and automatic ASIC and circuit board test generation. He has also consulted in many other areas.

Appendix A
Release Checklist

A simple checklist, such as the one here, can help you make certain that you're not overlooking any important items associated with the product release. Feel free to add or remove items, or to phrase the questions differently, as required for your environment.

Tracking Information

❑ Product: <insert name>
❑ Version: <x.y.z build>
❑ FCS Date: <FCS = first customer shipment>

Engineering/Development

❑ Are version strings updated with the final version information?
❑ Is all debugging and test code removed from the software?
❑ Are all seeded defects removed from the software?

Quality Assurance

❑ Is the final disposition and/or resolution of all defects complete? (No bugs with a status of open, unassigned, fixed but not yet verified, or nondeferred analyze)
❑ Is the appropriate testing on the final build complete? (Full regression, customer-specified, smoke, etc.)
❑ Is a program install from the release media onto a clean target machine complete? (CD-ROM, Web site, etc.)

❑ Is the program successfully installable (Files, registry updates, etc.)?

❑ Is a program uninstall from the target machine complete?

❑ If appropriate, is an upgrade install complete?

❑ Are the final help files included?

❑ Are the final read-me files included?

❑ Do all migration scripts pass?

❑ Have all supported platforms been tested and verified?

Technical Publications

❑ Release notes

❑ In-line help in products—documented in Readme, Release Note, and Quickstart

❑ Updated training materials reviewed by the tarchitect

Core Product Management

❑ Press release

❑ E-mail campaign to existing customers

❑ Sales training

❑ Pricing

❑ Launch plan

❑ Sales collateral (white papers, glossies, Web site)

Knowledge Transfer—Professional Services

❑ Can the customer install, upgrade, and integrate the system?

❑ How long will it take to install, upgrade, and/or integrate the system?

❑ Do any integrations need to be redone for the installation to work?

❑ Are all training materials current with the release?

Knowledge Transfer—Sales and the Channel

❑ Can your sales team articulate the benefits of the new release to their existing customers?

❑ Can your sales team explain the advantages of the new product to new customers?

❑ Do they understand the complete business model, including any changes to it from the previous release (such as price changes, promotional discounts, and so forth)?

❏ Can they explain the product in the context of the overall set of solutions offered by the company.

Knowledge Transfer—Technical Support

❏ Is technical support ready to support the product?

Release Activities

❏ Is a final list of the files in the released product available?

❏ Are the date and time stamps on the released files synchronized?

❏ Is the final (gold) distribution media available?

❏ Is a virus scan of the distribution media complete?

❏ Is a final verification of the correct files on the distribution media complete?

❏ Is a backup of the build development environment under change control?

❏ Is the Web site updated?

Appendix B

A Pattern Language for Strategic Product Management

This appendix introduces a pattern language for strategic product management (see Table B-1). What is unique about the patterns is that they help the marketect and the tarchitect to bridge any gap between their respective disciplines.

TABLE B-1 Strategic Product Management Patterns

Problem	Solution	Pattern
How do you segment your market?	Create a visual representation of the market(s) you're targeting.	Market Map
What is the right frame of reference for time in your problem domain?	Identify the events and rhythms of your market/market segments.	Market Events/Market Rhythms
How do you ensure that the right features and benefits are being created for your target market(s)?	Create a map of the proposed features and their benefits. Tie these to the market(s) you're targeting.	Feature/Benefit Map
How do you manage the evolution of your technical architecture?	Create a roadmap of known technology trends. Include specific and well-known changes you want to make to your architecture so that everyone can plan for them.	Tarchitecture Roadmap

Applying The Patterns

Figure B-1 captures the relationship between the patterns as they are applied. The order shown is one that has worked for me. Like most diagrams that suggest an ordering, the figure fails to show the dynamic way these maps were built. In most cases, I recommend starting with a Market Map, primarily because there is so much confusion among product development teams regarding the target market. However, if you're working in a mature market, or if your marketing communication department already has a precise calendar, you may find that starting with the market events and market rhythms pattern is the best way to begin.

The most important point is that instead of arguing which pattern should be first, you should simply pick one to get started. This is because the patterns are part of a

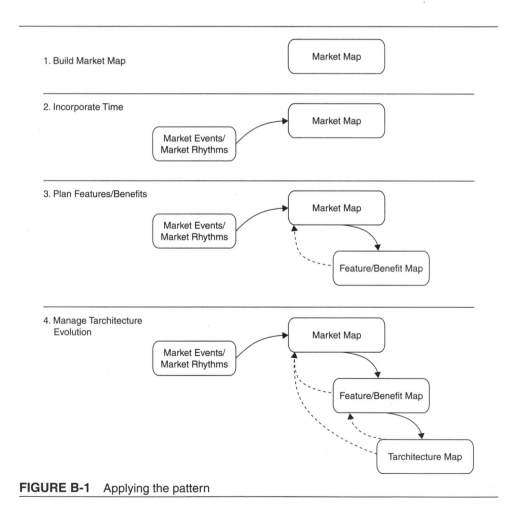

FIGURE B-1   Applying the pattern

system. Like all complex systems, this one is characterized by feedback loops, shown as a dotted line in the figure. It is almost guaranteed that the application of any given pattern will slightly modify the earlier application of another one. Instead of focusing your efforts on making a single diagram correct, start by identifying one market segment—just about any will do—and then add some market events or features. Try to increase your comfort that the data you need to make sound decisions will emerge, provided you keep iterating over the results.

Discontinuous events, such as a competitor releasing a new version faster than expected, a new conference forming around a new industry, or the introduction or maturation of an exciting technology, are likely to motivate a series of coordinated changes in all of these diagrams. For example, in applications that rely on voice technology, the maturation of Voice XML or SALT first captured on the tarchitecture map may cause upward ripples in all of the other maps. You might be able to reach a new market with an awareness of these new technologies, or you might be able to provide some "killer feature" by adding new support for these standards.

Capturing and Sharing the Result

I've found that the best way to capture the result of applying these patterns is through a series of large charts located in a publicly accessible dedicated space. A stylized, condensed example of such a display is shown in Figure B-2. The large question mark represents what happens when marketing identifies an unmet need requiring a technology or capability. The final row of the grid is the addition of the real schedule, or a schedule that has been communicated to customers and salespeople perhaps through

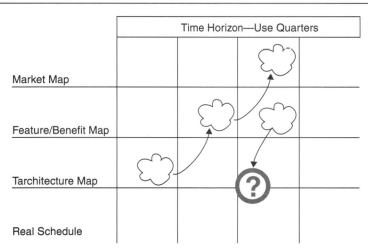

FIGURE B-2   Sharing the results

the product roadmap. Placing the real schedule along the bottom of the diagram ensures that everything is being considered pragmatically. Not shown in this example are market events/market rhythms. These should be added in your application of these patterns.

Market Map

Context

You have an idea for a new product and you're trying to understand its potential. You have an existing product and you want to make certain that you're marketing it in the most effective manner possible.

Problem

How do you segment your market?

Forces

- Market segmentation is hard because
  - Existing markets change.
  - Predicting emerging markets is as much art as it is science (who knew lasers were for playing music?).
- Market segmentation is critically important because
  - If you don't segment your market you run the risk of trying to serve all markets, which is almost certain failure.
  - Different market segments require different solutions. You need to focus to win.
- You can't identify the most profitable segments if you don't segment well.
- You can't meet the needs of every market.
- Usability requires an understanding of the market you're trying to serve.

Solution

Segment the market by creating classes or groupings of users who share similar characteristics and/or attributes. The characteristics include critical needs, buying patterns, and various attributes that are important to you. The attributes in a consumer market might be age, household income, Internet connectivity, and technical literacy. In a business market they might be revenue, number of employees, geography, and so forth. Name the segment on a piece of paper and then write down its most important descriptive characteristics. Large Post-It notes work well because they can be easily ordered.

Concentrate first on the actual users of your current product. (If the users are not the customers—people who have purchasing authority—you can address this at a later date.) In this process you will identify common "points of pain" or problems these users face. The results provide input to your Feature/Benefit Map. More important, though, is that you must solve your customers' problems.

When you begin this process try to make your segments as well-defined as possible. This will help you focus your efforts. As you examine each segment to make certain it is a viable (profitable) target, you may want to combine it with other segments. A fine-grained approach to market segmentation will give you more flexibility in combining segments should this be needed.

Once you have a reasonable number of segments (usually between 6 and 12) order them in terms of which segment you will be addressing first relative to the actual and/or contemplated features of your product. Even before the product is finished some segments will naturally emerge as "easier" to address than others. This may be because of existing relationships (such as channel and/or customer relationships) or because it is simply easier to build a product that pleases a certain segment. As you complete the other maps in this pattern language you can adjust the timeframes associated with the target segments.

Provide the market map to all team members, especially user interface designers and QA. User interface designers need the map to understand the needs of the customer. QA requires it to make certain that they are organizing testing according to key customer priorities.

Resulting Context

Your market is segmented at a sufficient level to support strategic planning. As the needs of one segment are addressed, the next segment can be more precisely analyzed in preparation for the product cycle.

Related Patterns

- Market Events/Market Rhythms
- Feature/Benefits Map

Market Events/Market Rhythms

Context

You are trying to establish the market window for a given release *or* an ongoing series of releases. You have a Market Map to help you explore specific market segments.

Problem

How do you choose a good target release date? How do you establish an ongoing cycle of releases?

Forces

- Customers usually can't accept a release at any time of year. For example, retailers won't accept new software releases during the holiday selling season.
- Customers can't absorb releases that occur too quickly, yet they get frustrated and concerned if releases happen too slowly.
- Developers hate arbitrary release dates.
- Sales activities require plenty of lead time.
- Releases that are too short are almost always bad—low in quality or incomplete.
- Releases that are too long are almost always bad—too many features and lost revenue and market opportunities.
- Organizations (developers, support, QA, release manufacturing, and others) that go too long without releasing a product lose valuable skills.
- Organizations that go too long without releasing aren't fun places to work.

Solution

Identify and record the key events and rhythms that drive your market. Every domain has them. For example, Comdex and CEBIT are important international conferences that drive many end-consumer computing devices. Consider the following when you're searching for important events.

- Conferences (technical, user group, and so forth)
- Competitors' press releases
- Topics of special issues in publications that focus on your domain and relate to your product or service

Events that are held periodically, such as Comdex, also create and establish the rhythm of the market. If you're a successful consumer electronics vendor, Comdex and CEBIT form the foundation of a yearly rhythm known by all market participants and driving all company activities. Other examples of marketplace rhythms include

- The end-of-year holiday season
- In the United States, the school year
- In Europe, summer vacations

Once you have identified marketplace events and rhythms use them to create the timing and rhythm of ongoing releases. I've had good luck with regular release cycles of between nine and twelve months. Broad software categories, such as high-end and enterprise systems, often have major releases every twelve months, with dot or maintenance releases following three to four months thereafter. Some software categories, such as operating systems, don't seem to have a rhythm.

The maturity of the market segment also affects the release cycle. Immature markets tend to have shorter release cycles and more events—a reflection of the learning going on among market participants. Mature markets tend to have longer release cycles and more established rhythms.

Resulting Context

Developers are happier because they know that marketing isn't making a date out of thin air. Commonly known dates have an energizing and engaging effect on the entire development organization. Customers are happier because they can engage in realistic strategic planning. They know that sometime in the third quarter they will be receiving a new release and can plan accordingly.

Related Patterns

- Market Map

Feature/Benefit Map

Context

You want to make certain that key marketing objectives match key development efforts. You have a Market Map to identify the key market segments you're targeting.

Problem

What is the best way to capture compelling features and their benefits for each market segment?

Forces

- People often think they understand the key features and benefits for a given market segment when they really don't.
- A feature may be a benefit to more than one market segment.
- Features that apply to multiple market segments may not provide the same perceived benefits to each one.
- Developers tend to think of features (cool), while marketing people tend to think of benefits (compelling advantages, reasons to purchase). This gap often results in poorly designed products and/or products that can't win in the market.

- Developers need to understand the nature and intent of *future* benefits so that they can be certain the tarchitecture is designed to meet them.

Solution

For each market segment capture the key features and benefits that motivate to purchase the product. It is crucial that you list features and benefits together. Omitting one gives the other inappropriate influence.

Choose an ordering for your map that makes the most sense. I've had good results ordering first by time and then by difficulty/complexity. Others get good results from ordering by what the market wants or what sales can sell. Paul Germeraad from Intellectual Assets, Inc., has organized features into a product tree where the edges of the tree are the features in the last release. The features of the next release are placed around those edges. Paul draws lines around the features proposed for the next release. One advantage of this visualization is that the entire company can feel good about the growth of their product. Another is very practical: The expanding size of the perimeter correlates with the growth of the product development organization. As the product tree grows, so do the needs of the team in caring for and feeding it (including the maintenance team).

Resulting Context

You have a representation of the key features and associated benefits needed to attack target market segments. This will provide the technical team with the data they need to update their tarchitecture map so they can realize these features.

Related Patterns

- Market Map
- Tarchitecture Roadmap

The Tarchitecture Roadmap

Context

You are building an application expected to have multiple, ongoing product releases. You have a Market Map and a Feature/Benefit Map to identify specific markets and the features/benefits that they want. You may have an existing architecture that supports one or more markets.

Problem

How do you manage/leverage technological change?

Forces

- No matter how well an application has been architected, changes in technology can invalidate prior assumptions.
- Technologies usually appear on the horizon with enough time to accommodate them if they're planned for.
- Developers like to understand where they are headed.
- Developers like to learn new things.
- Developers want a way to manage the tarchitectural evolution of poorly implemented features or capabilities. The want a way to make both the poor feature/capability known to others and register their desire to change it.
- Technology can enable new features that marketing may want.
- Marketing may demand features that can be supported only by adopting a new technology.
- Competitors' adoption of a new technology may put you in a disadvantageous, reactive state.
- Technical people will argue over emerging technologies. Sometimes the arguments are a way of learning more about the issues. Most of the time the only way to reach consensus is to allow them plenty of time for discussion.

Solution

Create a technology map that shows how your architecture will evolve. It should relate to the market map and feature/benefit map by showing how specific technologies produce benefits that are desired by key market segments.

Review this map whenever important milestones are realized and no less than once every six months. Examples of important internal milestones include code freeze, product shipment, and when 50% of current customers have upgraded to the most recent version. Examples of important external milestones can be a competitor issuing a new product release, new patent discoveries, whenever a member of the technical staff identifies a significant discontinuous technology, or whenever market events occur.

The creation and management of the tarchitecture roadmap requires that at least one member of the team scan the external environment for new developments in the field.

If marketing has identified a feature that cannot be supported by existing technologies (either directly or because of performance/cost curves) the tarchitecture roadmap can help the team maintain focus by periodically scanning the environment to see if any new technologies have emerged that meet this need.

Resulting Context

The good news is that you will identify promising technical futures for your product. The bad news is that unless your team has sufficient discipline they will want to explore every possible future—the dreaded "shiny new object" syndrome.

Related Patterns

- Market Map
- Feature/Benefits Map

References

Abdel-Hamid, T. K. and S. E. Madnick. *Software Project Dynamics: An Integrated Approach.* Englewood Cliffs, NJ: Prentice Hall, 1991.

Adelson, B. and E. Soloway. "The Role of Domain Experience in Software Design." *IEEE Transactions on Software Engineering*, Vol. SE-11, No. 11 (Nov. 1985): 1351–1360.

Allen, T. J. "Organizational Structure, Information Technology, and R&D Productivity." *IEEE Transactions on Engineering Management,* Vol. EM-33 No. 4 (Nov. 1986): 212–217.

Belady, L.A. and M. M. Lehman. "A Model of Large Program Development" *IBM Systems Journal*, Vol. 15, No. 3 (1976): 225–52.

Bently, J. and D. Knuth. "Literate Programming" *Comm. of the ACM*, Vol. 29, No. 5 (May 1986): 364–69.

Boehm, B. W. *Software Engineering Economics* Englewood Cliffs, NJ: Prentice Hall, 1981.

Christiansen, D. "On Good Designers." *IEEE Spectrum,* Vol. 24, No. 5 (May 1987).

COCKBURN, A. *Agile Software Development* Boston: Addison-Wesley, 2002.

Curtis, B., H. Krasner, and N. Iscoe. "A Field Study of the Software Design Process for Large Systems." *Comm. of the ACM,* Vol. 31, No. 11 (Nov. 1988).

Dijkstra, E. W. "The Humble Programmer" (1972) in *ACM Turing Award Lectures*, New York: ACM Press, 1987.

Free Software Foundation. http://www.fsf.org/

Gamma, E., R. Helm, R. Johnson, and J. Vlissides. *Design Patterns: Elements of Reusable Object-Oriented Software.* Reading, MA: Addison-Wesley, 1995.

Gause G., and G. Weinberg. *Exploring Requirements Quality Before Design.* New York: Dorset House, 1989.

Gilb, T. *Principles of Software Engineering Management.* Reading, MA: Addison-Wesley, 1988.

Goldberg, A., and K. Rubin *Succeeding With Objects: Decision Frameworks For Project Management.* Reading, MA: Addison-Wesley, 1995.

Hoare, C. "The Emperor's Old Clothes" (1981) in *ACM Turing Award Lectures.* New York: ACM Press, 1987.

Hunt, D. and D. Thomas. *The Pragmatic Programmer: From Journeyman to Master.* Boston: Addison-Wesley, 2000.

Humphrey, W. S. *A Discipline for Software Engineering.* Reading, MA: Addison-Wesley, 1995.

IEEE Standard Glossary of Software Engineering Terminology, IEEE Standard 729-1983.

Kawasaki, G. *The Macintosh Way.* San Francisco: HarperCollins, 1990.

Kruchten, P. See various papers on the 4+1 View of architecture at www.rational.com.

Koek, M. http://www.koek.net/pubs/fsl/proj.html (June 1999).

Lampson, B. "Hints for Computer System Design." *IEEE Software*, (Jan. 1984). pp. 11–30.

Lehmann, D. R. and R. S. Winer Product Management, 3rd ed. Boston: McGraw-Hill, 2002.

Mathis, R.F. "The Last 10 Percent." *IEEE Transactions on Software Engineering*, Vol. SE-12, No. 6 (June 1986): 705–712.

Meyers, S. *Effective C++.* Reading, MA: Addison-Wesley, 1992.

Nielsen, J. *Usability Engineering.* New York: Harcourt Brace, 1993.

Open Source: http://www.opensource.org/

Security: http://www.w3.org/Security/

Swartout, W. and R. Balzer. "On the Inevitable Intertwining of Specification and Implementation." *Comm. of the ACM,* (July 1982).

Usability http://www.sei.cmu.edu/pub/documents/01.reports/pdf/01tr005.pdf

Weick, K. *The Social Psychology of Organizing* 2nd ed. New York: Random House, 1979.

http://zdnet.com.com/2100-1105-877606.html

http://csrc.nist.gov/rbac/

Bibliography

Software Development—People and Project Management

Brooks, F. P., Jr. *The Mythical Man-Month: Essays on Software Engineering.* Anniversary ed. Reading, MA: Addison-Wesley, 1995.

> If you read only one book on software development, make it this one.

Hohmann, L. *Journey of the Software Professional: A Sociology of Software Development.* Prentice-Hall, 1996.

> A comprehensive examination of individual and team productivity, *Journey* provides both a strong theoretical model and practical advice for improving the effectiveness of individuals and teams.

Demarco, T., and T. Lister. *Peopleware: Productive People and Teams*, 2nd ed. New York: Dorset House, 1999.

> The timeless classic on creating more effective, more productive organizations, recently updated to include the newest thinking on how to create more effective teams.

Beck, K. *Extreme Programming Explained*. Boston: Addison-Wesley, 2000.

> XP is taking a lot of development shops by storm. It isn't right for every project, but it is worthwhile to learn more about this approach to project management.

Software Development—Configuration Management

Appleton, B. http://www.enteract.com/~bradapp/acme/

> Appleton maintains an incredibly thorough set of links on software development at his web site. The page listed above contains several useful papers, patterns, and other writings on software configuration management.

297

Babich, W. *Software Configuration Management*. Reading, MA: Addison-Wesley, 1986.

> Babich's book is a timeless classic. It is short, direct, and to the point. It provides a solid foundation for understanding configuration management issues.

Software Development—Code and Selected Technologies

McConnell, S. *Code Complete*. Redmond, WA: Microsoft Press, 1993.

> Software developers are paid to produce code and other stuff. Plenty of stuff has been written about the other stuff, much of which is fluff. This is the best book ever written on code. I remain hopeful that Steve updates the book to include modern techniques.

Fowler, M. *Refactoring: Improving the Design of Existing Code*. Reading, MA: Addison-Wesley, 1999.

> Martin's book contains a wealth of practical advice on how to engage in refactoring throughout a system.

Schneier, B. *Applied Cryptography: Protocols, Algorithms, and Source Code in C, 2nd Edition*. New York: John Wiley & Sons, 1995.

> Although somewhat dated, Schneier's book provides developers with a detailed understanding of many of the lowest set of protocols and standards that form the foundation of many security approaches.

Product Management / Marketing

Levitt, T. *The Marketing Imagination*. New York: Free Press, 1986.

> Arguably the most influential book on modern marketing that has ever been written. Levitt is the inventor of the whole product concept and the first person to focus marketing towards creating customer value.

Moore, G. A. *Crossing the Chasm: Marketing and Selling High-Tech Products to Mainstream Customers*. New York: Harper Business, 1999.

> This book spawned an entire new lexicon in product management. Forget to read this book and you can forget about advancing your career beyond some distressingly boring dead-end assignment.

Cooper, R. G. *Winning at New Products: Accelerating the Process from Idea to Launch*. Cambridge, MA: Perseus Books, 2001.

> Robert Cooper has written several books about how to create truly useful products. His approach combines common sense, market understanding, and flexibility with rigor and discipline.

Davidow, W. H. *Marketing High Technology: An Insider's View*. New York: Free Press, 1986.

> A classic and timeless book from a true veteran of silicon valley. What I like best about the book is Davidow's candid approach. According to Davidow, marketing is civilized warfare led by crusaders, not evangalists. Unless you play for keeps don't play at all.

Ries, L. and R. Ries. *The 22 Immutable Laws of Branding: How to Build a Product or Service into a World-Class Brand*. San Francisco: HarperCollins, 1998.

> This little book has a wealth of good advice on how to manage brands. If you want to know a lot about how marketing folks approach brand management, this is the book to read.

Business Classics

Porter, M. E. *Competitive Strategy: Techniques for Analyzing Industries and Competitors*. New York: Free Press, 1980.

> You can't be an effective marketect or tarchitect without an understanding of strategy.

Mintzber, H., and J. B. Quinn. *The Strategy Process—Concepts and Contexts*. Englewood Cliffs, NJ: Prentice Hall, 1992.

> Ditto.

Software Architecture

Buschmann, F., R. Meunier, H. Rohnert, P. Sommerlad, and M. Stal. *Pattern-Oriented Software Architecture, Volume 1: A System of Patterns*. New York: John Wiley & Sons, 1996.

> Collectively known as the "Gang of Five," this book contains several useful architectural and system-level patterns.

Bass, L., P. Clements and R. Kazman. *Software Architecture in Practice*. Reading, MA: Addison-Wesley, 1998.

> Although the case studies are either simplistic or not relevant to those of us creating real products, this book provides several excellent taxonomies on how to think about various issues in software architecture. Highly recommended.

Collins, D. *Designing Object-Oriented User Interfaces*. Redwood City, CA: Benjamin/Cummings, 1995.

> This book should be required reading for any developer given primary responsibility for the design of the user interface. Collins addresses the proper construction of the system model and shows how they should be implemented. What is especially important is the practical advice on separating the presentation from the underlying implementation details.

Fowler, M. *Patterns of Enterprise Application Architectures*. Boston: Addison-Wesley, 2003.

Martin's new book is destined to become a classic for any architect who is building enterprise applications. Martin's book is a great compliment to this book—which is among the reasons they are in the same series!

About Luke Hohmann

Luke Hohmann graduated from the University of Michigan in 1992 with an M.S.E. in computer science and engineering. While at Michigan, Luke was a member of the Highly Interactive Computing in Education (hi-ce) research group and was principal author of the GPCeditor, a lisp-based Macintosh programming environment that helped high school students learn Pascal.

Before attending the University of Michigan, Luke was a competitive pairs figure skater. During his 14-year career he garnered numerous honors and awards, and in 1985 he and his partner won the United States National Junior Pairs Championship. Luke has represented the United States in international competition and was a two-time competitor in the United States Olympic Sports Festival. Since then, he has focused on creating great software and winning solutions for customers and clients.

Luke has been invited to speak and teach at major industry conferences, including Software Development, OOPSLA, and UML World. A faculty member of the University of Santa Cruz, Extension, Luke's classes are in high demand because of his strong emphasis on learning by doing and his commitment to providing his students with individual coaching. Over the past 10 years, Luke has taught more than 5,000 students in a variety of topics ranging from C++ and Design Patterns to Project Management, Product Management, User Interface Design, and Software Architecture.

In 1997 Luke published *Journey of the Software Professional: A Sociology of Software Development* (Prentice Hall), which captures the deeper theories of cognitive psychology and organizational behavior that form the foundation of successful development teams. Critically acclaimed, *Journey* has sold more than 8,000 copies world-wide.

Luke is noted for his innovative use of low- and high-tech approaches to managing hi-tech products, the organizations that build them, and the customers they serve. Despite hectic work schedules, Luke has held daily meetings with key customers to make sure projects are properly synchronized. When issues of strategy surface Luke leads "sticky note" planning sessions that enable executive, product development, and engineering staffs to create simple, effective, and congruent strategic plans. When more thorough planning is required, Luke has asked that his team follow Stage-Gate development processes, with tough Go/Kill decision criteria built into all activities. Included in this process are the creation of business plans that clearly demonstrate the business value of the proposed project. Other techniques, such as project dashboards, ensure that management can quickly and accurately determine the status of every project.

When he began writing this book he lived in the heart of Silicon Valley with his wife and son, Jaren. By the time he finished, the family had grown to include Cres. He hopes that by the time you read his next book he and his wife will have added one or two more children. Luke maintains an active lifestyle, sharing long runs and trips to the gym with his wife and family. A member of the IEEE and ACM, he can be reached at luke@lukehohmann.com.

Index

X